Changing Lives

A volume in the series

Adolescent Development and Legal Policy

EDITED BY FRANKLIN E. ZIMRING

Also in the series:

Double Jeopardy: Adolescent Offenders with Mental Disorders
by Thomas Grisso

An American Travesty: Legal Responses to Adolescent Sexual Offending
by Franklin E. Zimring

Changing Lives

*Delinquency Prevention
as Crime-Control Policy*

Peter W. Greenwood

Foreword by Franklin E. Zimring

The University of Chicago Press | *Chicago & London*

Peter Greenwood has published widely in the areas of juvenile justice and delinquency prevention, criminal careers, sentencing, corrections, and law enforcement policy. Formerly the director of the RAND Corporation's criminal justice research program, Dr. Greenwood currently serves on the board of VisionQuest, a major provider of services for troubled youth.

The University of Chicago Press, Chicago 60637
The University of Chicago Press, Ltd., London
© 2006 by The University of Chicago
All rights reserved. Published 2006
Printed in the United States of America

15 14 13 12 11 10 09 08 07 06   1 2 3 4 5

ISBN:0-226-30719-0 (cloth)

Library of Congress Cataloging-in-Publication Data

Greenwood, Peter W.
    Changing lives : delinquency prevention as crime-control policy / Peter W. Green-wood ; foreword by Franklin E. Zimring.
        p.   cm. — (Adolescent development and legal policy)
    Includes bibliographical references and index.
    ISBN 0-226-30719-0 (cloth : alk. paper)
    1. Juvenile delinquency—United States—Prevention.   2. Juvenile delinquents—Rehabilitation—United States.   3. Crime prevention—United States.   I. Title.
    II. Series.

HV9104 . G685   2006
364.4—dc22   2005011954

♾ The paper used in this publication meets the minimum requirements of the American National Standard for Information Sciences—Permanence of Paper for Printed Library Materials, ANSI Z39.48-1992.

Contents

List of Illustrations | vii
Foreword | ix
Acknowledgments | xi

Part 1   **The Nature and Effectiveness of Crime Prevention**

Chapter 1   Delinquency Prevention as Crime Control | 3
Chapter 2   The Evolution of an Idea | 10
Chapter 3   Strategies for Measuring Program Impact | 28
Chapter 4   What Works | 49
Chapter 5   What Doesn't Work | 84

Part 2   **Prevention and Policy**

Chapter 6   The Uses and Limits of Cost Effectiveness in Allocating
Crime-Prevention Resources | 119
Chapter 7   Politics, Government, and Prevention | 155
Chapter 8   Programming in the Modern Juvenile Court | 183

References | 195
Index | 215

Illustrations

Tables

2.1   Types of response to crime | 11
2.2   Factors that distinguish between prevention and control | 15
3.1   Potential outcome measures for delinquency-prevention programs | 30
3.2   Victim costs by crime type | 38
4.1   Promising prevention programs for early childhood | 53
4.2   Promising prevention programs for elementary school children | 57
4.3   Promising prevention programs for adolescents | 63
4.4   Promising prevention programs for delinquent youth | 71
4.5   Costs and benefits of selected promising and proven programs | 80
5.1   Characteristics and outcomes of experimental boot camps | 99
6.1   Lower and upper range of net program benefits estimated by WSIPP | 143
6.2   Comparison of estimated cost of individual crimes | 145
6.3   Proven and promising programs ranked by effect size | 150

Figures

4.1   Program cost per youth | 74
4.2   Number of convictions prevented for typical participant | 75
4.3   Cost per conviction prevented | 76
4.4   Criminal justice compared with other savings | 78

4.5   Program costs and taxpayer benefits | 78

6.1   Distribution of annual expenditures on cocaine control in 1992 | 125

6.2   Comparative costs of decreasing cocaine consumption by 1 percent | 126

6.3   Structure of RAND three-strikes model | 131

6.4   Serious and violent crimes prevented by year | 133

6.5   Three Strikes vs. previous law: Projected prison populations | 133

6.6   Three Strikes vs. alternatives: Percent reduction in serious crime | 135

6.7   Three Strikes vs. alternatives: Percent increase in cost | 135

6.8   Three Strikes vs. alternatives: Cost per serious crime prevented | 136

6.9   Serious crimes prevented per $million invested | 139

7.1   Comparison of initial authorization and final funding for programs in the Omnibus Crime Bill of 1994 | 166

8.1   Trends in incarceration rates for juveniles and young adults | 185

8.2   Trends in juvenile arrests | 186

8.3   Disposition of juvenile arrests in 1999 | 186

Foreword

Changing Lives is the third in a series of books commissioned by the MacArthur Research Network to fill important gaps in our knowledge of the legal environment of adolescent development. The topic of Peter Greenwood's study, programs designed to prevent delinquency in children and adolescents, had earlier been pursued by a much larger body of literature and had greater involvement of government agencies than the previous topics in this series—analyses of mental health problems in juvenile justice and of adolescent sex offenders. But all the earlier enthusiasm generated about prevention as a goal in programming failed to produce clear notions of what constituted effective prevention in practice, how quality control could be integrated into the public investment in prevention programs, and where in government the administration and funding of government prevention programming should be located.

Part of the difficulty is the huge variety of programs that can properly be called "preventive" and the hybrid quality of the prevention enterprise itself. Programs that seek to change the life course of youth are a mix of education and pathology avoidance. Effective programs typically influence not simply one specific problem—criminal offending, educational attainment, job stability—but create a wide variety of different benefits that are usually the concern of different components within executive government. Where in government should these efforts be located? Many prevention programs can only be evaluated in the long term while most other types of crime control work much faster because they operate more closely to the immediate environment of offending.

The editorial board of this venture wanted to commission a book that would provide a rigorous structure for thinking about the prevention enterprise. While there was no perfect candidate for this difficult assignment to be found, our early discussions centered on a senior researcher who was nearly perfect. Peter W. Greenwood is a distinguished criminal-justice scholar with a broad portfolio of quantitative research achievements and a twenty-year career evaluating juvenile-prevention programs.

What Dr. Greenwood has produced is both rigorous and hopeful. The prescription for quality control that emerges from this study is careful attention to the replication of proven programs. With the accumulation of so many claims of effective programming, there is no substitute for reading the fine print in evaluating programs that work. Many of the most attractively packaged prevention programs don't meet scientific standards. Dr. Greenwood shows two distinct threats to proven-program adoption even in an age of scientific sophistication: copycat programs that may look like proven successes but may not work like them, and politically popular programs that persist as hardy perennials in prevention despite proven failure.

The first five chapters in this book provide a structure to material that has become familiar to prevention professionals. The last three chapters push into unfamiliar territory. Here the task is to outline a political economy of prevention programming in U.S. government. When and how can cost-effectiveness calculations move beyond sloganeering and help make choices in program policy? Where in government should most prevention programs be located and why? How can long-term programs for crime prevention ever compete with short-acting crime countermeasures? What kinds of prevention and intervention programs should be kept out of American juvenile courts and what kinds are necessary to the effective mission of the court in delinquency cases? These are all questions that have not yet been raised in the literature on prevention, and the field is better by far now that the governance of prevention has been addressed.

This book addresses a topic that lacks the well-defined borders of the first two ventures. Because Peter Greenwood's topic is vast, his treatment of it by necessity must be less comprehensive. There are hundreds of different types of prevention programs and any complete taxonomy would more resemble an encyclopedia than a monograph. But we anticipate that this is the first of many books on its topic, and expect there to be a much larger volume of future literature on prevention than on mentally ill juveniles or adolescent sex offenders.

So Peter Greenwood's mission is to stake out new territory, to inspire and to provoke a systematic literature on prevention.

Franklin E. Zimring

Acknowledgments

I have benefited from the help of many individuals and organizations in my coming to write this book. I would not have become interested in juvenile-crime prevention in the first place without experiencing the commitment and enthusiasm of juvenile-court judges Bill Gladstone and Sy Gelber in Miami.

The MacArthur Foundation Juvenile Justice Network provided the opportunity and financial support for my writing the book. Frank Zimring, chair of the Network's editorial board, has been a supportive mentor, astute guide, and challenging collaborator for much of my work on juvenile-justice issues over the past twenty-five years.

At RAND, the late Peter Rydell taught me how the methods of cost-effectiveness modeling could be applied to sentencing. The late Al Williams provided the funding to get the work started. Research grants from the Robert Wood Johnson, W. T. Grant, Smith Richardson and Culpepper Foundations provided the support required to develop the techniques of cost-benefit analysis more fully and to apply them to a variety of policy issues.

The investment possibilities presented in this book would not exist without the work of the therapists, scholars, researchers, and trainers who have developed the proven programs, and the techniques for transporting them to new locations. Jim Alexander, David Olds, Patti Chamberlin, and Scott Henggler have all been particularly helpful in sharing and explaining their work.

The attempt to describe the advantages of the best programs over those less proven relies heavily on the work of such individuals and organizations as Del Elliot and his Blueprints project; Steve Aos and his colleagues, who conduct the cost-benefit studies at the Washington State Institute for Public Policy; Marc Cohen's work in calculating the costs of crime; and Mark Lipsey's many meta-analyses of juvenile intervention programs.

Over the past few years Bob Burton, Pete Ranalli, and many other wonderful folks at VisionQuest have provided me with the opportunity to put what I preach into practice. I am grateful for all of their support and assistance in assembling and organizing the material presented in this book.

Part 1

The Nature and Effectiveness of Crime Prevention

Chapter 1

Delinquency Prevention as Crime Control

One of the most robust and consistent findings in criminological research is the connection between juvenile and adult crime. Almost all serious or chronic adult offenders have extensive juvenile records. The seriousness and extent of the juvenile record is one of the strongest risk factors for future criminality. So is arrest at an early age. A very high proportion of incarcerated felons were earlier in their lives placed by a juvenile court in what were meant to be therapeutic programs charged with the responsibility of looking out for their welfare, as well the safety of the community.

Each year more than 150,000 juvenile offenders are ordered into out-of-home placements at costs sometimes exceeding $300 per day. Several times that number are being "supervised" and provided with services in the community by agents of the juvenile court. Over the past decade state and local governments have also expended hundreds of millions of dollars on delinquency-prevention programs that promised to decrease the likelihood of its participants engaging in serious crime.

What have these expenditures bought us? Are we significantly safer than we would have been had they never been made? Is the juvenile-crime-prevention sector focused on improved results and driven by research findings, so that its improved performance is rewarded with increased funding? Or is it part of the local "pork barrel" system that rewards political connections more than merit?

For the past few decades the issue of violent street crime and what to do about it has been a dominant factor in national, state, and local politics. When concerns about the rising tide of violent crime first surfaced in the mid-1980s there were not any scientifically validated strategies or programs for dealing with it. Politicians almost universally fell back on the old tried and true approaches of passing tougher sentencing laws, for both juveniles and adults; building more prisons; and hiring more police. The Federal Crime Bill of 1994 supported all three of these approaches while the funding for prevention that was proposed in early drafts of the bill was completely cut out.

In recent years both the violent and property crime rates have dropped to historic lows. Although many public officials have tried to make the case that their tougher sentencing policies were responsible for the decline, comparisons across states and specifically targeted populations have shown that tougher sentencing was not the primary cause of the decline and accounted for only about one-fourth of the decline (Zimring et al., 2001; Greenwood & Hawken, 2001; Spellman, 2000).

As crime rates fell, researchers made considerable progress in identifying the connections between specific risk factors and criminal behavior. At the same time, program developers were busy developing and testing a wide array of intervention approaches, some more empirically grounded than others. The result at long last has been the demonstrated effectiveness of a small number of prevention models that appear to reduce crime much more cost effectively than any of the other approaches that have been tried—including tougher sentencing. The goal of this book is to describe the most promising of these prevention approaches, how they were developed, the quality of the evidence in support of their claimed effectiveness, the public policy problems involved in bringing them into wider use, and the potential for investments in developmental research to increase the range and quality of effective programs.

In theory, the adoption of any public policy or program for the purpose of reducing crime can be thought of as prevention. In practice, however, most discussions of crime-reduction strategies distinguish prevention from what are thought to be more direct means of crime control such as deterrence, incapacitation, rehabilitation, and increased security efforts. Delinquency prevention is generally characterized as a collection of theories and intervention techniques that attempt to redirect the life course of youth away from crime and toward more socially accepted behavioral norms.

Delinquency-prevention efforts in the United States date back more than 150 years, since the founding of the first reformatories and the New York House of Refuge in the 1820s. Over the years, new concepts and strategies have regularly emerged in this field and continue to do so today, though often without either a sound theoretical base or strong empirical evidence of their effectiveness. The conceptual bases for delinquency-prevention efforts have shifted over time. Starting with the cultural- and class-based theories of the early nineteenth century, they moved on to the more economically and psychologically based opportunity and control theories in the 1960s and 1970s. At the turn of the twenty-first century, the designs for delinquency-prevention programs sometimes reflect recent findings from social learning and developmental sciences, but they are also heavily influenced by the politically trendy concepts of the day.

Today, there is a growing disjunction between delinquency-prevention practice and the rapidly accumulating knowledge about patterns of delinquent behavior. Rarely have prevention efforts been framed in our understanding of the life-course trajectory of antisocial behavior and of the stages of child and adolescent development that contribute to the onset and persistence of delinquent behavior. The prevention field has also failed to integrate accumulating knowledge about the processes of desistance from antisocial behavior at each stage of development, which might be utilized in prevention programs to hasten the termination of delinquent careers. Instead, current prevention theory and practice reflects a vigorous but undisciplined marketplace of competing ideas, often without sound foundations in either theory or research.

There is general agreement among many policymakers and the wider public that delinquency and crime prevention are important activities, but there is little agreement concerning which agencies of government should direct them, or what these efforts should consist of, or how they should be run. Crime prevention is a field that cries out for rigorous definitions and precision in its terminology, especially at a time when simplistic sound bites and slogans prevail. It is a field in which rigorous evaluation is absolutely essential but rarely applied.

This book seeks to accomplish three tasks. The first is to define the key terms and organizational structures that are needed to support and advance the development and dissemination of effective prevention strategies and programs. The second is to carefully evaluate and organize the evidence for what works. The third is to identify key linkages between the accumulated body of evidence and public policy, both where it is now and where it should be headed in the future.

Prevention Defined

This book is about delinquency prevention—reducing the likelihood that young people will become delinquent or adult criminals. The word *prevention* is defined as "the act of preventing." To prevent something is "to act in anticipation of the event," "to keep it from happening," "to hinder," "to make impossible," or "to put some obstacle in the way." Prevention activities are undertaken with the aim of reducing the frequency or likelihood of particular undesirable events or situations from happening. Delinquency prevention shares a good deal of common turf with the related goals of crime prevention, violence prevention, and injury prevention.

Delinquency prevention involves reducing individual, long-term proclivities toward crime and violence, and is usually targeted at those youth or families that appear to be at elevated risk for participation in delinquent behavior. In attempting to redirect the life-course trajectory of delinquent youth away from crime, it differs from other crime-prevention strategies that aim to make particular crimes more difficult to successfully complete, through security measures (target hardening), changing the environment (street lighting, road barriers, etc.), or extra police attention. Violence-prevention strategies include both changing lives and altering the environment, but also include efforts to limit, reduce, or neutralize the agents of violence, which are usually identified as guns, alcohol, and illegal drugs. This perspective has led to efforts by the public health community to promote gun control, gun safety, and restrictions on alcohol outlets in high-crime neighborhoods. In the world of public health, violence-prevention efforts are seen as a subset of the larger field of injury prevention, which includes both deaths by homicide or suicide

In this book I restrict the definition of "prevention" to focus attention on those interventions that attempt to change the antisocial proclivity or life-course trajectory of individually targeted youth. I do not devote much space to other types of prevention, such as those that involve altering the environment (better lighting), improved security practices (use of metal detectors, better locks), or reducing access to such high-risk agents as guns or drugs. I show that the narrower focus is justified on the grounds that the life-course approach, when successful, appears to be far more effective than those other strategies, both because of its leveraged position at the start of the criminal career and because its effects are not usually negated or discounted by the replacement and displacement effects that occur with many other crime-control strategies.

What Kinds of Criminal Behavior Do We Most Want to Prevent?

All delinquent acts are not alike in their impact on the community or in what they have to say about the character of their perpetrator(s). In terms of community impact, there is a major distinction between crimes against the person and property crimes. The risk of being killed or seriously injured is many times greater in a robbery or aggravated assault than in a burglary, even when the victims are home at the time of the crime (Zimring & Hawkins, 1997). Studies of victim pain and suffering show that the costs associated with violent crimes are orders of magnitude greater than the costs of property crimes (Miller et al., 1996). Longitudinal studies have shown that there appears to be a pattern of progression in seriousness among delinquent youth, where the first offenses are minor property crimes. The more crimes a youth commits the more likely he is to escalate up to more serious property crimes and crimes of violence (Elliot et al., 1989; Tolan & Gorman-Smith, 1998). Thus a youth who commits a violent crime is much more likely to commit another than a youth whose record is clean. Therefore, the youth most at risk for future violent behavior include those already engaged in violence as well those at very high risk of chronic delinquency.

Although many of the programs and strategies this book reviews can be applied to a wide variety of deviant social behavior, I pay particular attention to how well they work in preventing criminal violence, particularly lethal criminal violence.

My focus is on programs that might change the life-course trajectories of those chronic youthful offenders who usually start young, account for a small fraction of those identified as delinquent by the police, but account for a majority of the crimes committed by their age group. Because the cost effectiveness of any program is heavily dependent on the risk level of its clients, it is important to understand the degree of accuracy with which we can predict trajectories for particular types of youth. Are those identified as high risk likely to commit many more offenses than their less-risky cohorts, or just a bit more?

Prevention and Government

One of the issues the book confronts in attempting to think about how delinquency-prevention programs should be stimulated, developed, operated, and monitored is the huge overlap in intentions and effect between prevention and education. Virtually everything the government does for youth is preventive in intention, although not always in effect. Prenatal healthcare, well-baby checkups, immunizations, home-visitation programs, and HeadStart are all programs designed to improve the well being and educational attainment of youth. And in doing so, they prevent a cluster of childhood problems including disease, abuse and neglect, malnutrition, learning problems, and conduct disorder. Since educational attainment and educational readiness appear to be so central to the healthy development of young people, determining where the preventive efforts of government leave off and the educational efforts begin is no easy task.

It may be that the distinction between education and delinquency-prevention activities is not one we are forced to make. Perhaps any activity that is part of the regular education curriculum can be considered educational, while those activities that get added on to help cope with the problems and challenges faced by high-risk youth can be though of as preventive. The problem with this simple distinction is that the best approaches to teaching and delinquency prevention in the schools have much in common between them. If we only count the benefits of programs on one side of the education/prevention ledger, we will ignore the significant contribution these "best practices" can make to improving the lives of children and their community.

This book represents a serious effort to provide the kind of interpretive and integrative structure that allows the kinds of discussions and developments that need to take place for the prevention field to prosper while becoming both accountable and coherently located in a larger government youth policy. At present, delinquency prevention is a subfield that suffers from a lack of definitions of its key terms. It also lacks a common language that allows representatives of law enforcement, juvenile justice, education, mental health, academics, and other professions to share their individual perspectives while working toward common solutions. Furthermore, it lacks an organizational structure that can effectively synthesize and integrate the efforts of these diverse groups. Finally, it lacks a rigorous evaluation of what we know and what we need to find out about the impacts of programs on high-risk youth. Filling these gaps is the ambition of this book.

The book is divided into two parts and eight chapters. The first part concerns the nature and impact of prevention programs; the second part concerns the many issues encountered when attempting to make prevention activities a part of American government. The first five chapters of the book are my attempt to survey the field of delinquency prevention as it is normally understood. In this first chapter I have introduced the concept of "prevention" and provided a map of the coverage of this effort. Chapter 2 provides a brief intellectual history of delinquency-prevention priorities and strategies. Chapter 3 details the building blocks of program evaluation. Chapters 4 provides a profile of effective programs while chapter 5 describes a number of ineffective programs and the reasons they nevertheless appear to thrive in the competition for scarce resources.

This analysis does not cover a number of specialized programs that do not target delinquent youth yet can still play important roles in personal development and crime prevention. Programs that provide job training and enhanced economic opportunity are very important but involve different strategies of development, evaluation, and dissemination than I cover here. Therapeutic programs for defined childhood or adolescent psychological problems are also beyond the scope of this undertaking, as are specialized treatment programs for juvenile sex offenders.

All of the topics covered in this book's first part have been addressed in professional and scholarly literature. The questions reviewed in part two have not received much attention in the prevention literature. Chapter 6 discusses how the concepts of cost effectiveness and cost-benefit analysis interact with questions of valuing the effects of prevention programs.

Chapter 7 addresses the issue regarding where in the government responsibility for delinquency prevention is most appropriately be lodged. Chapter 8 addresses the role of the juvenile court in treatment and prevention programs.

Chapter 2

The Evolution of an Idea

This chapter provides a brief intellectual history of key developments in delinquency-prevention concepts. In the first section, I locate the term *delinquency prevention* in the context of the extensive vocabulary used to describe governmental responses to crime. The second section traces the main ideas about delinquency prevention as they have evolved since a prevention-oriented juvenile court was first established.

Boundaries and Content

"Prevention" appears to be a fairly straightforward concept: efforts meant to stop some event or situation from happening. Less clear are the boundaries that are set to limit the concept's reach. A broad definition sacrifices focus, for it includes every kind of activity that might affect the future. A narrow definition, however, may exclude efforts at prevention that are policy relevant.

The field of delinquency prevention occupies the intersection of two overlapping spheres of public policy: crime control and youth development. It is a favored topic in neither, which goes a long way toward explaining why it is often treated like a political football rather than with the serious attention it deserves. Let's turn to the crime-control sphere first.

Concerns about crime occur in two different dimensions, as illustrated by the rows in table 2.1: the past and the future. One dimension is purely reactive and focuses on crime that has already occurred. Identifying and punishing the offender, assisting the victim, restoring order and peace to the community, and assigning blame for any lapses in security that allowed the crime to take place—all are aspects of this reactive approach. Traditional law enforcement investigation and prosecution efforts are largely focused

Table 2.1. **Types of response to crime**

Type of response	Level of focus	
	Environment or system	Individual
Reaction	Anger	Vengeance
	Blame	Punishment
	Fear	Restitution
	Flight	
	Restoration	
Anticipation	Increase security	Incapacitation
	Defensible space	Intervention
	Deterrence	
	Public health approach	

on this dimension, as are the more recently developed programs in "balanced and restorative justice" (Braithwaite, 1989).

The other dimension is anticipatory and proactive, and focuses on the future in the attempt to prevent or ameliorate crimes before they occur. All efforts to prevent crime fall within this latter category, but within it there is a broad array of different strategies and mechanisms. Some focus on the physical and social environment in which the crime might be committed, as indicated in the lower-left cell in table 2.1. Some involve direct investments in security systems or devices including locks, guards, and surveillance equipment or alarm systems. Others involve more indirect investments in making the environment safer, such as improved lighting, changing traffic patterns to make escapes more difficult, or removing shrubs and other obstructions where predators might hide (Clark, 1995; Taylor, 2002). The law-enforcement approach is to increase the likelihood of arrest and severity of penalties so that potential offenders will be deterred. The public-health approach to the prevention of violent crimes restricts access to alcohol, for example, which can increase the likelihood of a crime's taking place, or to guns, which increase the chances of a crime's being lethal (Mercy & O'Carrol, 1988).

Approaches that focus on preventing crimes by high-risk individuals include incapacitation and interventions. Incapacitation amounts to restrictive custody that effectively removes the offender from the community. Effective interventions, on the other hand, make individuals less likely to engage in crime in the first place. Following the public-health model, preventive interventions can be primary, focusing on the general population; secondary, focusing on those at higher risk; or tertiary, focusing on those who have already committed crimes. These interventions may be used for either adults or juveniles, or for both.

The narrow focus in this book is on those programs that provide preventive interventions for juveniles, whether in primary, secondary, or tertiary settings. I later justify this approach when discussing the issue of cost effectiveness. That discussion shows that a few, well-developed secondary and tertiary delinquency-prevention programs are far more cost effective, at current levels of funding, than any other crime-control strategy.

The two dimensions—reactive responses to past events on the one hand and, on the other, anticipatory proaction in view of possible future events—are important to distinguish because they often overlap. Some activities, such as long mandatory sentences, can help meet goals in both dimensions at the same time. One of the reasons that long mandatory sentences are so popular with elected officials is that they allow them to claim they are increasing the punishment of criminals while reducing the crime rate, through incapacitation and deterrence as well. A delinquency-prevention program that trains parents in techniques for monitoring and disciplining their children may be much more cost effective than mandatory sentences in preventing crime, but it does not provide the collateral benefits of punishment that appear often to be equally valued by society.

Within the policy sphere of youth development, delinquency prevention must vie for attention among all the other programs designed to benefit juvenile development. At the same time, it must deal with the array of problems that can interfere with its mission. Education, special education, healthcare, mental health, foster care, and welfare are the eight-hundred-pound gorillas in this particular policy sphere. Problem behaviors that are the focus of significant prevention funding and activity include school dropout, teen pregnancy, substance abuse, teen smoking, and delinquency. Not surprisingly, all these problem behaviors share a common set of antecedent risk factors (Elliot et al., 1989), and most can be ameliorated by similar types of interventions. But the devil is always in the details: whether a particular intervention designed to improve school performance will also reduce delinquency depends on what it contains, who it excludes, and what efforts are made to tailor its delivery to meet the needs of those particularly at risk for delinquency.

The evolution of delinquency-prevention policy and practice reflects changing perspectives and developments in both the crime-control and youth-development spheres. Again not surprisingly, policies and programs for dealing with serious delinquents have been most influenced by trends in criminal sentencing and corrections. Programs that attend to the needs and risk factors associated with younger children reflect more of the findings and trends in the youth-development field.

Education, health, and general welfare programs also attempt to change the life-course trajectory of juveniles in regard to other outcomes such as educational attainment, social development, and future income. For purposes of this analysis, I consider programs or activities to be attempts at delinquency prevention if crime prevention is a major purpose, and delinquency prevention per se if they do in fact have a significant crime-prevention effect. David Olds's Nurse Home Visiting Program was not initially designed as a delinquency-prevention program, but evaluations have shown that it has such effects (Olds, 1996; Karoly et al., 1998). The same holds true for the Perry Preschool Program (Schweinhart et al., 1993), the Syracuse Family Development Project (Lally et al., 1988), and Project PATHE (Gottfredson et al., 2002). Programs designed to better prepare disadvantaged children for entering elementary school, improve the care they receive, or improve school discipline and performance also have the effect of reducing delinquency. On the other hand, the Los Angeles Police Department's program Drug Awareness Resistance Education (DARE) was designed and marketed as a delinquency- and drug-prevention program, but evaluations have shown that it is clearly not effective (Sherman et al., 1997).

The last issue to be addressed in setting the boundaries of delinquency prevention asks who and what should reasonably be included. Are drug-treatment or education programs for inmates in prison still considered prevention? If not, how about for juveniles in training schools? Suppose they are in a group home? The three levels of prevention recognized by public health officials—primary, secondary, and tertiary—cover universal, at-risk, and involved populations. We could understand tertiary prevention to apply to youth in training schools, where the goal is to prevent their returning after being released. If we include work with institutionalized populations within our definition of prevention, however, it might overshadow the many other approaches for prevention, because institutionalized populations now consume the lion's share of resources devoted to dealing with delinquency in this population.

Let's assume we want to leave room, after prevention, for another form of response to delinquency—whether it be called "treatment," "intervention," or more classically, "rehabilitation." Where should the dividing line be placed? At first arrest? At first adjudication? At first placement? If the primary goal of delinquency prevention is reducing the costs of future crime (harm reduction), then seventeen-year-old serious and chronic offenders must be legitimate targets, because they represent the greatest threat of future criminal harm of any population group. One public-health view of the distinction between prevention and treatment holds that prevention intervenes before the three critical components discussed above come together. Treatment begins after they have coincided (Tolan, 2002; Dyal, 1995). According to Tolan, "From this perspective, prevention is limited to actions intended to prevent the onset of criminal activity in individuals." "Under this definition, most legal procedures and punishment-based actions should not be considered prevention. In essence, prevention works to block the formation of a pattern of delinquent activity among at-risk youth or in high crime locations" (Tolan, 2002). This definition of prevention would exclude our seventeen-year-old chronic offender as a potential target. In the field of injury prevention, however, the term prevention is used to refer to efforts to reduce the risk or severity of injury. This definition would clearly include our young offender. In injury prevention, treatment refers to post-event efforts to ameliorate the effects of an injury after it has occurred (Institute of Medicine, 1999).

The reason why it is difficult to distinguish between prevention and treatment in dealing with delinquency is that youth who have been delinquent in the past are the most likely to be delinquent in the future. If we think about treatment as dealing with the results of a crime, then treatment is something that is done for victims and injured communities, and looks a lot like restorative justice. Interventions that occur with juvenile delinquents after prevention has failed are oriented more toward immediate control rather than treatment. Later in this chapter I argue that institutions designed to handle delinquent youth invariably end up focusing on behavioral control. Table 2.2 lists a number of factors that help distinguish between efforts at prevention and those that are more properly understood to be directed at control.

Reflection on the factors listed in table 2.2 suggests a dividing line between prevention and more intensive forms of control interventions. Programs and services that engage youth and families voluntarily in their homes or other community settings for the purpose of reducing risk factors associated with delinquency can appropriately be categorized as delinquency prevention, no matter what the prior record of the participants. A youth placed in a close-custody institution in response to criminal acts may be receiving preventive services and treatment, but their effectiveness is usually secondary to that of the institution's need to maintain control.

Table 2.2. **Factors that distinguish between prevention and control**

	Prevention	Control
Setting	Home or community	Institution
Participation	Voluntary	Coerced / Required
Approach	Supportive, informative, empowering	Directive, disciplinary
Environment	Natural setting	Artificial, contrived
Affect	Flexible, adaptive	Authoritarian, rigid
Primary goal	Improved functioning	Control of individuals
Organizations providing	Public health, CBOs, social work, volunteers	Prisons, jails, training schools, institutions
Sponsorship	Public health, mental health, schools	Criminal and juvenile justice
Time frame	Long term	Short term

History and Evolution of Prevention Practice

Interest in preventive approaches to juvenile delinquency date back to the early nineteenth century. This interest spread with the establishment of the Juvenile Court at the beginning of the twentieth century, with the efforts at community development during the 1930s, with the establishment of the Office of Juvenile Justice and Delinquency Prevention during the 1970s, and finally with the surge in more scientifically rigorous delinquency research of the past two decades. Throughout this development, the attractiveness of various prevention strategies has cycled in and out of favor, in a somewhat predictable and reactive fashion. At the beginning of each new cycle, initial optimism about a new or rediscovered approach gives way to pessimism and outright opposition as the evidence for its effectiveness fails to live up to initial expectations. Orphanages, reform schools, rural camps, family group homes, deinstitutionalization, diversion, boot camps, and the DARE program mentioned above have all followed this pattern.

There have been four primary approaches to intervening with at-risk youth. One is to focus directly on individual juveniles—on altering their behavior, attitudes, beliefs, tastes, skills, thinking processes, and anything else that might contribute toward their delinquency. The problem with this approach is that outside authorities or intervenors have little influence over a youth unless a trusting relationship develops between them or they are in a close custody environment. But maintaining custody as a condition of intervention is very expensive, and the results do not appear to last long. Effective mentoring programs for low-risk youth, however, like that provided by Big Brothers and Big Sisters, do seem to provide a helpful structure for developing and protecting the necessary special relationships, and are cost effective as a result.

The second approach is to focus on the parents or guardians who provide the primary care and supervision for the youth. Jerry Patterson (1982) and others (Alexander, 1988) have shown that the families of disruptive and acting-out juveniles are strongly motivated to help them change their behavior but often do not have the skills or knowledge to do so. Working with the family to help them acquire the necessary skills and knowledge creates greater receptivity for the intervention on the part of the client, and the state does not have to pick up the tab for maintaining custody of the youth. Family-based interventions have turned out to be the most cost effective way to work with at-risk and acting-out youth (Aos et al., 2001).

The third approach to delinquency prevention is through the schools. Schools already have custody of youth for large parts of the day and are already in the business of helping them control their behavior and thinking processes. Delinquency-prevention efforts would therefore seem to be a natural extension of the educational function were it not for the fact that most schools have a difficult time carrying out their primary educational role as it is. Moreover, some effective prevention efforts that do take place in schools, such as substance awareness and resistance skill training, require extra resources or special instructors to be effective. However some involve changes in policies and practices that improve instructional effectiveness and academic attainment as well.

The fourth approach is to work toward changing the community or neighborhood in which the youth resides: to decrease crime and drug use while increasing supportive services (schools, healthcare, etc.) and opportunities for recreation or legitimate employment (community action), to get more adults involved in supervising adolescents (collective efficacy), or to change counterproductive or ineffective government policies (community mobilization and advocacy).

Whichever approach is currently in vogue—what grant seekers call "the flavor of the month"—those pursuing the other approaches tend to be disparaged or ignored, and yet are well positioned to be "rediscovered" after the currently fashionable approach loses its popularity.

Here is how delinquency prevention evolves. The first issue raised when authorities discover that a child lacks effective parents or guardians is to find some suitable placement. The best way to provide one is to create a shelter, which eventually becomes a Hall, Center, Institute, Camp, Ranch, or special school. A few of these "reform" institutions appear to be effective, have supportive champions, and may even slightly reduce recidivism rates (Greenwood & Turner, 1993). Most of these institutions, however, will become authoritarian "total institutions," with limited programming and reliance on locked rooms and special disciplinary units for controlling youth. Some will become corrupt to the point of abusing residents as part of their regular discipline or training procedures.

In a free society, institutionalization of any troublesome population eventually leads to demands for their deinstitutionalization. There is always some staff who will abuse the kids. There are always some administrators who let things get out of hand. Recidivism rates are found to be high. The notion of training schools and detention centers serving as "schools for crime" begins to make sense. In the delinquency field, one of the milestones along this path occurred in the first half of the nineteenth century, when critics turned against the New York Houses of Refuge within just a few years after it opened and called for the adoption of "family reform schools" like those being used in Europe (Schlossman, 1977). Another milestone was when Dr. Jerome Miller, the newly appointed head of the Massachusetts Department of Youth Services, ordered all youth in Massachusetts training schools removed and placed in more suitable, community-based programs., even though he did not have the power to close the institutions are get rid of any staff.

As soon as you start placing youth back in any high-risk neighborhood, you become aware of how poorly managed are the public services (such as schools and transportation) in that area. This observation may lead to the conclusion that the youth need enhanced services (afterschool programs, vocational training, etc.), or better yet, that the neighborhood as a whole needs special attention. The first observation gives rise to efforts directed at assessing risk and protective factors, assessing services to meet critical needs, and enhancing case management and coordination. The latter observation prompts calls for community action or some other task-force approach.

Eventually you are brought back to the decision that initiated this cycle, and you reconsider whether the "family"—as it is now or as it might be with some intervention—is the best place for the child. The interventions that appear most cost effective today, in preventing crime and other problem behaviors, are all family-based interventions that follow this logic.

Institutional Placements: Benevolent Custody or Junior Prisons?

In early colonial times, juvenile offenders were housed with adult offenders in prisons and jails, with all of the sordid consequences now associated with mixing younger offenders with older hardened criminals. The New York House of Refuge, and others like it, were created for less serious juvenile offenders in the 1820s as a preventive alternative to adult jails and poorhouses. There was at that time great optimism about the ability of education to improve individual behavior and quality of life. This reform movement was sponsored by the same people who were instrumental in simultaneous penal and educational reforms (Schlossman, 1977). The reformers hoped that the Houses of Refuge would carry out their mission by becoming exemplary educational institutions. Judges, concerned that the impoverished parents of many immigrant youth lacked the moral character and protective capacity to properly raise them, placed thousands of youth in these facilities with the aim of improving their prospects and reducing the likelihood that they would turn to crime.

By the mid-1800s, youth reformatories were no longer in favor with progressive reformers. They were seen as being too much like junior prisons, and those who supported them were thought to exaggerate their accomplishments. Less serious delinquents were still being mixed with more hardened, older juvenile offenders, and the same types of punishments and deprivations of liberty were being used to maintain overall control. Reformatories were already considered to be passé in Europe and so American reformers looked across the Atlantic for ideas about what might be tried next (Schlossman, 1977).

The new institutional model in use in Europe was the "family reform school," a much smaller facility than a reformatory, which was headed up by proxy parents. The family reform school was but the first of many successive attempts to capture the benefits of a family environment in an institutional setting. Each reincarnation was greeted with considerable optimism that a solution had been found to the recognized defects in older institutional models. The focus of the family-based models was less on educational progress than improving relationships among family members. The Massachusetts Industrial School for girls was one of the first institutions to adopt this model in the United States in the 1850s. At this time there was great optimism regarding the ability of phrenological psychology to manipulate "benevolent affections" to achieve "normal" emotional and mental adolescent development (Schlossman, 1977).

For young urban children who were not necessarily delinquent, but who were deemed by the courts to be in need of more adequate care and supervision, removal to foster families in more "healthful" rural settings became the intervention of choice. In the late nineteenth century, more than fifty thousand children were removed by "orphan trains" from New York City to more rural settings (Grossberg, 2002).

Although progressive reformers may have lost faith in training schools and similar types of custodial institutions for preventing delinquents from graduating to adult criminal careers, these institutions have continued to thrive and still account for the largest proportion of the funding available for working with delinquent youth.

Progressives and the Juvenile Court

The next major innovation in policy and practice for dealing with at-risk and delinquent youth was the establishment of the juvenile court at the beginning of the twentieth century. The first juvenile court in Chicago was founded in 1899 as a specialized institution for dealing with dependent, neglected, and delinquent minors. At that time, American cities were flooded with poor immigrants from Europe, whose values, behavior, and child-rearing practices were alien and frightening to middle-class moralists. They represented a challenge to the progressives, who took the lead in developing the new court (Empey, 1979).

The original guiding principle of the juvenile court was parens patriae, a medieval English doctrine that allowed the Crown to supplant natural family relations whenever a child's welfare was at stake—in other words, to become a substitute parent. The procedures of the court were purposefully informal and its intentions were presumed to be benign. Factfinding focused on the minor's underlying problems and special needs rather than the specific acts that brought him or her before the court. Dispositions were intended to reflect the "best interests" of the child, which were assumed to be the same as the public's (Tanenhaus, 2002).

The new court represented one aspect of a broad progressive movement to accommodate urban institutions to an increasingly immigrant population and to incorporate recent discoveries in the behavioral, social, and medical sciences into the rearing of children. The court was also a reflection of the philosophical movement of pragmatism, described as the "revolt against formalism." The new juvenile procedures reflected the ultimate pragmatic philosophy: "It's all right if it works."

Another innovative feature of the juvenile court was the appointment of juvenile probation officers to supervise youth in the community and to seek suitable placements when they were required. The concept of juvenile probation had been developed in Massachusetts after the Civil War, but it did not spread throughout the country until the states established their own juvenile courts.

During the decades after its establishment, the efforts of the juvenile court were supported by other government initiatives dealing with families and youth. In 1909, President Theodore Roosevelt presided over the first White House Conference on Dependent Children. In 1911, states first enacted laws providing for "mothers pensions" so that the "worthiest" of poor mothers would be able to keep their children at home rather than placing them in public orphanages. In part this reform was supported because it was a cost-effective alternative to increasing the number of juvenile institutions (Grossberg, 2002). The spread of compulsory education and child-labor laws were getting children off the streets, out of the workplace, and into schools.

In 1912, the federal Children's Bureau was formed and charged with the task of collecting data on the well-being of children. The Sheppard-Towner Act, passed in 1921, authorized matching grants to states to fund information and instruction on nutrition and hygiene, prenatal and child-health clinics, and visiting nurses for pregnant women and new mothers. Prevention was a primary motivating factor. This latter reform was vigorously opposed by the American Medical Association as an infringement on its turf and was repealed by Congress in 1929. Passage of the Social Security Act of 1935 included Aid to Families with Dependent Children (AFDC), which included fiscal incentives to care for troubled children in their own homes or private placements. Throughout these early decades, juvenile courts continued to function pretty much unchanged..

Although many progressive thinkers remained skeptical of the value of reform schools in curbing delinquency, there were periodic resurgences of optimism, such as when California's reform-minded Governor Hiram Johnson brought in Fred Nelles, an idealistic young Canadian businessman, to revitalize the Whittier School in 1912. Most of the original staff was replaced and the facility was completely remodeled to support its new therapeutic goals. Brutal punishments and make-work assignments were replaced by state-of-the-art educational and vocational training programs. Youth who were found to be mentally deficient and not amenable to treatment were transferred out and courts were encouraged to send predelinquents before they became established in criminal careers (Schlossman, 1983).

Throughout this period, a number of individuals contributed new concepts and research findings to the science of delinquency prevention. Feeble-mindedness and other inherited mental deficiencies were still seen as the leading cause of delinquency. The kinds of research being carried out in the more progressive reform schools of California and Ohio were designed to identify and screen out youth who could not be helped because they were mentally defective, and to identify the causes of predelinquency in the remaining youth, so that they could be cured.

Henry Goddard evolved from a leading proponent of the eugenicist view, during his time of service in New Jersey training schools, to one concerned with environmental causes of delinquency, when he worked in Ohio. During his twenty-five years as director of the Judge Baker Foundation in Boston, William Healy conducted studies leading him to conclude that the causes of delinquency were complex and varied from case to case. His prevention approach focused on treating "sick children" in the controlled environment of the psychological clinic.

Focus on Communities and Neighborhoods

All of the preventive innovations described above focus on the child and the family as the primary locus of intervention. Concurrent with these developments, however, and somewhat in reaction to the heavy-handedness of the juvenile court, was a growing appreciation for the role that neighborhoods might play in promoting or retarding the spread of delinquency. Benjamin Lindsey, the world-renowned judge of the juvenile court in Denver, viewed crime and its prevention as a communitywide responsibility and not the exclusive concern of courts and police. Lindsey sounded like a proponent of the modern multisystemic approach when he told a meeting of the National Education Association in 1909 that "[a]ll the courts or probation schemes on earth can never effectively correct the faults of the child as long as there remain the faults of those who deal with children in the home, schools, in neighborhoods—in the community itself."

Thomas Elliot, who conducted surveys for the National Probation Association, was another researcher who argued for keeping delinquent youth out of the juvenile justice system, and for expanding the competency and capacity of the educational system to provide for their socialization. From his studies of gang life in New York, Frederic Thrasher emphasized the need for coordinated professional social service agencies to meet the needs of slum youth.

Clifford Shaw and Henry McKay began studying the distribution of delinquent areas in Chicago in the 1920s, finding that rates of delinquency were highest in areas that exhibited the most "social disorganization"— high rates of poverty, ethnic heterogeneity, and residential mobility (Shaw & McKay, 1931, 1942). The outgrowth of this effort was the Chicago Area Project (CAP), a group of community-based organizations designed by indigenous community members that attempted to identify and address the community-level problems that were contributing to delinquency (Laub, 2002).

The Russell Square neighborhood in South Chicago, a community of recent Catholic immigrants, became the focus of the project. The strategy adopted by CAP was to train local leaders and volunteers to intervene on behalf of delinquent youth with the more formal agencies of social control—schools, police, probation, and parole. Unlike preceding reformers who assumed that delinquent youth were feeble-minded or otherwise mentally impaired, CAP operated from the premise that youth were simply inadequately socialized.

Shaw moved slowly in developing the project. He recognized that he had to win the support of key stakeholders in the community and give them a voice in designing the program. The development of this support had to be nurtured slowly, but it eventually was understood to be crucial for the project's continued existence. For many local participants, CAP came to be seen as an appendage of St. Michael's Church (Schlossman et al., 1984).

The CAP developed afterschool recreation programs and built weekend camping facilities to attract the participation of youth; volunteers developed contacts with all youth that had any contact with the police. Volunteers were trained to provide "curbside counseling" to gang-involved youth. They were also trained to act as mediators for neighborhood youth who were having troubles in school or who became involved with the police, were on probation, or were paroled. In this latter capacity, CAP developed an ambitious version of what we would today call a "reentry program." It kept track of all local youth sentenced to Illinois corrections facilities and maintained contact with the youth and their families. CAP interceded with the parole board to help set the conditions of release and worked with youth after they returned to the community to help them get back in school or acquire jobs.

Although CAP was undeniably a success in building an indigenous structure, fostering local leadership, eliciting widespread community support, and altering the way in which youth-serving agencies dealt with the neighborhood, knowledge about or reference to the lessons of CAP is almost totally lacking among those attempting to deal with delinquency at the community level today. Shaw's assessment of the project in 1944 was decidedly optimistic, however he recognized the statistical difficulties in attributing any decline in crime rates to the project. He chose specifically to downplay objective data showing a two-thirds decline in reported delinquency rates in the target area, even though comparison areas showed no similar decline (Schlossman et al., 1984).

Great Society Programs

By the 1960s, delinquency theorists were moving beyond the simple individual-deficit models that had been developed in previous decades to explain delinquency. New theories were developed that emphasized differences in opportunities (Cloward & Ohlin, 1960) and differential association with delinquent peers (Sutherland & Cressy, 1955). Delinquency was no longer seen as something inherent in individual character; rather it was something that risk-prone youth could catch from their exposure to others or could develop because of a lack of protective opportunities for advancement. The war on poverty that was central to President Johnson's Great Society had started out in Attorney General Robert Kennedy's office as a delinquency-prevention program. Its primary strategies included the improvement of education and opportunity structures, the reduction of poverty, and the general empowerment of impoverished communities (Edelman, 2002).

Diversion and Deinstitutionalization as Prevention Strategies

Frank Zimring (2002) reminds us that the original juvenile court had two rationales: one diversionary, the other interventionist. Many thought that the primary purpose of the juvenile court was to divert children away from the harmful effects of criminal court involvement—stigma, association with hardened criminals, exploitation by adults, and so on. Others, including many judges, thought the court's primary goal was to turn delinquents' lives around for the better. The first aim is relatively simple. The latter is more difficult and requires granting the courts much more power and control.

In its 1967 decision In re Gault, the Supreme Court dealt the interventionist goal of the juvenile court a serious blow by requiring the court to provide full due-process protection to accused youth and by restricting its powers of intervention over nondelinquent youth (Zimring, 2002). In Gault, the Court found that actions taken in pursuit of the interventionist goals were interfering with the diversionary goals of the court, which included the aim of minimizing harm. In the years that followed Gault, this interest in minimizing the harm done to minors by their involvement in the justice system became the primary goal of juvenile-justice reformers. "Diversion" and "deinstitutionalization" became the watchwords of the movement.

OJJDP

The Juvenile Justice and Delinquency Prevention Act of 1974 established the Office of Juvenile Justice and Delinquency Prevention (OJJDP) and charged it with pursuing two preventive/diversionary goals: removal of children from prisons and jails, and the deinstitutionalization of status offenders—children who were disobedient, truants, or runaways, but who had not committed any crimes. Millions of dollars were provided to state and local government to fund programs in support of these goals. Joan McCord used long-term, follow-up data from the Cambridge-Somerville experimental program (which provided mentors, counseling, and recreational opportunities for at-risk youth) to show that even the most benign interventions could have iatrogenic effects (1992, 1997). In 1978, a special committee of the National Research Council concluded that there was little evidence in support of deterrence effects of punishment (Blumstein et al., 1978). If deterrence and rehabilitation are both found not to work and other forms of intervention are potentially harmful, diversion and deinstitutionalization begin to look like pretty good goals.

Prevention in the 1980s and 1990s

Juvenile crime rates reached a low point in 1984 and then began to rise steadily, particularly juvenile violence. Homicide was identified as the leading cause of death for young African American males, bringing the Centers for Disease Control into the picture with its own unique approaches to injury prevention and public health. There were also increasing trends for such adolescent high-risk behaviors as drug and alcohol use, smoking, teen pregnancy, and early school dropout. Among interventionists, the search for effective prevention strategies was on. Funding for research on these problems increased considerably, including block funding to states and funding for more rigorous, large-scale longitudinal studies that tracked sample cohorts over extended periods. Both the research and policy communities had accepted the fact that some children are more predisposed to delinquency or violence than others by risk factors associated with their physiology, families, behavior, or neighborhood environment (Hawkins et al., 1998; Lipsey & Derzon, 1998).

Current theories of delinquency prevention stress the interaction among the many different risk and protective factors in the process of determining the developmental course. Prevention programs are seen to work by reducing changeable or dynamic risk factors and enhancing protective factors. For instance, malleable or changeable risk factors at the individual level associated with delinquency and violence include pregnancy and delivery complications of the mother; hyperactivity, concentration problems, restlessness, and risk taking; early initiation of violent behavior; involvement in other forms of antisocial behavior; and beliefs and attitudes favorable to deviant or antisocial behavior. Family related risk factors include living with a criminal parent, harsh discipline, physical abuse, and neglect, poor family management practices, low levels of parent involvement with the child, high levels of family conflict, parental attitudes favorable to violence and separation from the family. Other risk factors include academic failure, low commitment to schooling, truancy, early drop-out, and frequent school transitions; delinquent siblings, delinquent peers or gang membership. Community level risk factors for violence include poverty, community disorganization, availability of drugs, neighborhood adults involved in crime, and exposure to violence and racial prejudice (Lipsey & Derzon, 1998; Hawkins et al., 1998). In modern delinquency theory, interventions that reduce these risk factors for specific groups of at-risk youth should lead to lower rates of delinquency within those groups. It is the design and testing of potential interventions, and the refinement of knowledge about how these risk factors interact over the life-course development, that represent the current frontiers of delinquency-prevention research.

In the 1992 reauthorization of the Juvenile Justice and Delinquency Prevention Act of 1974, Congress added a new Title V (Incentive Grants for Local Delinquency Prevention Programs) to fund "collaborative, community-based delinquency prevention efforts" that incorporated six underlying principles: (1) community control and decisionmaking, (2) research-based planning, (3) comprehensive and multiple disciplinary solutions, (4) leverage of resources and systems, (5) evaluation, and (6) a long-term perspective (OJJDP Report to Congress 1997). The grants program was based on the risk-and protection-focused approach to delinquency prevention represented by the Communities That Care model (Hawkins & Catalano, 1992). Following that model, OJJDP provided Key Leader Orientation and Risk and Resource Assessment training for hundreds of communities. Unfortunately, the weak spot in this reinvigoration of the government's interest in delinquency prevention has been the weakness of the evaluations used to assess the programs, and therefore the limited evidence base from which to make program selections.

In 1994, the report of a National Research Council panel on youth violence concluded that there was not enough evidence to recommend any one particular strategy or approach for reducing youth violence (Reiss & Roth, 1993). This lack of evidence did not stop funds from flowing to a wide assortment of demonstration and experimental interventions. However, in addition to being poorly designed from a theoretical standpoint, most of the evaluation designs for these experimental programs were also so poorly implemented that the accumulation of new evidence on what works and what doesn't has been painfully and unnecessarily slow (Sherman et al., 1997).

Each of the perspectives noted above has produced its own approach to the delinquency- and violence-prevention problem. The more traditional criminal-justice approach has emphasized harsher penalties and intervention at all levels of behavior, from the mandatory waiver to adult courts for serious offenders to the strict enforcement of truancy and curfew laws, and zero tolerance for weapons in schools. Public-health professionals have focused on the agents of violence, primarily guns and alcohol, and emphasized public education and political action to restrict their availability to youth. Community-action proponents have encouraged foundations and government funding agencies to make substantial grants to local community and neighborhood coalitions, in the hope that they will find a way of identifying their community's risk factors and adopt effective strategies for dealing with them.

Most surprisingly, many of the more significant prevention breakthroughs have come from disciplines not primarily concerned with delinquency, crime, or violence. School reformers' experimenting with strategies to improve educational effectiveness have discovered that some of these approaches also improve outcomes for troubled youth as well (Gottfredson et al., 2002). Programs designed by pediatricians and early-childhood specialists to improve the health status or school readiness of at-risk children have also been found to decrease their involvement in delinquency. The biggest breakthroughs have come from the fields of psychology and family counseling, where researchers have developed effective techniques for teaching adolescents how to anticipate and deal with potentially negative influences from their peers; in addition, parents and guardians have received training in how to deal with the behavior of acting-out youth. The last two decades have produced a whole new literature on effective strategies for intervening with delinquent youth that has been developed by experts in fields other than criminology and juvenile justice.

The policy trends and practices in delinquency prevention over the past 150 years have been driven largely by fads and wishful thinking rather than careful research and analysis. Yet the fashionable reforms and programs for juvenile delinquents have seldom had the impacts that their proponents promised. Even when an approach has demonstrated some degree of success, like the community-based work of Shaw and McKay described earlier in this chapter, it has often been discarded in the search for new and more innovative approaches.

It is only in recent years that a diligent process of research and development on the part of a few individual investigators and public agencies has begun to produce clearly effective and transportable programs. In the next chapter, I propose a framework for evaluating this literature and assembling its findings into a coherent and reliable framework. Succeeding chapters explore the most promising approaches and program models, and demonstrate that improving delinquency science is no longer the most difficult part of the delinquency-prevention research and development process. The hard part is getting policymakers and practitioners to embrace and accurately reflect the findings of science in the strategies and programs they adopt and support for working with delinquent youth.

Chapter 3

Strategies for Measuring Program Impact

One of the problems with using prevention as a strategy for intervention when dealing with youth behavior is that the effectiveness of the preventive steps that have been taken is often difficult to observe or measure. The impact of preventive measures doesn't "happen" as a discrete event in the world. How do we know that brushing teeth prevents cavities or that getting flu shots reduces the likelihood of getting the flu? In both cases the determination as to whether the preventive intervention works, at least to hard science standards, requires some form of experiment. One group has to be given the intervention while another similar group is not. Both groups must then be followed to determine whether the targeted events (tooth decay or the flu) are less prevalent in the treated group.

Experiments using randomized samples are the gold standard in social sciences as well (Shadish et al., 2002), but are much less frequently encountered. As Sherman et al. (1997) found in their review conducted for the U.S. Department of Justice, randomized field experiments in criminal justice are few and far between, and unfortunately not increasing in their frequency of use.

Imagine how much easier it is to determine whether an intervention is successful in repairing tooth decay after the problem has started. The decay is present and progressing before the intervention is attempted. If the rehabilitative intervention is successful, the progress of the decay will be arrested and the damaged part of the tooth repaired. The outcome of the intervention can be directly observed in every case. But now consider, in contrast, how much harder it is to detect the effect of preventive interventions for delinquency. Because we are now dealing with behavior that is usually covert, and therefore difficult to detect, we must rely on proxy outcome measures such as arrests or self-reports, neither of which is completely correlated with crime. Because both the onset and desistance of delinquency occur at fairly steep rates, we need to have very closely matched comparison groups to ensure that whatever differences we observe are due to the intervention and not just the passage of time.

Because delinquent acts are fairly rare events, even among active delinquents, we must track samples for follow-up data collection over extended periods of time if we hope to obtain an accurate measure of their behavior. Finally, because delinquency is not randomly distributed throughout the population, but concentrated among the most impoverished and disorganized communities and families, data collection for longitudinal follow-up studies are further hampered by frequent changes in residence, which often results in more homes without telephones and irregular school attendance—reducing participation rates in telephone or classroom surveys.

In this chapter, I review a number of measures and their attributes that have been used as outcome measures of delinquency prevention. I then take a critical look at the traditional types of research designs used to assess impacts of interventions in order to see how well they do in delinquency-prevention settings. Finally, the chapter examines a variety of strategies and techniques for summarizing and categorizing the existing research literature, and restating the results—an undertaking that has become a growth industry within the prevention field, producing an alphabet soup of conflicting claims and results.

Outcome Measures

Bad outcomes are the ultimate events, characteristics, or states that a preventive intervention hopes to avoid. The ultimate goal of delinquency- and violence-prevention programs is a reduction in delinquent and criminal behavior. The usual proxy measures for crime or delinquency are arrests, referrals, convictions, or placements, whichever is deemed to be most accurately captured by the most comprehensive juvenile record system serving the area being studied. More complete but also much more expensive measures that are sometimes used are based on self-reports or on the reports of observers (such as teachers) of behaviors that include criminal or delinquent acts, fighting, drug use, and so on.

While crime reduction is the ultimate goal, reductions in future confinement and other juvenile- and criminal-justice system costs are also often explicit goals, as are improvements in academic or vocational performance and other measures of social functioning (e.g., reduced depression, dependency, alcoholism). Table 3.1 lists the various measures commonly used to evaluate the impact of delinquency-prevention programs, along with comments on their usual source, reliability, and usefulness as a measure of crime-prevention effectiveness.

Self-reported data is by far the most detailed and accurate, but also the most expensive to collect (Elliot & Ageton, 1980; Blumstein et al., 1986). Tracking and follow-up procedures usually bring the cost up to well over $300 per interview. If appropriate tracking and retention procedures are not maintained, selective attrition will quickly and severely affect the accuracy and reliability of the resulting data. Severity measures that can be derived from self-report data include:

- Fraction reporting commission of any crime.
- Fraction reporting commission of designated violent crime.

Table 3.1. Potential outcome measures for delinquency-prevention programs

Measure	Source	Reliability	Usefulness
Self-reported crime and drug use	Personal interviews	High if done correctly	Much greater detail than from records
Arrest	Police	Fairly high	Most frequently recorded event; proxy for crime
Referral	Probation	Some screening for accurancy; does not apply to adults	Similar to arrests for juveniles but does not apply to adults
Conviction	Court or probation	Misses diverted cases, may be delayed and affected by plea bargaining	Not as good as arrests or referral because of delay and case attrition
Placement or incarceration	Probation, court, or rap sheet	Affected by local sentencing policies	Good screen on seriousness of offense; also reflects costs to system
Academic performance	School records	Fair degree of correlation with crime	Risk factor plus cost of services
Behavior	Teacher or parent observation	Fair degree of correlation with crime	Risk factor
Costs and benefits	System data	Wide margin of error	Important criteria for decisions

- Fraction reporting commission of property crime.
- Fraction reporting use of designated drug within specified time period.
- Offense rate = average number of offenses of a specified type committed during periods not confined or incarcerated.
- Frequency of drug use.

Without substantial outside funding for research and evaluation purposes, which can pay for self-report surveys, the next best alternative is arrest and/or referral data, whichever combination is most reliable. An arrest is deemed to have occurred when police take a juvenile into custody. However, only some fraction of all juvenile arrests results in a *referral* to probation or the juvenile court for further action. Less serious offenses may be dismissed or diverted to some other system such as Mental Health or Family Services (Greenwood, 2002).

As a starting point, arrests can be used as a reasonable proxy for offenses, adjusting appropriately for differences in probability of arrest across offense categories and age groups. For instance, the probability of arrest is higher for robbery offenses than larcenies because of the personal contact between victim and offender. A robbery arrest will therefore represent fewer offenses committed than are represented by each larceny arrest. Given these qualifications, arrest and referral history data can be used to construct almost all of the same summary outcome measures described above for self-reported data except those dealing with drug use.

Percentage of time incarcerated is a good proxy for the amount of criminal-justice resources consumed by an offender, or expended on his or her account. Juvenile residential facilities operate at a cost between $35,000 and $60,000 annually for each youth. Adult prisons and jails operate at a cost of more than $20,000 per year for each inmate. Time incarcerated is also required to arrive at an estimate of *active street time* as the denominator in estimates of offense rate—crimes committed per month or per year of active street time.

Apart from the types of crime and periods of required confinement, the other primary candidates for proxy outcome measures are the risk and protective factors thought to be the primary influences on antisocial behavior. For older youth, these include various measures of performance and success in school and characteristics of their peers. Rule breaking, truancy, lack of interest, and poor performance in school are all seen as risk factors. So is association with antisocial peers. Association with gang members or membership in a gang poses even greater risk than that of deviant peers.

For younger children, measures of family characteristics and parenting process are thought to play a more influential role (Lipsey & Derzon, 1998). Deviant or mentally ill parents, abuse, neglect, failure to monitor, and inconsistent parenting are all thought to put children at risk (Hawkins et al., 1998). Prevention programs can address the dynamic risk factors associated with parenting, peers, and school, and thus measure their success to some degree by these indirect performance measures. Vocational attainment and marriage/stable relationship are protective factors for older youth and young adults (Lipsey & Derzon), and thus appropriate proximate measures for this age group.

Drug use and gang affiliation are both dynamic risk factors in that they can be changed by an intervention, and thus appropriate impact measures. Unfortunately, they require self-reports to measure with any degree of accuracy and thus are very expensive to obtain. A further problem with any self-report measure is that the intervention might change willingness to report a particular behavior (drug use) as well as change the behavior itself (Thornberry, 1998).

Another set of possible outcome measures worth mentioning includes various behavior rating scales such as the Aggression and Social Withdrawal subscales of the Achenback Child Behavior Checklist (Achenback, 1991) or the Adaptive and Maladaptive Teacher Rating Scales developed by Walker, Severson, and Feil (1995). In a review of predictors of violent or serious delinquency, Lipsey and Derzon (1998) found that when using predictors from ages six to eleven to predict risk at ages fifteen to twenty-five, "prior antisocial behavior was the best overall predictor of subsequent antisocial behavior."

The final and most compelling delinquency-prevention outcome measure for many, particularly those with a background in business or economics, is *return on investment*. If expenditures on delinquency-prevention programs are thought of as investments in crime prevention, it is possible to compute the expected return from investments on a particular program in terms of future savings to taxpayers, and possibly the costs avoided by victims. This approach of converting all significant outcomes into monetary terms has been much better developed by economists working in the health and environmental fields than the few who work in criminal justice. But even here, the approach is beginning to take hold. The Washington State Institute for Public Policy has begun calculating costs and benefits for the prevention programs they deem to be "proven," and for all of the other delinquency-prevention programs on which the state is spending money (Aos et al., 2001). This information is published on their web site at www.wa.gov/wsipp.

Evaluation Designs

The impacts of a particular program are not easily observable but must be estimated through some evaluation procedure. An evaluation design using random assignment—a true experimental design—is in many situations the optimal way to establish the causal effect of a prevention program directed at youth crime. This type of design requires the researcher to randomly assign participants to either the treatment program or the comparison group. There are several different experimental designs to choose from, including those that allow for only posttreatment measures, that allow for both pre- and posttest measures, that use multiple groups to combine the preceding designs, and that allow each subject to undergo each type of experimental treatment if more than one is offered.

Randomized experiments do have several drawbacks, however. The most important include an inability to generalize results to other populations, settings, and times, and the fact that in some situations they are impractical, too time-consuming, or prohibitively expensive. In fact, in situations in delinquency prevention, and all the other social sciences as well, the randomized experiment is not the evaluation design selected. Most evaluation of crime-prevention efforts employ so-called quasi-experimental, nonexperimental, or more judgmental designs. The fundamental distinction between quasi-experimental and randomized experimental designs is that there is no random assignment of participants to either the treatment or comparison group. Instead, the comparisons between treatment and nontreatment conditions must always be made with the assumption that the groups are not equivalent. As a result, the internal validity of these designs is threatened, and causal inferences about the effects of the programs are more difficult to make. There are many different kinds of quasi-experimental designs, including those that incorporate control groups (either matched, statistically equated, or generic population norms), those that use both pre- and posttests, regression-discontinuity designs, and repeated-measures designs that use numerous pre- and posttests.

The random assignment of participants to treatment and comparison groups ensures that other factors that might influence the outcomes are also randomly assigned across these conditions, thus allowing the researcher to assume that the only systematic differences between the treatment and control groups are found in the treatments or interventions that are applied. In nonrandomized studies, two methods can be used for distinguishing the treatment or program effects from the effects of other factors. Quasi-experiments attempt to mimic true experiments by using matching or other methods to establish an equivalent comparison group. Nonexperimental studies rely primarily on statistical methods to distinguish the effects of the intervention from other confounding causes. Quasi-experimental studies may use such statistical techniques as well to increase the equivalence between groups.

Other research design types include nonexperimental designs and judgmental approaches. Nonexperimental designs do not include comparison groups. They use panel designs instead, and simple before-and-after studies. While comparisons are not made directly to a control group, the treatment group may still be compared with itself, for example, at multiple points before and after the participants enter the program. Judgmental approaches are those in which the opinions and assessments of program administrators, key stakeholders, official records, and participants themselves are utilized to estimate program impacts.

While quasi-experimental and nonexperimental designs are usually more practical in field settings than are randomized designs, it is important to note that none of them produce findings that are completely immune to alternative explanations for differences between treatment and comparison observations. None of them can invest the researcher with as much confidence in reaching causal conclusions as the randomized experiemental design. Furthermore, nonrandomized designs have been shown to systematically overestimate the positive impacts of intervention programs in criminal justice settings (Weisburd et al., 2001).

There are several characteristics of the field of delinquency prevention that must be considered when deciding how vigorous an evaluation design to use. Two are problems of perverse incentives. If a program wants to look good in comparison to others, it can use a selection process called "creaming"—selecting only the least risky youth to participate in the program, or rejecting the most risky.

If screening out high-risk candidates is a form of frontend creaming, then the process of flunking out noncompliant or problem youth and escalating them up to more restrictive placements often results in backdoor creaming—the degeneration of assignments to experimental or control conditions, if the escalated youth are removed from the study.

The last problem that is somewhat unique to delinquency-prevention efforts is the one of leverage. Delinquency prevention offers tremendous leverage compared to most other crime-prevention strategies. Just a small change stretched out over a potentially long criminal career can have quite large effects. Small impacts are therefore important if they are sustained over time. Detecting small impacts takes stronger designs, and tracking impacts over time is expensive.

The Impact of Research Design on Outcomes

While there is general agreement that experimental studies are more likely to ensure higher internal validity than quasi-experimental or nonexperimental studies, reviews of the literature have not produced consistent findings on the issue of whether there is a consistent bias produced by nonrandomized research designs. Lipsey (1992) concluded on the basis of his first meta-analysis that nonrandomized studies are not likely to strongly bias conclusions regarding program and treatment effects. Similar conclusions were reached by Shadish and Ragsdale (1996).

In recent years, the concept of "evidence-based medicine" has gained strong support within government and professional circles (Milenson, 1997; Zuger, 1997). A central component of this movement is reliance on systematic reviews of prior research and evaluation (Davies, 1999). The Campbell Collaboration (C2) was recently established by a group of social scientists to develop systematic reviews of research evidence in the areas of social and educational interventions (Boruch et al., 1999). A special coordinating group was created by the Campbell Collaboration to deal with crime and justice issues (Farrington & Petrosino, 2000).

While recognizing that random assignment of subjects to alternative interventions provides the highest level of internal validity for causal statements, the C2 concluded that it is unrealistic at this time to restrict systematic reviews on the effects of interventions relevant to crime and justice, to randomized experimental studies, because they are so infrequently found in this field.

Shortly thereafter, Weisburd et al. (2001) used the database and Scientific Methods Score developed by researchers at the University of Maryland (Sherman et al., 1997), discussed later in this chapter, to reexamine this issue. They concluded that research design does have a systematic effect on outcomes in criminal-justice studies. The weaker a design, the more likely it is to report a result in favor of treatment and the less likely it is to report a harmful effect of treatment. This effect was found even when limiting the comparison to randomized studies and those with strong quasi-experimental designs.

More recently, a Research Design Policy Brief prepared for the C2 steering committee by Shadish and Meyers (2002) proposed:

- C2 systematic reviews not be undertaken unless randomized experiments are available to be included in the review.
- When both randomized and nonrandomized studies are included, C2 reviews must separate estimates of intervention effects for randomized versus nonrandomized studies in all important analyses.

Key Decisions in Analyzing Outcomes

For any outcome measure, it is necessary to decide how widely impacts will be searched for, how they will be identified and described, and how long a follow-up period to use. In the best of all worlds we would like to identify all of the impacts of an intervention, no matter where or how far in the future they occur. Many evaluations, however, report only outcomes for the participating youth up to the time of their exit from the program, but nothing thereafter.

The simplest way to report the impacts of an intervention is the straightforward binary method of statistical significance. Did the intervention produce impacts that are significant as measured by standardized statistical tests, using a sufficiently rigorous research design? This is the outcome measure that has been traditionally used by academic reviewers of the literature (Hawkins et al., 1995; Tolan & Guerra, 1994) and is the method used by Hawkins and Catalano (1992) and Hawkins et al. (2002) in compiling the list of promising programs for their Communities That Care program; it is the method used as well by Sherman et al. (1997) in their evaluation of prevention programs for the U.S. Department of Justice.

The problem with reporting only the binary outcomes provided by significance tests is that this method fails to capture the large differences in the magnitude of impacts that are known to exist between interventions. The standard measure of impact that has been adopted by many reviewers and review groups, including the Campbell Collaborative, is the effect size, typically defined as the difference between the treatment and control group means, on the selected recidivism measure, standardized (divided) by the pooled standard deviation. This *standardized mean difference effect size* is commonly used to represent the results of experimental comparisons in meta-analyses and other quantitative studies (Cooper & Hedges, 1994; Lipsey & Wilson, 1998).

In the delinquency field, where environment and situational factors appear to play a critical role in shaping behavior, some interventions have been shown to produce significant effects while participating youth are in the program, but no differences between experimental and control youth soon after program completion (Ellickson et al., 1993). This phenomenon of transient behavioral change has led the so-called Blueprints project at the University of Colorado, one of the program-rating groups discussed later in this chapter, to require evidence of impacts that last beyond the point of program exit before including that program on their list of proven models (Elliot, 1997).

The issue of how far into the future to measure results depends on what we expect the future to hold. If many of the benefits of a program are not expected to appear until some years down the road, then observations will be required until their presence is verified. If current trends and tendencies can be assumed to continue uninterrupted, then shorter follow-up periods will do. The Washington State Institute for Public Policy (WSIPP) uses ten years as the cut-off point in their estimates of program benefits. The Perry Preschool, a program for three and four year olds that includes home visits by the teacher, is only cost effective, however, if you include reductions in crime and enhanced income that occur more than a decade after participating youth leave the program (Karoly et al., 1998).

Another issue that must be resolved in any effort to compare the effectiveness of alternative crime-prevention strategies is where to draw the boundary between the benefits or savings that will be considered and those that will not be. All programs must be compared on an equal footing. In some analyses, the only savings considered are those expected within the criminal-justice system. Another approach is to move past the various agencies of government and consider the taxpayer as the appropriate perspective from which to view this issue (Karoly et al., 1998). Costs are costs and savings are benefits, no matter where they are experienced. This approach requires the collection of outcome measures reflecting the more global impact of an intervention on all the various elements of government. David Old's Nurse Home Visitation Program is not cost effective as a delinquency-prevention program alone, but when crime-reduction benefits are combined with reduced welfare and schooling costs, benefits exceed costs by several orders of magnitude (Karoly et al., 1998).

A final financial issue to be resolved is whether to include the benefits of less crime to potential victims, their families, and friends. It is in estimating benefits to victims that the criminal-justice system has lagged behind efforts to monetize benefits in such fields as health and the environment

(Cook & Ludwig, 2000). Victim surveys provide fairly good estimates of direct out-of-pocket costs such as the value of lost or damaged property, medical costs, and lost wages. As Cook and Ludwig have shown, however, these direct costs are only a small proportion of the total victim costs imposed by crimes against persons. The difficult part of the valuation problem is in estimating the indirect costs of pain and suffering, security expenses, and restricted life-style, costs that can be quite large.

For many years, economists have argued about the proper method of placing a monetary value on matters relating to "quality of life," such as clean air or a safer environment. One approach is to try and find markets that reflect these values, such as the wage premium demanded by workers engaged in dangerous professions. But there are not many professions in which being robbed, raped, or shot is a substantial risk. Furthermore, the wages for those that do engage in such professions (drug dealers, smugglers, prostitutes, etc.) are difficult to assess (Reuter et al., 1990).

Economists Ted Miller, Mark Cohen, and Brian Wiersema (1996) used jury awards to obtain estimates of the total costs to victims for various crimes, as shown in table 3.2. In the Washington State Institute's cost-effectiveness analysis of proven and existing programs (Aos et al., 2001), estimates of savings to victims are based on these findings of Miller et al. and are several orders of magnitude larger than just the savings to taxpayers alone.

Cook and Ludwig (2000) used a method advocated by Harvard economist Tom Schelling called "contingent valuation" to develop estimates of potential victims' "willingness to pay" to reduce gun violence. They surveyed a representative sample of citizens about how they would vote on a referendum to raise taxes a specified amount, which would be used to fund a prevention program to reduce gun violence by a specified percent. Both the amount of the tax and the amount of gun violence it would prevent were randomly varied for each respondent. Their findings suggest

Table 3.2. **Victim costs by crime type**

Crime type	Cost to victim ($)
Fatal assault	3 million
Nonfatal sexual or physical assault	87,000
Drunk driving	18,000
Robbery or attempt	8,000

Source: Miller et al., 1996.

that taxpayers would collectively pay about $900,000 to prevent each act of gun violence. Cook and Ludwig argued that the higher value they obtained, in comparison to the earlier findings of Miller et al. (1996), stemmed from the fact that we are in general an altruistic society, and are willing to pay to reduce gun-shot injuries to others as well as ourselves. Families and friends are the easiest case, but even the victimization of complete strangers is something that most of us would pay some amount to reduce. According to the Cook and Ludwig study, the annual cost of gun violence in this country is on the order of $100 billion.

Cohen et al. (2004) were funded by the National Institute of Justice to use contingent valuation in determining how much a nationally representative sample of thirteen hundred residents would be willing to pay to reduce specific types of crimes. Their estimates of the Public's willingness to pay were, in the aggregate, 1.5 to 10 times higher than the estimates reported in their previous work using jury verdicts (Miller et al., 1996).

If the only question being asked is how much to spend on prevention, then critics of the Miller et al. data are right to point out the heroic assumptions required to extrapolate their data from jury verdicts to ordinary crime victims, and the huge margins of error that are involved. But if the purpose is to decide which of several proposed interventions is most cost effective, then victim costs need not be considered. Instead, the preferred metric is the number of crimes prevented for a specific amount invested in either program, assuming that both programs prevent the same relative mix of crime types. Victim costs would become relevant only if one approach prevented mainly property crimes while the alternative prevented mainly crimes against persons.

At this fledgling stage in the development of appropriate victim-cost data for evaluating the cost effectiveness of preventive-crime interventions, there are not many choices. We can ignore victim costs altogether, and seriously undervalue interventions that prevent crimes, particularly violent crimes. We can use the Miller et al. data as the analysts at WSIPP have; or we can use the even higher estimates for the social costs of crime produced by contingent valuation. Until there is more of a consensus on this issue, the prudent approach for any cost-effectiveness study is to use all three methods, reporting separately the results from each. In that way the readers of the study will be free to come to their own conclusions regarding the appropriate method.

In summary, determining the impacts of a delinquency-prevention program is considerably expensive. Only a rigorous experimental design with long-term follow-up can accurately assess the lasting impacts. Such evaluations are now all too rare and not always applied to the most promising programs. If the process of producing proven models is to be accelerated, there will have to be some kind of change in the funding or incentives for conducting such experiments, either setting up a new federal agency with the responsibility of conducting such trials or requiring that much more of current delinquency spending be shifted from unproven to proven programs, thereby increasing the value of the latter.

Methods of Categorizing the Literature and Restating the Findings

For most of us, our opinions about the effectiveness of any one particular model or approach to delinquency prevention are based on the findings of one or more recent reviews of the pertinent evaluation literature. The dawn of the modern trend in certified lists of promising or exemplary programs can be traced back to the publication of Mark Lipsey's meta-analysis of juvenile programs in 1992. Lipsey's analysis did not identify specific programs but rather specific approaches that were more likely to be effective than others.

The next major event in this development, also in 1992, was publication of the Communities That Care (CTC) material by David Hawkins and Richard Catalano, which provided a list of specific programs that the authors found promising. Although they addressed risk and protective factors associated primarily with alcohol and drug use, delinquency prevention was included as well. CTC also provided guidance and technical assistance on community engagement and mobilization of support.

The next step was the publication of the National Academy of Science's report on violence edited by Albert Reiss and Jeff Roth (1993). This review claimed, at least implicitly, that there were no exemplary prevention programs for which positive outcomes could be confidently predicted

One year later, another less widely circulated report was prepared by Patrick Tolan and Nancy Guerra (1994) for Del Elliot's Center for the Study and Prevention of Violence at the University of Colorado in Boulder. Their report, entitled *What Works in Reducing Adolescent Violence*, asserted that there were a number of exemplary program models in which confidence could be placed. Multisystemic Therapy (MST) and Functional Family Therapy (FFT) were at the top of their list. Also in 1994, a young researcher at Yale, Hirokazu Yoshikawa, published a review and summary of early-childhood interventions, some of which appeared to have significant crime-prevention effects.

In 1994, my colleagues at RAND and I published a cost-effectiveness analysis of California's draconian "Three Strikes and You're Out" law, predicting large increases in cost with anything like full compliance. Two years later, Greenwood et al. (1996) published a cost-effectiveness study showing that parenting programs and the Quantum Opportunities Program sponsored by the Ford Foundation to be much more cost effective than the long prison sentences mandated by "Three Strikes." A third RAND report (Karoly et al., 1998) demonstrated that even expensive early-childhood programs such as David Olds's Nurse Home Visitation Program and the Perry Preschool could be cost-effective strategies for preventing crime if you factored in the value of benefits in other areas as well (school, unemployment, health, etc.).

A major development in the evolution of the program-certification process was the 1997 publication by the Department of Criminology at the University of Maryland, supported by the U.S. Department of Justice, of an in-depth review of all crime-prevention strategies. *Preventing Crime: What Works, What Doesn't, and What's Promising* (Sherman et al., 1997) reached a large and eager audience that was being encouraged and funded to think creatively about how to deal with crime. The original report listed dozens of programs that appeared to be effective and specifically identified some that were not. One of the Maryland researchers' major contributions to the field was the development of a five-level Scientific Methods Score (SMS), which was used to rate the internal validity of the evaluations they reviewed. Programs categorized as "working" were supported by at least two evaluations of Level 3 or higher, and a preponderance of any other evidence.

Another major development that same year was the publication of the first set of the so-called Blueprints (Elliot, 1997) by the Center for the Study and Prevention of Violence at the University of Colorado. The original group of programs rated "proven" by the Blueprints included ten programs that met rigorous criteria for proving their effectiveness and were prepared to help others to replicate their models. As indicated previously, a program is not considered to be proven by Blueprints until it has demonstrated its impact on problem behaviors with a rigorous experimental design, the impacts have been shown to persist after youth leave the program, and the program has been successfully replicated in another site. Del Elliot, the founder of Blueprints, chose to go deep and narrow where many of his predecessors had gone shallow and wide. The focus of Blueprints is on bringing a small number of well-designed and tested programs up to scale with multiple replications. They appear to have succeeded remarkably well. The current Blueprints web site lists eleven model programs and twenty that are considered promising. The design, research evidence, and implementation requirements for each model are available on the site (www.colorado.edu/cspu/blueprints). A decision tool helps visitors identify the programs that are most suitable to their needs. In the first few years of the Blueprints project, funding was available from the center to support the technical assistance needs of a number of sites attempting to implement each Blueprint. The center has published a report describing the lessons learned from these early implementation efforts (Mihalic et al., 2002).

Once we had both wide-angle (Sherman et al., 1997) and highly focused (Blueprints) ongoing reviews of the literature, the next step was for someone to undertake cost-benefit studies of them all. As noted earlier, the field of delinquency prevention was indeed fortunate when the Washington State Institute for Public Policy (WSIPP) took on this task. Steve Aos and his colleagues (1999) developed a model for estimating the costs and benefits for many of the Blueprint programs and a number of others that they found to be promising. They used the program cost and effect sizes reported in the literature, follow-up arrest and placement data for cohorts of Washington youth, and victim cost data estimated by Miller et al. (1996). Some of the programs that dealt with the families of delinquents appeared to produce tax payer savings seven to ten times the program costs.

The most recent development in the evolution of delinquency prevention is a report of the Surgeon General on youth violence (U.S. Department of Health and Human Services, 2001). In addition to reviewing recent trends, developmental pathways, risk and protective factors, and common myths, the report also reviewed the research on preventing youth violence. Its principal findings and conclusions include the following:

- A number of prevention programs have demonstrated their effectiveness.
- Most highly effective programs combine components that address both individual and environmental conditions.
- Nearly half of the most thoroughly evaluated strategies have been shown to be ineffective.
- Program effectiveness depends as much on the quality of implementation as on the type of intervention.

The Surgeon General's Report made note of "the numerous agencies and organizations" that have "published recommendations on 'what works' in youth violence prevention" with "little consistency regarding the specific programs they recommend." The report attributed this lack of consistency to "lack of uniformly applied scientific standards for what works."

A summary listing of the reviews is provided by Mihalic and Aultman-Bettridge (2002) and includes the American Youth Policy Forum, Center for Mental Health Services (Greenberg et al., 1999), Center for Substance Abuse Prevention (CSAP), the Department of Education's Safe Schools, the National Institute of Drug Abuse (NIDA), Strengthening America's Families, and Title V of the Juvenile Justice and Delinquency Prevention Act.

The system used in the Surgeon General's Report to grade or score the programs was as follows:

- Strategies and programs were first classified as "Effective" or "Ineffective."
- Effective strategies and programs were further subdivided into "Model" and "Promising" categories depending on whether they met "very high standards of demonstrated effectiveness" or "minimum standards."
- Within the model and promising categories, a further distinction was made between strategies and programs that demonstrated effects on violence and serious delinquency (Level 1) and those that demonstrated effectiveness on known risk factors (Level 2).

In order to be identified as effective, a program had to have been evaluated with an experimental or quasi-experimental design that would place it at Level 4 or 5 on the University of Maryland's Scientific Methods Score, described above. That grading system placed a program in one of four categories: "Model," "Promising," "Does Not Work," and "Unevaluated." In a way, the Surgeon General's Report is even more selective in its screening than Blueprints. Several of the Blueprints proven programs are listed as only "promising" by the Surgeon General's Report, which also grades one "promising" Blueprints program only as a "model."

Some of the other reviews, like those we have already described, simply organize and summarize the information contained in the literature, grouping studies together to arrive at conclusions about particular models or approaches (Posey et al., 1996; Sherman et al., 1997; Greenberg et al., 1999; Mendel, 2001). Some use statistical meta-analysis techniques to develop more rigorous estimates of outcomes for interventions for which there are many reported studies (Lipsey & Wilson, 1998). Finally some rating or certification systems use expert panels or some other screening process to assess the integrity of individual evaluations, and specific criteria to identify proven, promising, or exemplary programs (Elliot, 1997;

U.S. Department of Health and Human Services, 2001; Mihalic & Aultman-Bettridge, 2002). These reviews also differ from one another in the particular outcomes they emphasize, such as delinquency, drug use, mental health or school-related behaviors, their criteria for selection, and the rigor with which the evidence is screened and reviewed.

Why Reviewers Come to Different Conclusions

A cursory review of the various program-rating systems noted above might lead one to conclude that there is very little consistency among them, as the Surgeon General's Report suggested. Some lists of recommended programs are long (Posey et al., 1996) and others are very short (Elliot, 1997). Some reviews have several different tiers of validation (U.S. Department of Health and Human Services, 2001) while others distinguish only between those that are effective and those that have not demonstrated their effectiveness (Posey et al., 1996). Only a few of the reviewers include a rating category for those programs that have been demonstrated not to work (Sherman et al., 1997; U.S. Department of Health and Human Services, 2001). While identifying a program as ineffective or possibly harmful does not win a reviewer any friends, and may generate some angry mail from supporters of the flunking program (the controversy over DARE, mentioned in chapter 2, comes to mind), such reviews do provide a useful service by providing activists the data they need to help put more effective alternative programs into place.

On closer examination, however, the differences between reviewers and lists can largely be explained and reconciled by noting differences in their goals and in the criteria that programs must meet to be selected. Differences in purpose or focus among reviewers lead to the selection of different outcome measures or screening criteria for inclusion in the various reviews. For instance, the University of Maryland review (Sherman et al., 1997) looked at the full range of crime-prevention strategies, including police and correctional programs, while the Blueprints project only includes program models that have been shown to reduce delinquency or drug use among youth, with fairly rigorous evaluation designs. Other reviews among those mentioned above have focused on school-based strategies (Mihalic & Aultman-Bettridge, 2002), programs that make schools safer (Department of Education's Safe Schools), reducing drug use (CSAP, NIDA), or reducing mental health problems (Center for Mental Health Services). Since many evaluations focus only on a limited number of outcome measures, a shift in the outcome measures of interest will invariably result in a shift in the set of program evaluations that can be included in a review.

The less obvious difference among the reviews is the criteria they use to screen and assess the effectiveness of available studies. Different reviewers use different screening criteria for determining which evaluation designs are acceptable and what kind of results are required to establish a program strategy as promising. Sherman et al. (1997) developed a five-point Scientific Methods Score to rate the strength of the various designs they reviewed. They required at least two evaluations of Level 3 (measures of crime before and after the program in experimental and comparable control conditions) or higher, showing statistically significant and desirable results, with the preponderance of all available evidence showing effectiveness in order for an intervention to be classified as "working." "Promising" interventions were those with only one Level 3 or higher evaluation indicating positive results, with the preponderance of the evidence pointing in the same direction.

In order to be selected as a model program for the Blueprints (Elliot, 1997), there must be evidence of a deterrent effect on problem behavior, based on a strong research design; evidence of sustained effects after youth leave the program; and replication with a high degree of fidelity in at least one site, demonstrating continued program effectiveness (Mihalick et al., 2002). The type and level of screening used in identifying model programs will have an impact on the number of programs identified and on the confidence that practitioners can have in their ability to replicate the reported results. Strict screening produces fewer model programs but greater confidence in their ability to be replicated.

How much evidence should be required before a program is rated as "proven" or before a community or agency decides to adopt it? Being very demanding results in a high degree of confidence that the program will work but a limited number of program options. Not being demanding enough results in many more choices but lower confidence in their effectiveness. Communities and individual agencies will differ over what they think the appropriate balance to be. At the current time, most behave as if they require very little confidence.

Consider the end points of this "degree-of-proof" measure. At the very lowest level would be a program that has never been evaluated or even clearly described. At the highest level would be a program that is fully specified as to its design and protocols, has been evaluated with strong experimental designs, and consistently achieved sustained and positive impacts on the outcome measures of interest.

Many, but not all, reviews start with the requirement that the programs to be included have at least one fairly rigorous outcome evaluation. The conclusion reached by almost all those who have undertaken serious reviews of the crime-prevention literature is that the majority of existing prevention programs have not been evaluated, and among those that have, most of the evaluations are of fairly low rigor (Sherman et al., 1997; U.S. Department of Health and Human Services, 2001). Only a few models have been carefully evaluated and only a very few have been evaluated in multiple settings. This conclusion suggests the need for a degree-of-proof measure that has room for some differentiation at the lower end of the scale, to encourage the many models currently in the lower range to begin moving upward. Some of the indications that a particular program is making progress in this respect include the following:

1. *Use of a theoretically sound design for addressing specific risk factors.* The first step in evaluating the likely impact of a proposed program should be its face validity—is it logically sound? Is there a plausible case for believing that the activities of the program will lead to the desired outcomes?
2. *Use of proven practices.* The results of recent reviews suggest that programs that are based on proven practices are more likely to produce significant impacts than those without such a foundation. All of the most effective programs are of this type.
3. *Use of an outcome evaluation showing significant positive impacts on targeted risk factors.* This requirement is often the starting point for many reviews of the literature. Minimum standards for the experimental design usually require some kind of control group, which is designed to be comparable to the experimental group, at least with statistical controls. Risk factors can include performance at school, relations with peers or family members, drug use, and so on.
4. *Evidence from an experimental design of posttreatment or sustainable impact on delinquency.* Many programs show positive impacts while youth remain in the program but provide no evidence that those impacts translate into reduced delinquency in the community. This marker requiring such evidence is used by the Blueprints project and is part of the Surgeon General's Report.
5. *Evidence from multiple experimental trials of posttreatment impact on delinquency.* One successful demonstration might be lucky happenstance. A repeat performance is much more convincing. This step is also a requirement of the Blueprints project and the report of the Surgeon General.

6. *Replication of model and impacts in natural setting.* It is one thing for a diligent principal investigator—along with devoted graduate students, clinical interns, and other academic associates—to achieve positive results with a model. It is another thing entirely to get similar results when the program is delivered by a community-based organization or government agency. This marker is not just a test of the program model, but also the means by which it is disseminated to adopting sites. MST and FFT have been undergoing this type of testing in Washington (Aos, 2002) and New York.

7. *Multiple replications of model and impacts in natural settings.* This is the final step in demonstrating transportability.

Where a program registers in measuring its effectiveness as indicated by these seven markers indicates the degree to which it can be expected to produce positive impacts for communities considering adopting it.

A final matter having to do with how a program is rated concerns how its impact is to be reported: as simply effective or not, in terms of its impact on future crime, or in financial terms. A case can be made for all three. The most frequently reported outcome on review of a program is simply whether or not it has produced any significant impact on the outcomes of interest. For instance, that is the only outcome reported for programs in the Communities That Care (Hawkins & Catalano, 1992; Posey et al., 1996) list. This single pass-or-fail measure, however, fails to distinguish between programs according to the magnitude of their impacts.

A second way to go about reporting program effectiveness is to provide some measure of impact. For delinquency-prevention programs, this would be the reduction in delinquent behavior for the targeted group during the follow-up period. The generally accepted measure of this impact—"effect size"—is usually defined in delinquency studies as the mean difference in outcomes, between the experimental and control samples, divided by their pooled standard deviation (Lipsey & Wilson, 2001). Properly designed evaluations produce an estimate of effect size, which in turn can be used to project impacts on crime (Aos et al., 2001). Large differences and smaller standard deviations produce larger effect sizes.

The third way to report program effectiveness, now required by some decisionmakers charged with allocating resources, is in terms of return on investment or the ratio of benefits to costs. The cost per youth for some of the more promising interventions ranges from a few hundred dollars for a few training sessions (Aggression Replacement Training [Aos et al., 1998]) to more than $10,000 for extensive services over an extended period of time for such programs as David Olds's Nurse Home Visitation Program (Karoly et al., 1998) or the Quantum Opportunities Program (Lattimore et al., 1998). Measures of effect size tell us nothing about what it costs to achieve those effects or what they are worth.

Based on the characteristics of the treatment sample, and the reported effect size achieved, it is possible to project how many criminal acts would be committed by the sample both with and without the program intervention (Greenwood et al., 1996; Welsh et al., 2000; Aos et al., 2001). Using these estimates of future crime rates, it is also possible to estimate the number of arrests and sanctions of various types that these youth will experience with and without participation in the program. By attaching cost estimates to crimes (Miller et al., 1996), arrests, and sanctions (Aos et al., 2001), it is possible to estimate the costs saved by taxpayers and victims alike through an effective intervention. Finally, dividing the cost of the intervention into the total expected benefits provides an estimate of the returns from investing funds in the program.

In summary, different reviewers produce different lists of proven and promising programs because they focus on different outcomes and apply different criteria in screening programs. On the upper end of everyone's promising-program scale are the very small number of thoroughly evaluated programs that have consistently demonstrated significant positive effects and developed effective strategies for dissemination and replication. At the bottom end are the vast number of programs that have never been evaluated. Arrayed across the scale between the upper and bottom ends are those programs that have some evidence to support their claims of effectiveness in a single trial.

Chapter 4

What Works

In chapter 2, I reviewed how ideas about what constitutes effective delinquency-prevention strategies have changed over time, albeit in a somewhat cyclical fashion, with what were at one point popular strategies passing out of favor only to later regain their acceptance in the field. In chapter 3, I provided an overview of how methods for assessing and organizing information about the effectiveness of prevention programs and strategies have developed over time. The goals of the present chapter are to examine those programs and strategies that have been identified in the literature as most effective in preventing delinquency; assess the quality of evidence on which these designations are based; show how this information can be used to guide communities in selecting programs; and suggest where further research and program development efforts might be most productively pursued.

Given the wide range of risk factors that have been found to predispose youth to serious or chronic offending, it should not be surprising that there are a wide range of programs designed to address these factors at various stages in the life-course development. At the earliest stage are those programs designed to help expectant mothers improve the health of their baby, cope with their new childcare responsibilities and improve parent-child attachment. Few if any of these programs were designed specifically as crime- or delinquency-prevention efforts, but as we will see later, some of them, in pursuing their other objectives, do contribute substantially to reducing later delinquency and violence.

At the other end of the spectrum are those programs designed specifically to deal with youth who have been adjudicated for violent or serious delinquent acts. Many of these programs were designed to serve as a final effort for establishing delinquent youth on a prosocial development path before they become further immersed in the trappings of the formal juvenile- and criminal-justice systems.

In between these two extremes lie a broad range of programs designed to address particular risk factors and developmental stages. Some of these programs are "universal" in that they are applied to the entire population of a classroom, school, or neighborhood. Such programs usually address community risk factors that are indirectly related to violent offending— for example, drug use, communications skills, or low socioeconomic status (SES). Targeted or selective programs are designed to identify and inter- vene with youth who are at higher levels of risk than their peers, or who already have demonstrated some degree of antisocial behavior. Since universal programs are less likely to label or stigmatize their participants, they are often preferred by community leaders. However, as this chapter's review will show, it is those programs that target the highest risk groups that have demonstrated the greatest returns on taxpayer investments.

Before conducting this review, two procedural questions must be addressed: how to identify the most promising programs, and how to organize and categorize the programs that we are to examine. The process of searching through appropriate databases to identify potential candidates for designation as promising programs, and then reviewing all of the research on each program, is a large and time-consuming undertaking. Fortunately, several organizations have begun to conduct this type of systematic review and publish the results of their efforts on a regular basis. For the purposes of this chapter, I rely on the ongoing screening and review efforts of the Blueprints Program administered by the Center for the Study and Prevention of Violence at the University of Colorado, and the review of prevention strategies and programs contained in the surgeon general's report on youth violence (U.S. Department of Health and Human Services, 2001, hereafter Surgeon General's Report), both of which were considered in chapter 3. I selected these two resources because they are comprehensive and reliable, focus on violence and delinquency outcomes, and apply similar criteria for rating the strength of the evidence. As I argued in the previous chapter, these two review efforts have applied the most stringent screening of the evidence available at this time.

My approach in this chapter follows the convention used in the Surgeon General's Report of including, but distinguishing among, general strategies and specific program models. Positive outcomes from rigorous evaluations and successful replications lead to the identification of specific models as "promis- ing" or "proven." Positive outcomes from several different models using many of the same basic techniques lead to the identification of promising strategies.

Prevention strategies and programs are usually categorized by some combination of their setting, the methods they utilize, and the characteristics of the individuals they target. For instance, programs can target the at-risk youth, their families, or their communities. Interventions can take place in the home, schools, special centers, and community or juvenile-justice settings. Youth can be targeted when they are infants, in early or late childhood, or adolescence. Intervention methods can include cognitive, behavioral, or clinical approaches; skill development; various incentives; and supportive services. Programs can be universal and involve all children of a specified age (primary prevention), or be selectively focused on youth who exhibit one or more risk factors (secondary prevention) or who are already delinquent (tertiary prevention).

One approach to organizing the various programs is by age or developmental stage of the cohort of subjects of each program. Another is to organize programs around the methods they use, the kind of population they are designed to address, or where they take place. A third approach is to organize them according to the degree of confidence one has in estimates of their impacts, and the ability of individual communities and agencies to successfully replicate them in a variety of settings. A final strategy is to organize programs according to the magnitude of impact they can be expected to achieve for a given investment—that is, their cost effectiveness.

In the first part of this chapter, I follow the first two of these strategies. Programs are initially organized by age and developmental stage. Then, within each of these groups, they are organized by where the program takes place and the intervention methods utilized. After reviewing all the programs listed as "promising" by Blueprints and/or the Surgeon General's Report, we will reorganize and review the programs again, this time according to the strength of the evidence and their expected impact on crime and taxpayer costs. This last step will utilize the limited number of cost-benefit analyses that have been completed to date.

Programs for Infancy and Early Childhood

Since many children come into the world with characteristics or in situations that place them at risk for a variety of problems, including delinquency and violence, a number of strategies have been developed to identify and address these risk factors as soon as they can be detected. All of these programs target children or families with one or more risk factors and are therefore classified as "secondary" prevention in the lexicon of public health. Table 4.1 lists the delinquency-prevention programs that focus on this developmental period and that are identified as "proven" or "promising" by the Surgeon General's Report or by Blueprints. The six programs within this category can be further divided into two subcategories based on their general approach: home-visitation programs for mothers with infants, with or without additional services; and various combinations of parent training, daycare, and preschool for parents with preschool children.

Home-visitation programs work with at-risk mothers to improve their prenatal health status, reduce birth complications, and provide guidance and support in caring for the infant and improving the quality of their own lives. Programs differ in how they identify at-risk mothers, when the home visits begin and end, who the visitors are, what the visits cover, and what other services are provided.

The preeminent program in this category is David Olds's Nurse Home Visitation Project, mentioned in chapter 3, which trains and supervises registered nurses as the home visitors. This program is found on just about every list of promising strategies based on the strength of its evidence regarding significant long-term effects and portability. It attempts to identify young, poor, first-time mothers early in their pregnancy. The sequence of approximately twenty home visits begins during the prenatal period and continues over the first two years of their child's life, with decreasing frequency. In addition to providing transportation and linkage to other services, the nurse home visitors also follow a detailed protocol that provides childcare training and social skills development for the mother. A fifteen-year follow-up of the Prenatal/Early Infancy Project in Elmira, New York showed that the nurse home visits significantly reduced child abuse and neglect in the participating families, and that there was a measurable decline in arrest rates for the children and mothers (Olds et al., 1997). The women who were part of the program also spent much less time on welfare and, among those who were poor and unmarried, experienced significantly fewer subsequent births.

A number of less expensive and less structured home-visitation models have been tested, using social workers or other types of visitors rather than nurses; they have not, however, been successful in achieving the same level of success or consistency as the Olds program with nurses (Olds et al., 2003). The Olds model has been successfully replicated and evaluated in several other sites and is now being replicated on a national scale. Retitled as the "Nurse Family Partnership," the strategy has been identified as a

Table 4.1. Promising prevention programs for early childhood

Strategy	Program	Setting	Age range	Risk factors	Duration	Methods	Surg. Gen. rating	Blueprint rating
Home visits by nurses	Nurse Home Visitation	Home	Prenatal to 2 yrs	Low SES, 1st birth	2 yrs	Home visits, child care, personal skill development	Model 1	Proven
Day care and homevisits	Syracuse Family Development	Daycare and home	Birth to 5 yrs	Low SES	5 yrs	Day care, child skills development, home visits	Prom 1	Prom
Multicontextual	Yale Child Welfare Project		Prenatal to 2 yrs	Low income, inner city, 1st birth	30 mos	Home visits, parent training, services	Prom 2	Prom
Preschool and home visits	Perry Preschool	Preschool and home	3 to 4 yrs	Low SES	2 yrs	Parent training	Prom 1	Prom
Parent training	Parent-Child Development Center Programs	Center	2 mos to 3 yrs	Low income	2 to 3 yrs	Parent and other skills training, structured play	Prom 2	Prom
Parent training	Parent-Child Interaction Training	Group	Preschool	Low SES, conduct, or emotional problem	5 sessions	Parent training	Prom 2	n.a.

"proven" model by Blueprints (Olds et al., 1998) and the Surgeon General's Report, as well as by many other reviews of programs in this field (Mihalic et al., 2002).

Two other promising home-visitation programs are the Syracuse University Family Development Research Project and the Yale Child Welfare Project. In addition to weekly home visits by paraprofessional child-development trainers, the more expensive Syracuse program includes five years of individualized day care that includes child training on social and cognitive skills and child behavior management. The program has demonstrated significant impacts on delinquent behavior in long-term, follow-up studies (Lally et al., 1988) and is rated "promising" by both Blueprints and the Surgeon General's Report. It has not, however, been replicated to the degree that the Olds program has been, possibly because of its higher cost.

The Yale Child Welfare Project is a thirty-month program that targets first-born infants of low-income mothers, and also uses in-home visitation (usually by a social worker) and day care to deliver parent training and other family and child services. Ten-year follow-up studies showed positive impacts on academic achievement and antisocial behavior (Seitz et al., 1985), but, like the Syracuse project, these evaluation results have not been replicated. The Yale project is rated "promising" by Blueprints and the Surgeon General's Report, the latter at Level 2.

Various combinations of early-childhood education, day care, and parent training make up the other strategy that has shown promise for young children in high-risk families. These programs attempt to advance cognitive and social development of the children, as well as the parenting skills of their caregivers, so that participants will be better prepared and more successful when they enter regular school. Some programs include home visits as well. The Perry Preschool Program put into practice in Ypsilanti, Michigan is the best known of these efforts (Schweinhart et al., 1993). Children aged three to four from low-income families participated in two years of high-quality early-childhood education. In addition they received weekly home visits from their teachers and referrals for social services when needed. In follow-up studies through age nineteen, participants demonstrated significant reductions in police contacts, antisocial behavior, serious fights, and school dropout rates (Berruta-Clement et al., 1984). The Perry Preschool program is rated as "promising" by both the Surgeon General's Report and Blueprints.

The least intensive program in this category, which targets low-income parents of preschool children with at least one behavioral or emotional problem is the Parent-Child Interaction Training Program. Parents enrolled in the program participate in four or five small group sessions in which they learn a variety of parenting skills. No preschool or childcare services are provided. One-year follow-up data from a randomized trial show children who participated in the program improved significantly more than those in the control group on teacher ratings of attention deficit, hyperactive, aggressive, and anxious behavior (Strayhorn & Weidman, 1991).

The last program in this category is the parent training offered through Parent-Child Development Center Programs. These efforts target low-income families with children from two months to three years of age. The training focuses on mothers as the primary caregivers and includes child-development, home-management, and family-communication skills. Evaluations of the program have demonstrated improved school achievement in grades two and three, improved parenting skills, and reduced aggressive behavior by children at ages four to seven and eight to eleven (Johnson & Walker, 1987). These evaluations of the program, however, are somewhat compromised by high attrition rates (U.S. Department of Health and Human Services, 2001).

In reviewing this category of programs, several conclusions may be drawn:

- Infancy and early-childhood programs that prevent delinquency can also prevent a number of other developmental and family problems such as unemployment, unwanted births, and arrests for the mother and school or health problems for the child. A cost-benefit study of the Olds Nurse Home Visitation Project found it produced $5 savings in future governmental expenses for every $1 invested in the program, when applied to high-risk families (Karoly et al., 1998). Reduced criminality and criminal-justice system costs accounted for only about one-fourth of the savings.
- Because of their relatively high cost, on an individual case basis, promising delinquency-prevention programs for very young children appear to require that they target at-risk families in order to be cost effective.
- Only one of the programs in this group, the Olds program, is currently a serious contender for widespread replication. It is the only program rated as "proven" by the most authoritative reviewers and is the only one that has developed a detailed training, data-collection, and monitoring process to assist sites in replicating the model.
- Although home visits, parent training, and enriched preschool programs all appear to make some contribution to improving school performance and reducing antisocial behavior, the challenge for program developers

attempting to have a significant positive impact on this age group is to find a cost-effective combination of these services that local service providers and funders will find attractive. The Nurse Family Partnership appears to have met this challenge in at least seven states, but is still getting stiff competition from less expensive home-visitation programs that do not have the same track record of proven success. I say more about this issue in chapter 5.

Programs for Elementary-School-Age Children

After working with the parents of very young children in their homes, at preschool, or some other family-friendly setting, the next developmental opportunity for further delinquency-prevention efforts occurs in the elementary schools. Of course, home visitation and parent training still remain viable options. Some promising approaches for elementary-school-age children involve schoolwide reforms or capacity enhancements. Some focus on skill building or management changes in the classroom alone. Others combine interventions in the classroom or school with various forms of parent education, training, or visits to the home. Many of these programs are universal in that they address all of the children in a particular classroom or school. Others target children who are disruptive in class or are at risk of academic failure. All of the programs and strategies identified by the Surgeon General's Report or Blueprints as at least "promising" are listed in table 4.2. Blueprints has designated two of the programs in this group as "proven" models, while the Surgeon General's Report designated only one as "proven," which is not one of the Blueprints model programs.

The first category of programs that might be considered for children in elementary school are schoolwide-enhancement or capacity-building efforts that have been shown to reduce behavior problems and increase academic performance. Denise Gottfredson has led several extensive reviews of such efforts (Gottfredson, 2001; Gottfredson et al., 2002), several of which are listed as "promising" strategies in the Surgeon General's Report, including Continuous Progress Programs (universal) in which students are allowed to progress through material at their own pace (U.S. Department of Health and Human Services, 2001); Cooperative Learning Programs (universal), which place students of varying skill levels together in small groups, allowing them to help each other learn (Slavin, 1989, 1990); and Compensatory Education Programs, which are selective interventions for children at risk of academic failure, such as cross-age or adult tutoring (U.S. Department of Health and Human Services, 2001).

Table 4.2. Promising prevention programs for elementary school children

Strategy	Program	Setting	Age range	Risk factors	Duration	Methods	Surg. Gen. rating	Blueprint rating
School capacity building	Continuous Progress Programs	Classroom	6 to 13 yrs	Universal	Ongoing	Individualized curriculum and pacing	Prom 2	n.a.
School capacity building	Cooperative Learning	Classroom	6 to 13 yrs	Universal	Ongoing	Small groups with mixed skill levels	Prom 2	n.a.
School enhancement	Peer to peer tutoring	Classroom	6 to 13 yrs	Academic failure	Ongoing	Peer to peer tutoring	Prom 2	n.a.
Classroom management	Good Behavior Game	Classroom	6 to 10 yrs	Universal	Ongoing	Classroom behavior management	Prom 2	Prom
Skill building	I Can Problem Solve	Classroom	4 to 12 yrs	Universal	12 sessions	Training in interpersonal problemsolving	Prom 2	Prom
Skill building	PATHS	School	5 to 10 yrs	Universal	3 mos	Self-control and problemsolving	Prom 2	Proven
Skills and parent training	LIFT	Classroom and home	6 to 10 yrs + parents	Universal	10 weeks	Skill training and parent training	Prom 2	Prom
Skill building	Preventive Treatment Program	Home and school	7 to 9 yrs	Disruptive boys from low SES	17 sessions	School-based social skills training	Prom 1	Prom
Multicontextual	FAST Track	Classroom and home	5 to 10 yrs	Disruptive in kindergarten	Ongoing	Social skills and parent training, home visits, tutoring, behavior management	Prom 2	Prom
Multicontextual	The Incredible Years	Classroom and home	3 to 8 yrs	Conduct problems	Ongoing	Parent training, behavior management	Prom 2	Proven
Multicontextual	Seattle Social Development Program	Classroom and home	7 to 12 yrs	Universal	5 yrs	Skills training, parent training	Model 1	Prom

The next category of programs to be considered after schoolwide-enhancement or capacity-building efforts are those involving management techniques in the classroom. The Good Behavior Game is a classroom-management program designed to reduce aggressive/disruptive classroom behavior and prevent later delinquency. The program targets entire classrooms of younger elementary school children by improving teachers' ability to define tasks, set rules, and discipline students, and allowing students to work in teams in which each member is responsible for the rest of the group. The Good Behavior Game produces its greatest impacts on those children demonstrating early, high-risk behavior (Dolan et al., 1989). Evaluations at the end of the first grade have found less aggressive and shy behaviors according to teachers and reduced aggressiveness according to peer ratings. Follow-up evaluations in the sixth grade have found decreases in levels of aggression for males who were rated highest for aggression when in the first grade (Barrish et al., 1969). Classroom management techniques play a central role in two more multifaceted programs—FAST Track and the Seattle Social Development Program—that deal with this same age group. They are reviewed below.

Moving on from school and classroom management changes we find a number of promising skill-development programs that focus on enhancing students' social skills and problemsolving abilities. I Can Problem Solve is a universal program that can be applied at any elementary grade level. The instructional materials and problemsolving exercises that make up this program are presented in twelve sessions over a three-month period. Evaluations have found reduced impulsive and inhibited classroom behavior and improved problemsolving skills after one year for kindergarten students (Shure & Spivack, 1982) and improvements in classroom behavior and problemsolving three to four years after program completion for fifth and sixth graders (Shure, 1993). Both the Good Behavior Game and I Can Problem Solve have been rated as "promising" by Blueprints and as Level 2 of "promising" by the Surgeon General's Report, meaning that they have demonstrated long-term or consistent effects on important risk factors for violence.

The next program in this category is Promoting Alternative Thinking Strategies (PATHS), a universal program taught by regular elementary classroom teachers who have participated in three days of training. The aim of PATHS is to increase student self-control, emotional competence, and problemsolving skills. The curriculum is implemented with entire classrooms of children ranging from kindergarten to fifth grade. The curriculum includes separate units that deal with feelings and interpersonal cognitive problemsolving. There is a strong focus on encouraging students to apply the newly learned skills in their everyday lives.

Evaluations of PATHS have shown that it improves self-control and planning skills and produces reductions in hyperactivity, peer aggression, and conduct problems. For students with special needs, it was found to reduce symptoms of anxiety, depression, and conduct problems (Greenberg et al., 1998; Sherman et al., 1997). PATHS is rated "promising" at Level 2 by the Surgeon General's Report and is a Blueprint "model" program.

The next step in the progression of program types for this age range is to add home visitation and/or parent training to skill development and behavior management in the classroom. The five programs described below combine these elements, with some adding additional elements as well.

Two programs that combine parent training with classroom interventions are Linking the Interests of Families and Teachers (LIFT) and the Montreal Preventive Treatment Program (PTP). Both are rated as "promising" by the Surgeon General's Report (Level 2) and Blueprints. The classroom component of LIFT, which includes twenty one-hour sessions delivered over a ten-week period, targets students in the first and fifth grade. Each session includes lecture, roleplaying, structured group-skills practice, and daily rewards. Parent training takes place in groups at the school. LIFT also includes a peer component that focuses on encouraging positive social behavior during playground activities, using a modified version of the Good Behavior Game. An evaluation of immediate posttest results indicated decreased physical aggression on the playground, reductions in aversive behavior by mothers, and increase in teacher ratings of positive social skills (Eddy et al., 2000).

PTP, developed by Richard Tremblay and his colleagues in Montreal, is a two-year intervention for disruptive kindergarten boys that combines home-based parent training with school-based social-skills training (Tremblay et al., 1992). Evaluations have found that by age twelve, experimental youth were 50 percent less likely to have serious school adjustment problems and significantly less likely to have initiated delinquent behaviors (Tremblay et al., 1996).

The remaining three programs combine activities designed to improve teacher and parent responses to disruptive youth, and to improve the skills and behavior of the youth as well. FAST Track is a comprehensive, long-term prevention program that spans grades one through six (Conduct Problems Prevention Group, 1992). It particularly targets youth who are disruptive in kindergarten. Parent training and home visitations during the first year focus on improving parenting skills and supporting the child's academic performance. Social Skills Training and a special PATHS curriculum enhance students' emotional awareness and problemsolving skills. Academic tutoring is offered three times per week to improve reading skills.

FAST Track is rated "promising" by the Surgeon General's Report (Level 2) and Blueprints. Short-term, follow-up studies for several cohorts of students have shown that FAST Track students have better behavioral ratings from parents, teachers, and observers; nominate fewer peers as being aggressive; and have parents who are more involved in their school activities and use more appropriate discipline techniques (Conduct Problems Prevention Group, 1999).

The parent, teacher, and child training series that are part of The Incredible Years Program targets children between the ages of three and eight with conduct problems. Its two primary goals are to provide cost effective, early-intervention programs that all families and teachers of young children can use to promote social, emotional, and academic competence; and to provide comprehensive interventions for teachers and parents to deal with the early onset of conduct problems in young children (Webster-Stratton, 2001). The training for parents includes a series of three separate programs to foster parenting and personal skills. The training for teachers emphasizes effective classroom-management skills, the use of incentives for difficult behavior problems, and proactive teaching strategies. It also shows how to teach empathy, social skills, and problemsolving in the classroom. The Dinosaur curriculum for children emphasizes training children in skills such as emotional literacy, empathy, and anger management.

Parts of The Incredible Years have been subjected to different levels of evaluation. The BASIC program for parents has been demonstrated through six randomized studies to result in improved parental attitudes and parent-child interaction, reduction in parents use of violent discipline, and reduced child conduct problems (Webster-Stratton, 2001). These effects have been sustained up to three years after intervention. BASIC has also been demonstrated to be an effective selective prevention program for multi-ethnic Head Start families in two randomized trials (Webster-Stratton, 1998) and subsequent independent replications (Webster-Stratton, 2001).

Evaluations have demonstrated that the ADVANCE component of the parent training program increases effective problemsolving and communication skills for both parents and children (Webster-Stratton & Hammond, 1997). Several randomized trials have demonstrated that the teacher-training program resulted in teachers being less critical, less harsh, using more praise, and being more nurturing; participating children were less aggressive with peers and more cooperative with teachers (Webster-Stratton & Reid, 1999).

Two randomized trials have demonstrated that the twenty- to twenty-two-week child-training program using the Dinosaur curriculum results in improved peer interactions and improved conflict-management skills, over and above those achieved with use of the parent or teacher components alone (Webster-Stratton & Hammond, 1997). The Incredible Years is rated as "promising" (Level 2) by the Surgeon General's Report and is the most recent program elevated to "model" status by Blueprints.

Last but not least in this category is another multicomponent intervention, the Seattle Social Development Program (SSDP). The goal of SSDP is to increase elementary school student bonds to school and family while decreasing other risk factors (U.S. Department of Health and Human Services, 2001). Intervention methods include classroom-behavior management, child-skills training, and parent training over five years of student participation. Follow-up studies at age eighteen have shown lower rates of violence, less heavy drinking and sexual activity, and better school performance than controls (Hawkins et al., 1998). SSDP is rated as "promising" by Blueprints and is listed as a "model" program in the Surgeon General's Report.

Altogether the category of promising or proven delinquency-prevention programs that focus on elementary-school-age children includes three general strategies—Continuous Progress Programs, Cooperative Learning, and Compensatory Education—and eight specific program models. One of the programs in this group, the SSDP, has been designated a "model" program by the Surgeon General's Report. Two other programs, The Incredible Years and PATHS, have been selected as Blueprints "model" programs. Some of the programs are no more than specialized curricula that can be inserted into regular school programs and provided on a universal basis. Others, including two of the three model programs (SSDP and The Incredible Years), require extensive involvement and training of both parents and teachers and can only afford to be implemented on a selective basis. All of the "proven" programs utilize multiple strategies and methods to achieve their results.

Programs for Adolescents

Promising programs for adolescents include many of the same approaches used with elementary-school-aged children—school enhancements or capacity building, parent training, and skill building. Where they differ is in the attention they pay to the critical choices faced by adolescents: the use of alcohol, tobacco and drugs; engaging in other risky behaviors (sex, selling drugs, joining a gang, etc.); and staying in school. Table 4.3 contains basic information for all of the delinquency-prevention programs that target adolescents and that are considered "proven" or "promising" by the Surgeon General's Report or Blueprints.

The first set of programs and strategies in this category calls for enhancing or reorganizing the more traditional services and programs typically found within schools. Project PATHE is a comprehensive program for secondary schools that is directed at reducing school disorder and increasing student bonding with the school. The entire school community works together to design and implement improvement programs. Schoolwide academic and disciplinary problems are identified and resolved through innovative teaching techniques, student team learning, and the development of clear but fair rules. School climate is enhanced through extracurricular activities, peer-counseling services, and school pride campaigns. Career attainment is emphasized by adding job-seeking skills and career exploration programs. At-risk students receive additional monitoring, tutoring, and counseling aimed at improving their self-concept, academic success, and bonds with the social order. Evaluations of program effectiveness show reduced self-reported delinquency and school alienation, increased attachment to school, and improved school climate (Gottfredson, 1990). Both Blueprints and the Surgeon General's Report consider PATHE a "promising" program.

Project STATUS is another school-based program designed to improve the climate of junior and senior high schools and to reduce delinquency and dropout. The two primary strategies utilized are collaborative efforts for improving school climate and a year-long English/social studies class focused on key social institutions. An evaluation of Project STATUS found less total delinquency, drug use, and negative peer pressure and greater academic success and social bonding (Gottfredson, 1990). Project STATUS is rated "promising" by Blueprints but not by the Surgeon General's Report.

While the two preceding programs are "universal" interventions in the sense they involve all of the students in a school, the next group of programs specifically target students at high risk for behavioral problems and/or dropout. The School Transitional Environmental Program (STEP) aims to reduce the complexity of school environments, increase peer and teacher support, and decrease student vulnerability to academic and emotional difficulties by reducing school disorganization and restructuring the role of the homeroom teacher. It specifically targets those students at

Table 4.3. Promising prevention programs for adolescents

Strategy	Program	Setting	Age range	Risk factors	Duration	Methods	Surg. Gen. rating	Blueprint rating
School enhancement	PATHE	School	11 to 14 yrs	Universal	Multiyear	School reform, careered, extra for at-risk students	Prom 2	Prom
School enhancement	STATUS	School	11 to 18 yrs	Universal, school dropout	Multiyear	School climate change, integrated social studies class	n.a.	Prom
School reorganization	STEP	School	11 to 18 yrs	Behavior problems	Multiyear	Enhanced homeroom, grouping STEP participants	Prom 1	Prom
School enhancement	Preventive Intervention	School	11 to 13 yrs	Low academic motivation, family or behavior problems	1 yr	Behavior monitoring, reinforcement, parent communication	Prom 2	Prom
School enhancement	QOP	School	15 to 18 yrs	Dropout	4 yrs	Incentives, counseling	Prom 2	Proven
School capacity building	Positive Youth Development	Community, school	10 to 14 yrs	Low income, lack of opportunity	Multiyear	Extracurricular and afterschool activities targeting at-risk youth	Prom 2	n.a.

(continued)

Table 4.3. (*continued*)

Strategy	Program	Setting	Age range	Risk factors	Duration	Methods	Surg. Gen. rating	Blueprint rating
Mentor	BBBS	Community	11 to 16 yrs	Single parent	1 yr	Screening and training of mentors	n.a.	Proven
Skills training	Life Skills Training	Classroom	10 to 12 yrs	Gateway drug use	3 yrs, 15 sessions 1st year	Self-management and social skills, info and skills re drug use	Model 2	Proven
Skills training	ATLAS	Classroom, gym	14 to 18 yrs male athletes	Universal	8 wks	Drug info and resist training, weight training	n.a.	Prom
Parent training	Preparing for the Drug Free Years	Community	11 to 12 yrs	Gateway drug use	7 wks	Family competency training	Prom 2	Prom
Parent training	Iowa Strengthening Families	Classroom	11 yrs + parents	Conduct disorder	7 sessions, 7 wks	Parent skills and family communication training	Prom 2	Prom
Family therapy	Brief Strategic Family Therapy	Home	8 to 17 yrs	Behavior problems	12 to 15 sessions	Motivation, assessment, restructuring	n.a.	Prom

Multicontextual	Bullying Prevention Project	School	10 to 16 yrs	Universal, aggression, physical abuse	Multiyear	Assessment, parent/teacher problemsolving, classroom behavior management	Prom 2	Proven
Multicontextual	CASASTART	Community	11 to 13 yrs	Distressed neighborhood	2 yrs	Law enforcement, case management, services, after school	Prom 1	Prom
Multicontextual	Project Northland	School, community	11 to 13 yrs	Universal, early alcohol use	3 yrs, 15 sessions 1st yr	Family communication, resistance skills, community action	n.a.	Prom
Multicontextual	Midwestern Prevention Project	Classroom, school and community	10 to 12 yrs	Universal, gateway drug use	3 years	Mass media, parent education and organization, community organization and health policy	Model 2	Proven

greatest risk for behavioral problems. STEP students are grouped in home-
rooms in which the teachers are trained to assume the additional role of
guidance counselor. All project students are assigned to the same core
classes. Evaluations have demonstrated decreased absenteeism and dropout, increased academic success, and more positive feelings about school
(Reyes & Jason, 1991). Both Blueprints and the Surgeon General's Report
consider STEP a "promising" program.

The limited evidence regarding the effectiveness of any one of these
programs (one or two evaluations of pilot programs) suggests that they are
best implemented along with activities already identified with improved
school effectiveness. These include collaborative planning and problemsolving involving teachers, parents, students, community members, and
administrators; grouping of students into small self-contained clusters;
career education; integrated curriculums; and student involvement in
establishing and enforcing rules. Likewise, the next two programs might
best be thought to represent a strategy that uses various policies and
practices designed to increase student attachment to schooling and reduce
dropout.

Preventive Intervention is a two-year, school-based behavioral rein-
forcement program that begins in the seventh grade and targets students
with low academic motivation, family problems, or disciplinary problems.
The intervention includes behavior monitoring, classroom reinforcement,
and enhanced communications among teachers, parents, and students
(U.S. Department of Health and Human Services, 2001). Preventive
Intervention is considered "promising" by both Blueprints and the
Surgeon General's Report.

The Quantum Opportunities Program (QOP) is a more comprehensive
approach that works with small groups of high-risk youth from poor
families and neighborhoods. The program provides an opportunity for
education, development, and service activities. Students remain part of the
same group through four years of high school. This continuity is meant to
provide a sustained relationship with a positive peer group and a caring
adult leader. All of the program activities take place outside of regular
school hours. The participants receive 250 hours per year of competency-
based, basic-skills training; development opportunities such as cultural
enrichment; and service opportunities in their communities. Financial
incentives are used to increase participation and completion. Results of a
multisite evaluation indicated that participants were less likely to be arrested
during their high-school years than a control group of similar high-risk
teens. In addition, QOP participants were more likely to complete high

school and continue on to college than the control group (Lattimore et al., 1998). QOP was selected as one of the original Blueprints "model" programs in 1998, but was removed from the list in 2003 because of disappointing results from more recent Department of Labor replication efforts. QOP is rated "promising" (Level 2) by the Surgeon General's Report.

The next two programs involve efforts to expose at-risk youth to more prosocial relationships and activities. Positive Youth Development is a general category of afterschool activities such as those run by the Boys and Girls Clubs, the Big Brothers and Big Sisters of America programs, and a Canadian afterschool program that targets at-risk youth in particular housing projects. Although the critical components of these programs are not defined well enough for them to be listed as "promising" or "model" programs, evaluations of these activities have demonstrated significant declines in vandalism, drug trafficking, and delinquency (U.S. Department of Health and Human Services, 2001; Jones & Offord, 1989).

The mentoring program of the Big Brothers and Big Sisters is a Blueprints "model" program, but was not listed as "promising" in the Surgeon General's Report. Local program affiliates carefully match adult volunteers to youth in the program. Although it is not a requirement of the program, a large portion of youth participants are from disadvantaged, single-parent households. The mentor meets with his or her youth partner at least three times per month for three to five hours at a time. The one-to-one relationship is meant to promote the development of a caring relationship between the pair. Studies of the program have shown that participants are less likely to start using drugs, to hit someone, or to be truant than a control group of youth on a waiting list to enter the program. Improvements in attitudes, school performance, and family relationships were also noted for the treatment group (Tierney & Resch, 1995).

The next two programs in this category involve different kinds of skills training to prevent early drug use. In addition to being a problem behavior in its own right, early experimentation with drugs is a risk factor for later serious delinquency and violence (Lipsey & Derzon, 1998). Life Skills Training is a drug-use-prevention program targeted at children in junior high or middle schools. In the first year of the program, teachers conduct fifteen sessions focusing on general life skills and strategies for social resistance. Booster sessions are provided in years two and three of the program (ten and five sessions, respectively). Teachers use a variety of techniques including instruction, demonstration, feedback, reinforcement, and practice to train students in the three core areas of self-management skills, social skills, and information and skills related to drug use.

Multiple evaluations of LST have shown it to reduce the use of alcohol, cigarettes, and marijuana among participants. The reductions in alcohol and cigarette use are sustained through the end of high school (Botvin et al., 1990, 1995). Life Skills Training is rated a "model" program by both Blueprints and the Surgeon General's Report, and appears on most other lists of "proven" programs (Mihalic et al., 2002). The program has been widely disseminated throughout the United States over the past decade with funding from government agencies and private foundations.

ATLAS (Athletes Training and Learning to Avoid Steroids) is a drug-prevention and health-promotion program that emphasizes the impact of anabolic steroids, alcohol, and other drugs on athletic performance. The program, which can be implemented in schools or recreation centers with male athletes, is integrated into team practice sessions and consists of a classroom curriculum and weight-room skill training sessions (Goldberg et al., 1996). An evaluation involving random assignment of over 3,200 athletes in three cohorts and thirty-one schools found less use of steroids, alcohol, and other drugs (Goldberg et al., 1996). ATLAS is listed as "promising" by Blueprints, but not by the Surgeon General's Report.

The next three programs directed at adolescents involve various forms of parent training and family therapy. All three are rated as "promising" by Blueprints, as are the first two by the Surgeon General's Report.

Preparing for the Drug Free Years (PDFY) is a family competency-training program that focuses on improving parenting skills and parents' self-efficacy. It also provides students with peer-pressure-refusal skills. The program has been implemented with families of middle-school students living in rural, economically distressed areas of the Midwest. Evaluations of PDFY have demonstrated: improvements in general child-management skills and ratings of self-efficacy on the part of parents; less initiation of alcohol use; and positive trends in reducing tobacco and marijuana use among their children (Park et al., 2000).

Iowa Strengthening Families Program (ISFP) is another universal, family-based intervention. Over the course of seven weeks, the program helps children and parents learn individual skills that improve daily family communication. ISFP has been successfully implemented in thirty-three rural, Midwestern schools. Follow-up evaluations show improved child management practices, increased parent-child communication, and lower rates of alcohol initiation and use (Spoth et al., 1998).

Brief Strategic Family Therapy (BSFT) is a short-term, problem-focused intervention with an emphasis on modifying maladaptive patterns of interaction among family members. It targets families of children between the ages of eight and seventeen who display or are at risk for behavior problems. The program consists of twelve to fifteen one-hour sessions delivered over a three-month period. Individual components include understanding resistance and motivating families to join in the effort; identifying interaction patterns that support problem behavior; and developing a specific plan to restructure maladaptive interaction patterns by reframing and working with boundaries and alliances. An evaluation of posttreatment impacts showed significant reductions in Conduct Disorder and Socialized Aggression for BSFT adolescents compared to controls participating in group therapy (Szapocznik & Williams, 2000).

The final four programs in this category are all multicontextual, combining a number of strategies and approaches into a coherent program approach. The Bullying Prevention Program (BPP) was developed for use with students in elementary and junior high schools in Bergen, Norway. The program involves the collaboration of teachers and parents in setting and enforcing clear rules against bullying behavior. Two years after the intervention, bullying problems decreased by 50 percent in schools with BPP. Other forms of delinquency declined as well and school climate improved (Olweus et al., 1998). BPP is one of the eleven Blueprints "model" programs and is listed as "promising" in the Surgeon General's Report.

CASASTART is a multidimensional program that targets at-risk youth in impoverished neighborhoods with a combination of specialized law enforcement, case management, social services, and afterschool activities. Evaluations of the diverse programs comprising this multisite strategy demonstrated significant positive effects on drug use immediately following participation, and on violent crime and drug selling one year later (Harrell et al., 1998). CASASTART is rated as "promising" by both Blueprints and the Surgeon General's Report.

Project Northland is another communitywide intervention designed to reduce adolescent alcohol use. The program spans three years and incorporates training of individuals, parents, peers, and the community. Communications between sixth graders and their parents are enhanced by having them work on homework assignments together and participate in group discussions. Seventh graders participate in a peer- and teacher-led curriculum that focuses on resistance skills and normative expectations. Eighth graders are encouraged to become active citizens by interviewing community members about their beliefs and activities concerning adolescent drinking, and by conducting town meetings to make recommendations for community action and assistance in reducing teen drinking. An evaluation at the end of the third year demonstrated reduced alcohol use and improved parent communication. Project Northland is listed as "promising" by Blueprints, but not by the Surgeon General's Report.

The Midwestern Prevention Project (MPP) is another communitywide intervention that attempts to reduce gateway drug use by targeting sixth and seventh graders. The five major components of the program, implemented in a stepwise fashion over a four-year period, are a mass-media program; a school program; parent education and organization; community organization; and local health policy. Evaluations have found reduced use of tobacco and marijuana, and reduced hard-drug use through age twenty-three (Pentz et al., 1998). The program is listed as a "model" program by both the Surgeon General's Report and Blueprints.

Within this category of adolescent programs, Blueprints has designated four as "models" while the Surgeon General's Report only designated two of those four as "proven." The proven programs include schoolwide, classroom, and individual levels of focus. All of the proven programs are relatively inexpensive on a per-capita basis.

Programs for Adjudicated Delinquents

In chapter 2, I argued that efforts to prevent further delinquency could be particularly effective when applied to youth whose behavior brought them to the attention of law enforcement or the juvenile court. This is because they would remain highly likely to demonstrate continued involvement in crime over an extended period of time. The final group of programs to be considered here includes those that are defined to deal with just such juveniles.

There are only four such programs of this type, as is shown in table 4.4. Three have been selected as "model" programs by both the Surgeon General's Report and Blueprints, while the fourth is deemed to be "promising" by Blueprints, but not by the Surgeon General's Report. The three "model" programs are Functional Family Therapy, Multisystemic Therapy, and Multidimensional Treatment Foster Care. All three involve recruiting and motivating families to participate in the intervention, working with families to identify problems and develop solutions, and extensive monitoring of adherence to the model and intervention protocols.

Functional Family Therapy (FFT) targets youth between eleven and eighteen years of age who have problems with delinquency, substance abuse, or violence. The program focuses on altering interactions between family members, and seeks to improve the functioning of the family unit by honing the family's skills at problemsolving, enhancing emotional

Table 4.4. Promising prevention programs for delinquent youth

Strategy	Program	Setting	Age range	Risk factors	Duration	Methods	Surg. Gen. rating	Blueprint rating
Enhanced probation	Intensive Protective Supervision	Home, community	12 to 17 yrs	Delinquency	6 mos	Assessment, monitoring, home visits	Prom I	Prom
Clinical family intervention	Functional Family Therapy	Home or office	12 to 17 yrs	Chronic and serious delinquency	4 mos	Motivation and engagement, assessment, communications Behavioral change skills training	Model I	Proven
Therapeutic foster care	Multidimensional Treatment Foster Care	Foster home	12 to 17 yrs	Chronic and serious delinquency	9 mos	Recruitment, screening, parent training, respite care	Model I	Proven
Multisystemic	Multisystemic Therapy	Home, school, community	12 to 17 yrs	Chronic and serious delinquency	4 mos	Assessment, parent training, service coordination, emergency response	Model I	Proven

connections between family members, and strengthening parental ability to provide appropriate structure, guidance, and limits to their children (Alexander et al., 1998). FFT is a relatively short-term program that is delivered by individual therapists, usually in the home. Each team of four to eight therapists works under the direct supervision and monitoring of several more experienced therapist/trainers. The effectiveness of the program has been demonstrated for a wide range of problem youth in numerous trials over the past twenty-five years, using different types of therapists, ranging from paraprofessionals to trainees, in a variety of social work and counseling professions. The program is well documented and readily transportable.

The second model program included in the category of adjudicated youth is Multisystemic Therapy or MST. The overriding purpose of this approach is to help parents deal effectively with their youth's behavior problems, including disengagement from deviant peers and poor school performance. To accomplish family empowerment, MST also addresses barriers to effective parenting and helps family members build an indigenous network for social support. To increase family collaboration and treatment generalization, MST is typically provided in the home, school, and other community locations. Master's-level counselors provide fifty hours of face-to-face contact spread over four months.

MST takes about as long to work with an individual family as FFT, but it is more intensive and more expensive. In addition to working with parents, MST will locate and attempt to involve other family members in supervising the youth, as well as seek the participation of teachers, school administrators, and other adults who interact with the youth. MST therapists, unlike those in the FFT program, are also on call for emergency services. Evaluations of the program demonstrate that the therapy is effective in reducing re-arrest rates and out-of-home placements for a wide variety of problem youth enmeshed in both the juvenile-justice and social-service systems (Henggler et al., 1998).

The third model program in this group is Multidimensional Treatment Foster Care. MTFC is a cost-effective alternative to group residential treatment for adolescents who have problems with chronic delinquency and antisocial behavior. Based on concepts having to do with social learning, community families are recruited, trained, and closely supervised to provide MTFC treatment oversight for participating adolescents. MTFC parent training emphasizes methods of behavior management to provide youth with a structure and therapeutic living environment. After completing a preservice training, MTFC parents attend a weekly group meeting run by a program case manager, which provides ongoing supervision. Support is also provided to MTFC parents by means of daily telephone calls, and family therapy is also provided for the youth's biological family. Evaluations with random assignment have demonstrated the MFTC model, in comparison to youth assigned to traditional group homes, to be effective in reducing arrests among participants (Chamberlain & Mihalic, 1998; Chamberlain & Reed, 1997).

The fourth program in this category, Intensive Protective Supervision (IPS), targets nonserious status offenders. Offenders assigned to IPS are closely monitored by counselors who carry reduced caseloads and interact more extensively with the youth and his family than traditional parole officers. The counselors make frequent home visitations, provide support for parents, develop individualized service plans, and arrange for professional or therapeutic services as needed. A follow-up evaluation of the program at one year found that youth assigned to IPS were less likely to be referred to juvenile court and were more likely to have successfully completed treatment than youth assigned to regular protective supervision (Sontheimer & Goodstein, 1993; MacKenzie, 1997). IPS is rated as "promising" by both Blueprints and the Surgeon General's Report.

The presence of three proven models and one promising one within this category suggests that there is a low level of investment in developing and testing such models. It is strange that this should be the case where the models that have been proven turn out to be so cost effective.

Costs and Benefits of the Most Promising Programs

The programs and strategies for delinquency prevention reviewed above make it clear that there is a great deal of variation among programs in the resources and skills required to implement them effectively. Some require just the training of teachers or the purchase of special curriculum materials. Others require specially trained staff to work with parents and children. Some require staff with special qualifications or access to additional services as well. Other programs require a limited number of sessions spread over a period of several months. Still others require ongoing intervention with parents and children for a number of years. Several of the proven program models require ongoing supervision and training for therapists working with families, and the periodic collection of quality assurance data to ensure that the program model is being implemented consistently.

In this section, I compare program characteristics by looking at the issue of costs. The costs of a program are the up-front investment that a

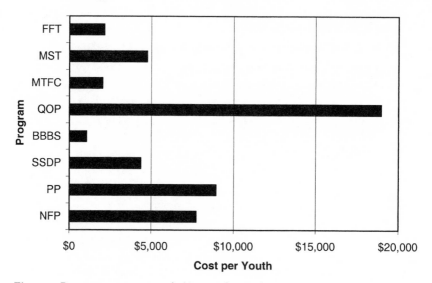

Fig. 4.1. Program cost per youth (Aos et al., 2001)

community must make in order to begin reaping program benefits. Program costs provide a kind of proxy for the intensity, complexity, and duration of the program. Those with low per-capita costs are generally more inclusive than those that involve higher costs per case. The latter are also usually associated with greater requirements for staff training and supervision, and less reliance on standardized curriculum materials.

Figure 4.1 displays cost-per-case data for the seven model or promising programs for which such data is available. Most of the cost estimates were developed by the Washington State Institute for Public Policy (WSIPP) (Aos et al., 2001), based on the reported costs of implementing the model less the costs of the control-group program, appropriately discounted for the base year of comparison. In cases where no program costs were reported in the evaluation literature, WSIPP used descriptions of staffing needs, program duration, and intensity to estimate likely per-capita program costs based on wage rates being paid in similar types of programs.

The first thing to be noticed is the range of variability. The mentoring program of Big Brothers and Big Sisters (BBBS) costs less than $2,000 per youth served while the Quantum Opportunities Program (QOP) costs almost $19,000 for each youth served. Although a youth may be involved in a mentoring program for a year or more, the costs are relatively lower because not many resources are required to train or supervise the mentors. QOP, on the other hand, is an expensive program because each youth is

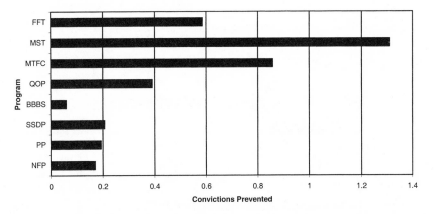

Fig. 4.2. Number of convictions prevented for typical participant (Aos et al., 2001)

involved for four years and the program requires a full-time staff. The median cost per youth for all the programs in this group is about $5,000.

The next thing we might notice about the pattern of costs is how they are distributed. With the exception of QOP, those programs serving older, more high-risk youth (FFT, MST, MTFC) tend to be less costly, on a per-capita base, than those serving younger children, particularly the Nurse Family Partnership (NFP) and Perry Preschool (PP). Both of the latter programs serve each youth and family for two years and require highly trained staff. Programs that serve older youth, primarily through training their families, have a shorter duration. They also serve youth that might have been served by other programs as well. The program cost figures estimated by WSIPP subtract the costs of any current programming that the promising programs replace.

Prevention programs differ not only in costs but also in the risk-level of youth they serve and the impact they have on risk. These two characteristics are summarized in figure 4.2, which shows the expected number of felony convictions that each program prevents for a typical participant. These estimates were developed by WSIPP by multiplying the estimated effect size for each program by the average number of convictions experienced by youth in Washington who are similar to those served by each program. An appropriate discount rate is applied to all costs and benefits to make the figures current (Aos et al., 2001). The estimates vary from less than one felony conviction prevented for every ten youth participating in a mentoring program (BBBS) to 1.3 felony convictions prevented for each youth served by MST. MST serves high-risk populations and has a large effect size. BBBS

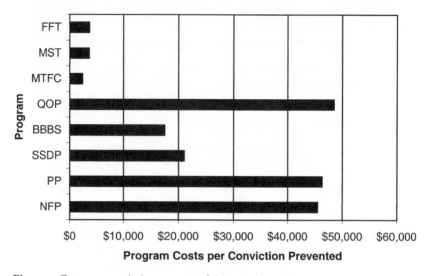

Fig. 4.3. Cost per conviction prevented (Aos et al., 2001)

serves lower-risk youth and does not have a large effect size. All of the model programs that serve older high-risk youth are estimated to prevent more than one felony conviction for every two youth that they serve. Preschool (PP) and NFPs do not prevent as many convictions per youth served, not because they do not have a large effect size, but because they are focused on families at high-risk for poor child outcomes, of which crime is only one part.

Of course each felony conviction represents a much larger number of underlying offenses. With probabilities of arrest for crimes against persons at around 10 percent, and probabilities of conviction approximately 50 percent, each conviction for a felony crime against persons represents something like twenty actual offenses (Blumstein et al., 1986). For property crimes, the ratio of crimes to convictions is even higher.

Having looked at the variation in costs and impacts across the most promising delinquency-prevention programs, the next characteristic of interest is the cost of each conviction prevented—what many would consider to be an appropriate cost-effectiveness measure for delinquency-prevention programs. This data is displayed in figure 4.3 for each of the seven programs.

One of the first things to notice in figure 4.3 is that the cost per each conviction prevented is much lower for the three programs that target actual delinquents (FFT, MST, MTFC) than for those programs that deal with younger at-risk children. Each conviction prevented by PP or NFP programs costs more than $40,000 to achieve, compared to less than

$5,000 for each conviction prevented by FFT, MST, or MTFC. Once again, the cost effectiveness of these latter programs is due to their large effect sizes, modest cost, and ability to target very high-risk youth.

Do the outcomes in figure 4.3 suggest that primary and secondary delinquency-prevention efforts directed at younger children are not cost effective, and that all prevention resources should be devoted to model programs for delinquents already identified by the juvenile justice system? Not necessarily. Delinquency is closely associated with many other developmental problems. Many youth who have reached the stage of delinquency development where they require placement in an FFT or MST program have already developed substance abuse and smoking habits, fallen behind in their schoolwork, developed relationships with other delinquents, and failed to develop good work habits. Prevention programs that occur earlier in the developmental cycle provide an opportunity for avoiding or reducing many of these related problems.

Long-term, follow-up studies of the NFP and PP programs have demonstrated the wide range of benefits this type of early-prevention program can have. In addition to a substantial reduction in future arrests, the preschool program produced taxpayer savings in education costs by reducing special-education needs and the number of students held back a grade, in welfare costs by improving employment, and in increased tax receipts due to higher earnings. The Nurse Home Visitation Project in Elmira, New York produced significant savings in welfare costs for the mothers and healthcare costs for the children, increased tax receipts from the mothers' employment, and decreased arrests for both mothers and children. The estimated savings for these two programs is illustrated in figure 4.4, which compares the savings they produce in criminal-justice costs with taxpayer savings in other areas. Note that the "other" related savings are quite large relative to the criminal-justice savings. Of course, if we added in the savings in pain and suffering to potential crime victims the crime-related savings would increase by several orders of magnitude.

The low cost effectiveness of these early-childhood programs in preventing crimes, and the relatively large potential savings in noncriminal-justice costs, should not eliminate consideration of these programs as part of a community-based approach to crime prevention. They do suggest, however, that programs of this type should be housed in agencies affiliated with the local health, social service, or educational systems, rather than a criminal-justice agency that tends to focus on more immediate threats to public safety.

Taking into account the noncriminal-justice savings generated by some of the early-childhood programs, figure 4.5 shows how the expected

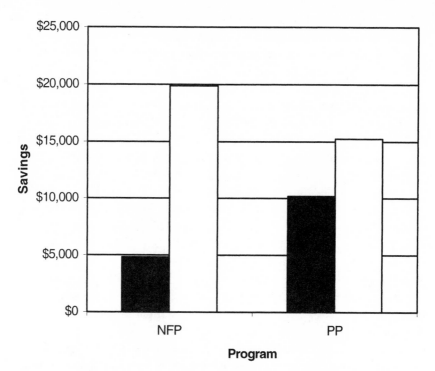

Fig. 4.4. Criminal justice compared with other savings (Karoly et al., 1998)

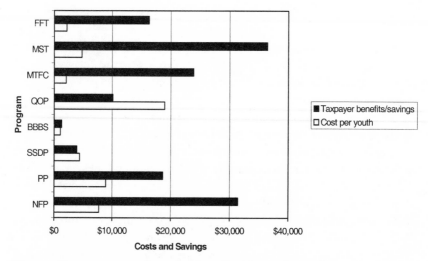

Fig. 4.5. Program costs and taxpayer benefits (Aos et al., 2001)

program costs and taxpayer benefits compare for each of the programs on which we have focused. The highest ratio of benefits to costs is achieved by MTFC at 11.6 to 1. MST and FFT are not far behind at 7.7 and 7.5 to 1, respectively. NFP comes in at 4.1 to 1 and PP at 2.1 to 1. The BBBS mentoring program just about breaks even at 1.2 to 1, while the SSDP and QOP both now cost more than they return in savings.

For most of the programs, the taxpayer benefits reflect the direct savings in government criminal-justice expenditures estimated by WSIPP, using the reported effect size for that program and the expected criminal-justice costs for a cohort of youths like those served by the program, less the costs of the program. For the Nurse Family Partnership and Perry Preschool programs, the net benefits for taxpayers include government saving in other areas in addition to criminal justice, as estimated by Karoly et al. (1998) in a cost-benefit study of those two programs.

One of the model programs not included on this list, Life Skills Training, has also been shown to return $2 in savings for every dollar invested in the program. However, according to a recent analysis by Caulkins, Chiesa, and Everingham (2002), most of the savings are associated with reduced use of tobacco and alcohol rather than reductions in crime.

Table 4.5 contains all the data required for cost-benefit calculations for each of the programs, including estimates of the saving to potential victims. Once again, the programs with the highest ratio of taxpayer benefits to costs are the three that focus primarily on training, empowering, and in some cases assisting the families that will serve in the immediate future as the primary guardians, caregivers, monitors, and disciplinarians for the youth. MTFC recruits, trains, assists, and monitors foster parents who are willing to allow the kind of troubled teen who would normally be placed in a group setting to reside in their home. WSIPP estimates that MTFC will return more than $11 in taxpayer savings for every dollar invested in the program, and another $30 or so to possible victims in reduced pain and suffering—a total of more than $40 as a return on an investment of $1. This is a very good investment indeed.

The return on investment for taxpayer investments in well-managed MST and FFT programs is around $7.50 for every dollar invested, which is also a pretty good deal. In order to be considered well managed, responses on questionnaires administered periodically to key family members must indicate that the program is being delivered with a high degree of fidelity to the proven model. FFT first engages, motivates, and then assists families in identifying and solving problems affecting the troubled youth. MST does all that and also works with the youth's teachers, probation officer, and other

Table 4.5. Costs and benefits of selected promising and proven programs

Program name	Age range (yrs)	Surg. Gen. rating	Blueprint rating	Effect size	Cost per youth ($)	Net benefits per case, taxpayers only ($)	Taxpayer benefits/ costs	Net benefits per case, taxpayers and victims ($)	Taxpayer and victim benefits/ costs	Total victim benefit/ total taxpayer benefit
Nurse Home Visitation	Prenatal to 2	Model 1	Proven	−0.29	7,733	23,663	4.1	41,848	6.4	1.57
Perry Preschool	3 to 4	Prom 1	Prom	−0.1	8,936	9,740	2.1	21,466	3.4	1.63
Seattle Social Development Program	7 to 12	Model 1	Prom	−0.13	4,355	−456	0.9	14,169	4.3	4.75
Life Skills Training	10 to 12	Model 2	Proven	−0.07	147	150	2.0	150	2.0	1.00
Big Brothers Big Sisters	11 to 16	Proven	Proven	−0.04	1,054	225	1.2	4,524	5.3	4.36
Quantum Opportunities	15 to 18	Prom 2	Proven	−0.31	18,964	−8,855	0.5	16,428	1.9	3.50
Intensive Protective Supervision	12 to 17	Prom 1	Prom	−0.05	2,234	176	1.1	6,816	4.1	3.76
Multi-dimensional Treatment Foster Care	12 to 17	Model 1	Proven	−0.37	2,052	21,836	11.6	87,622	43.7	3.75
Multi-Systemic Therapy	12 to 17	Model 1	Proven	−0.31	4,743	31,661	7.7	131,198	28.7	3.73
Functional Family Therapy	12 to 17	Model 1	Proven	−0.25	2,161	14,149	7.5	59,067	28.3	3.75

Source: Aos et al., 2001; Karoly et al., 1998.

service providers to resolve problems impeding the youth's prosocial development. MST programs also have greater emergency-response capability and are more likely to assist the family in obtaining additional services. The delinquency-prevention programs that offer the best return on taxpayer investments were all designed by psychologists and supported with funding from the National Institute of Mental Health (NIMH) during their development.

The next most cost-effective program for delinquency prevention, the Nurse Family Partnership, was developed by pediatrician David Olds. Taxpayer investments in programs that provide NFP to high-risk, first-time mothers should return about $4.10 for every dollar invested. This assertion assumes that the mix of government services and assistance usually expended on such mothers is not substantially different from what it was in Elmira, New York in the 1960s and 1970s, when the original experimental sample of families were raising their children. Most of the home-visitation programs currently in operation do not use nurses as the primary home visitors because of their higher cost and frequent lack of availability. As I indicated previously, home-visiting programs that do not use nurses do not produce significant effects, even when they follow the Olds protocols (Olds et al., 2003).

The next most cost-effective program intended to prevent delinquency is the Perry Preschool, developed by early-childhood educators. PP returns $2 to taxpayers for every dollar invested. Next in order of return on taxpayer investment comes LST (2 to 1), the mentoring model of BBBS (1.2 to 1), and finally IPS (1.1 to 1). SSDP is estimated by WSIPP to return only ninety cents on the dollar of taxpayer investment because of its modest effect size, significant cost, and inclusion of many fairly low-risk students. QOP would only return fifty cents on the dollar if we were sure to achieve the relatively large effect size reported from the first round of demonstration programs, despite the program's high cost and inclusion of low-risk participants. However, recent testing of QOP by the Department of Labor suggests such impacts are not easily achieved (private communication from Blueprints).

Reliability of the Evidence

Up to this point, I have sorted programs by how they were rated by Blueprints and the Surgeon General's Report, the age group they target, which evidenced-based techniques they use, and their cost effectiveness. The next question that any potential adopter or supporter of these programs might want to ask is how easily transportable the programs are. How sure can an adopting site be that that they will obtain results similar to those reported in the literature. Neither the Surgeon General's Report nor Blueprints required more than one successful replication of their proven models. Thus there is a good deal of ground to cover between having the originator of a successful program replicate it in another setting and being confident that many different types of organizations will be able to achieve similar effects with the model. Here I look at how the top-rated programs compare in this regard.

The program with the largest number of evaluations, in various types of settings, is Functional Family Therapy. At the time the FFT Blueprint was published in 1998 there had been fourteen evaluations of the model demonstrating its effectiveness. Since that time, FFT has been replicated in hundreds of sites, with the state of Washington conducting a statewide randomized trial involving thirty-six therapists (Barnowski, 2002).

In second place comes the much less expensive drug-prevention program Life Skills Training. During the past two decades, Gilbert Botvin and his colleagues have conducted at least seven pilot studies and several large-scale trials demonstrating the effectiveness of the basic LST model and several variations, all with random assignment and large effect sizes. With strong support from the U.S. Department of Education, CSAP, and OJJDP, LST has been implemented in a significant fraction of American middle schools (Ringwalt et al., 2002).

The programs in third and forth place in terms of evaluations and replications are NFP and MST. MST is being replicated in more than eighty sites, including Canada and Norway, and has been evaluated in four randomized trials. NFP is being replicated in more than sixty sites and has been evaluated in three randomized trials. These programs have developed detailed training protocols and data-collection procedures for monitoring fidelity of implementation.

In fifth place in the replication competition is MTFC, which has been the subject of four randomized trials and several replications. As of this writing, the developers of MTFC, Patti Chamberlain and her colleagues at the Oregon Social Learning Center, have just begun to set up the kind of separate dissemination, training, and licensing organization that the previous four programs have had in place for several years. Each new replication of MTFC is still something of a major event, whereas the four programs noted above already have trouble keeping track of all of their replication sites.

Sixth place probably goes to The Incredible Years. Although some components of the model (BASIC) have been the subject of multiple randomized trials and at least five independent replications, some have been tested only twice.

Beyond The Incredible Years, the strength of the evidence in support of any one particular program model is pretty well described by how it ranks on the Blueprints and Surgeon General's Report lists. If it is a "model" program, then it has successfully demonstrated long-term impacts and been successfully replicated at least once. If it is rated "promising," then evidence for its success rests on just one or two randomized trials.

The ranking of any particular program involves assessing the strengths of the individual program components, the developer's skill in integrating them together, their cost, and the efforts that have gone into demonstrating their effectiveness. The field of delinquency prevention has come a long way in the past few decades. There is no doubt that additional programs will be added to the lists of proven or cost-effective programs. Some will come from the "promising" lists. Others may be adaptations or extensions of current model programs, such as an MST PLUS, which could include the use of short-term residential placement.

In the meantime, the program rankings shown in this chapter provide the best source of information for communities or agencies that are interested in improving the effectiveness of their delinquency-prevention efforts. These same rankings should also be used as a guide by delinquency-research funders to identify target groups and program strategies that have the possibility of being cost effective.

Chapter 5

What Doesn't Work

In the previous chapter I reviewed a number of delinquency-prevention programs and strategies that have met generally agreed-on evidentiary standards to be qualified either as "proven" or "promising" program models. These models provide concrete examples or blueprints for effective interventions that prevention organizations can adopt or adapt to their own specific needs. But recent reviews of the delinquency-prevention literature have also identified a number of strategies and programs that do not appear to work or that may even backfire, increasing the likelihood of further delinquency rather than reducing it. There have been literally hundreds of different prevention programs implemented in the past two decades. If each state had generated only ten, that would make for a total of five hundred. Some meta-analyses currently contain more than four hundred evaluations. If we make the conservative assumption that five hundred different programs have been implemented, then we can get a feel for the likelihood of any one becoming designated as "promising" or "proven." Since there are but ten proven models, only 10/500 or 2 percent of all programs have achieved proven status. By the same reasoning, only 30/500 or 6 percent have achieved promising status.

The vast majority of all prevention programs, more than 90 percent, have no evidentiary support at all. They have either not been evaluated or have been evaluated with a research design that was too weak or flawed to detect the presence or absence of significant treatment effects. Finally, there is a remaining 2 percent of all programs that have been evaluated sufficiently well to determine that they either have no effect or have negative or iatrogenic effects; making participants more likely to engage in crime.

In this chapter, I focus more closely on these failed approaches for several reasons. One is that many jurisdictions have continued to support some of these programs long after they were found to be ineffective or harmful. The history of the program Scared Straight provides such an example. Examination of such instances can inform us about the motives and conflicting demands on those who control prevention programs and their purse strings.

Another reason for looking at these failed programs is that a number of them are fairly close copies, reproductions, or adaptations of other programs. Many jurisdictions appear to pick and choose components for their delinquency-prevention efforts like a diner at a buffet table, rather than relying on a few proven models. Many assume that if they stay fairly close to the basic ideas and concepts incorporated into a proven program, they will obtain similar outcomes. But how close is close enough when adapting a successful model program to local conditions? The evidence-based literature can assist communities by steering them toward programs and strategies that appear to work, and away from strategies and programs that do not.

There is a further important reason to dedicate a chapter to the careers of failed programs. We can learn much about why some programs seem to thrive despite evidence of ineffectiveness. Our special focus in this chapter is on programs that demonstrate this capacity.

Delinquency-Prevention Programs and Strategies That Do Not Work

In order to identify programs that do not work, the screening criteria might have to be modified from that used to identify proven programs. This is because the first evaluation of an effective program is likely to generate additional evaluations, while an unsuccessful program is unlikely to be subjected to additional rigorous evaluation. This is not always the case, however, if the ineffective program continues to be replicated, as was the case with DARE (the Los Angeles Police Department's Drug Abuse Resistance Education program) and with military-style boot camps, both of which are reviewed in this chapter.

The criteria in the Surgeon General's Report (U.S. Department of Health and Human Services, 2001) used to identify programs that do not work include:

- Rigorous experimental design (experimental or quasi-experimental).
- Significant evidence of null or negative effects.
- Replication, with preponderance of evidence suggesting that the program is ineffective or harmful.

The Surgeon General's Report focused on the effectiveness of programs for preventing youth violence. This chapter describes strategies that have been identified as ineffective in reducing either violence, delinquency, or their related risk factors on the basis of multiple evaluations. In addition to the Surgeon General's Report, the chapter we will draw primarily on the meta-analyses of Mark Lipsey and David Wilson (1998) for delinquency-focused interventions and Denise Gottfredson et al. (2002) in the area of school-based programs.

Primary Programs That Do Not Work

Four strategies frequently employed with adolescents and teenagers have been demonstrated ineffective in multiple settings: peer counseling, mediation, or leadership; alternative recreation; social competency instruction that does not use appropriate cognitive behavioral methods; and school-based drug testing. The first of these, peer-led programs, involve counseling, mediation, or leadership. They are quite popular despite having been shown to be ineffective in reducing youth violence and related risk factors as early as 1987 (Gottfredson, 1987). More recent meta-analyses have confirmed this finding and found that adults are equally or more effective than peers in these various roles (U.S. Department of Health and Human Services, 2001).

A second popular delinquency-prevention strategy involves providing alternative recreation and leisure-time opportunities for disadvantaged youth. While research does support the effectiveness of adult supervision for high-risk juveniles, programs designed to provide alternative recreation opportunities have not been found effective in reducing drug use, either because they failed to attract the appropriate youth or were ineffective in countering the criminogenic effect of bringing at-risk youth together. These programs have not been evaluated for their effect on crime (Gottfredson et al., 2002).

The third primary prevention strategy that is both ineffective yet widely implemented involves social-competency training without using the cognitive-behavioral approaches that have proven successful in other area. This strategy is popular by virtue of its being the central focus of DARE, which was developed by the Los Angeles Police Department and the Los Angeles Unified School District in 1983.

The core seventeen-lesson curriculum delivered by uniformed officers to fifth- and sixth-grade students in their classrooms is the most frequently used form of the program. The curriculum focuses on teaching students the skills needed to recognize and resist social pressures to use drugs. It also contains material about the consequences of drug use. However, the preponderance of the evidence from numerous evaluations and several careful reviews suggest that this strategy does not work in reducing crime, drug use, truancy, or related risk factors (U.S. Department of Health and Human Services. 2001, Gottfredson et al., 2002). In addition to its failure to use modeling, roleplaying, and other cognitive-behavioral approaches, it is also argued that the fifth- and sixth-grade versions of DARE are ineffective because they are developmentally inappropriate. Students at that age are not yet concerned with peer pressure, drug use, and the impression they make on members of the opposite sex (U.S. Department of Health and Human Services, 2001).

About 19 percent of all secondary schools in the United States conduct some form of student drug testing (Juvenile Justice Update, 2004), the fourth strategy mentioned above. A recent study using Monitoring - the Future data found that rates of student drug use were virtually identical in schools that required drug testing and those that did not (Yamaguchi et al., 2003).

Secondary Programs That Do Not Work

Two strategies that have been frequently employed to prevent further delinquency on the part of high-risk youth involve attempting to shift or redirect peer-group norms, especially for gang members, and activities designed to increase the deterrent effect for the risks of being arrested or shot. In the first of these approaches, efforts to shift peer-group norms involve bringing at-risk youth together for some intervention or working with naturally occurring groups such as gangs. Evaluations have shown that these efforts are not effective in reducing delinquency (U.S. Department of Health and Human Services, 2001; Welsh & Hoshi, 2002), and can even make matters worse (Dishion et al., 1999).

A second notoriously ineffective preventive strategy has been implemented through a program that carries one of the most wonderful labels in the history of juvenile programming: Scared Straight. Aiming to increase the *deterrent effect* of arrest and imprisonment, the Scared Straight program arranges for at-risk juveniles to meet with hardened criminals, who are coached to "get in their face" and drive home the negative aspects of a criminal life-style. To emphasize the risks of being injured or killed, at-risk youth are taken to view dead bodies in the morgue. Evaluations have shown that neither of these approaches has any effect on subsequent delinquency (MacKenzie, 2002). More will be said about this program below.

Tertiary Programs That Do Not Work

The largest category of ineffective strategies and programs contains those developed to work with more serious delinquent youth. It includes residential programs, boot camps, individual counseling, milieu therapy, social casework, waiver to adult court, behavioral token programs, early release to probation or parole, vocational programs, and wilderness challenge programs. The primary downside to residential, as opposed to individualized, community-based programs is that by bringing delinquent youth together the overall rate of delinquency increases through a process called "deviant peer contagion." This interpersonal processes by which deviant youth encourage and reinforce each other's negative behavior has been studied through observational methods and is associated with escalations in substance use, delinquency, and violent behavior (Dishion et al., 2001).

Another problem with most residential programs is that they take place in artificial settings away from the high-risk situations that youth will encounter when they return to the community. It is difficult to help youth in such settings develop the motivation and skills they will need to deal with the risk factors that are unique to their lives back in their home communities. A third problem with residential programs is that they are expensive, costing anywhere from $100 to $250 per day—at least three times the cost of intensive nonresidential programs.

It is for all these reasons that residential programs have been found less effective than community-based programs in imposing any particular form of intervention (Lipsey & Wilson, 1998; MacKenzie, 2002). However, once it is decided that a serious or chronic juvenile offender must be placed in a residential program, short programs are less effective than longer ones (Lipsey & Wilson, 1998). This phenomenon probably explains the ineffectiveness of boot camps and early release from residential placements on probation or parole.

Other strategies that have been shown to be ineffective but still are utilized as components of many residential placements include:

- Milieu therapy in which the entire environment of the program is designed to be therapeutic.
- Behavioral token economies through which youth can earn points, which can be redeemed for special privileges (snacks, extra TV time, etc.), for doing their chores and meeting the expectations of the program.

- Wilderness challenge programs that require youth to participate in challenging physical activities like hiking, rock climbing, or running marathons.
- Vocational training, individual counseling, and social casework, which are frequently utilized in both residential and community settings and are core components of many reentry and aftercare programs.

If the total number of delinquency-prevention programs and program components is approximately five hundred, then only 2 percent of these programs have achieved proven status; 6 percent are promising; and 3 percent have been shown not to work or may even lead to negative consequences. The great mass of programs and strategies being used to combat delinquency in American communities are unevaluated and produce uncertain impacts.

There are several ways of responding to this situation. The reaction of most researchers and academics is to call for more evaluations—more government funding for evaluations and more efforts devoted to evaluation by local program providers. Another response, which appears to be that of the many local funding agencies, is one of resignation. Since 90 percent of all prevention programs are unevaluated, anyone funding an unevaluated program has plenty of company and need not worry about being called to account. Everyone is using unevaluated programs. Furthermore, since there are some forty proven or promising programs and strategies and only fourteen that have been shown not to work, the odds should be in favor of any unevaluated program turning out to be promising rather than being found not to work—shouldn't they?

The appropriate conclusion drawn from the pattern of evidence described above is to recognize that all of the proven programs were developed through repeated cycles of design, testing, redesign, and retesting—a process that gradually increased the impact they were able to achieve. Without undergoing this time-consuming developmental process, it is extremely unlikely that very many of the large number of untested programs would produce worthwhile results, even if they were to be tested. The one exception may be the case of community-based approaches. Starting with the early work of sociologist Clifford Shaw in Chicago (Schlossman et al., 1984) and continuing through the recent efforts of the public-health community (Mercy & O'Carrol, 1988), there always have been those who have argued that improving conditions and services in high-risk communities is the best way to combat delinquency. Although many such community-focused interventions have been attempted, we know very little about their long-term impacts because the appropriate research designs are so difficult to implement. The lack of more community-based approaches on the proven and promising lists may be due more to the difficulties of evaluating them rather than to their underlying effectiveness.

Programs That Persist Despite Evidence They Do Not Work

It should not be surprising that many programs fail to achieve the impacts on delinquency that were hoped for, despite the best intentions of their developers. Adolescent development is a complex process and the influence and interaction of a multitude of factors is still poorly understood. What may be surprising is the fact that a number of programs continue to be utilized despite consistent evidence that they do not work. In this section of the chapter, I review the history and evaluation of four such programs as a way of developing insights into why this phenomenon occurs: DARE, Scared Straight, boot camps, and a particular form of home visitation. The close study of such paradoxical "successes" can teach as much about the practical reality of prevention in modern America as the detailed study of their more evidence-based competitors.

DARE

The Drug Abuse Resistance Training program, or DARE, provides one of the most dramatic examples of how a program can be put into practice nationwide with little in the way of supportive evidence, and then continue to flourish and prosper despite mounting evidence that it is ineffective in reducing drug use. A comparison of the DARE marketing campaign with those used by its more proven competitors also provides some insights into how such marketing campaigns should be run and might be regulated.

Some of the earliest attempts at preventing adolescent use of tobacco, alcohol, and other drugs used standard techniques of information dissemination and scare tactics designed to emphasize the dramatic risks associated with the use of these substances (Botvin, 1990). Another approach in the late 1970s and early 1980s combined information dissemination with preaching, appeals to morality, and advocacy of temperance. Although evaluations demonstrated that programs based on these traditional approaches were effective in increasing participants' knowledge base, none of these approaches was shown to be effective in reducing drug use (Botvin; Schaps et al., 1981).

In the mid-1970s, drug education was reconceptualized by some of the leading researchers as a process designed to increase affective skills

(Swisher, 1979; Botvin, 1990). The affective-education approach put less emphasis on factual information and more emphasis on the personal and social development of students through such activities as values clarification, communication skills, peer counseling, and assertiveness training (Botvin, 1990). Still other researchers advocated the development of pro-social alternatives to drug use such as youth centers, community service, or Outward Bound types of challenge activities (Swisher & Hu, 1983). Some evaluations of these approaches found impacts on intermediary risk factors but, like the more traditional approaches discussed above, neither was found to affect substance use (Botvin, 1990).

The approach to substance-abuse prevention that has been identified as most promising utilizes psychosocial approaches that include training in personal, social, and resistance skills. The intent of these programs is to teach the kind of generic skills for coping with life that will have a fairly broad application. By the mid-1980s, most of the studies testing the use of skills-training approaches began to demonstrate significant and large behavioral effects, showing reductions in experimental drug use ranging from 45 to 75 percent (Botvin, 1990; Botvin & Eng, 1982; Schinke & Gilchrist, 1983).

The DARE program was not developed by researchers directly involved in the developmental work described above. Rather, DARE was the product of a collaborative effort between the Los Angeles Police Department (LAPD) and the Los Angeles Unified School District curriculum specialists. The program they developed was a slightly modified version of one that had been developed by William Hansen at the University of Southern California called Project SMART (Boyle, 2001). The version of SMART that DARE adopted had already been dropped by Hansen because it was found not to work. It did not utilize the kind of cognitive-behavioral approaches to resistance training and social-skills development that recent evaluations had identified as most effective in changing antisocial behavior (Botvin, 1990; Ellickson et al., 1993). For whatever reasons, DARE chose to focus its core curriculum for drug-abuse prevention on fifth and sixth graders, who are believed by many prevention experts to be too young to appreciate or cope with the kinds of peer pressure they will encounter in the next few grades. The program also failed to provide for any credible evaluations of its approach.

A newly trained cadre of uniformed LAPD officers first presented the DARE curriculum to students in 1983. The pilot test included fifty Los Angeles elementary schools. Despite the shortcomings listed above, the program proved so popular with school officials, parents, and students that it was rapidly expanded throughout the school district. Prior to the development of DARE, the LAPD's most visible form of school-based drug prevention was assigning youthful-looking undercover officers to pass themselves off as students, so that they could identify and help arrest those involved in drug sales on school campuses. This approach was not well received by students and many of their parents.

With the public-relations success of the DARE program, the LAPD began offering free training sessions for other law-enforcement agencies throughout the state. Soon the state Office of Criminal Justice Planning began funding DARE training efforts. A nonprofit organization, DARE America, was created by former LAPD officials to mount an international fundraising, dissemination, and training effort. All of these efforts were moving ahead with little in the way of solid evaluation results to document the effectiveness of the program.

DARE eventually evolved into a series of school-based programs for preventing drug use and violence for youth in kindergarten through the twelfth grade. The core DARE curriculum remains focused on children in the fifth and sixth grades, comprising seventeen class sessions taught by specially trained uniformed police officers. In earlier grades, the program consists of classroom visits by uniformed DARE officers who warn children about risky behaviors. In later grades, it consists of booster sessions that build on what was taught in the basic curriculum.

The DARE approach is deeply rooted in the social skills and social influence model of drug education. It includes such measures as psychological inoculation and training in resistance skills in addition to personal and social skills (Botvin, 1990; Rosenbaum & Hanson, 1998). The basic assumption implicit in DARE is as follows:

- Classroom instruction by trained police officers will result in enhanced self-esteem, self-understanding, and assertiveness, a clearer sense of values, and more responsible decisionmaking habits;
- that in turn will make students less vulnerable to the enticements and pressures to use drugs and alcohol (Rosenbaum & Hanson).

DARE America developed a network of alliances among professional organizations, training centers, prominent public officials, and business leaders to help guide the evolution and dissemination of the program. Within a few years of its beginning in 1983, DARE programs were operating in many localities and most of the states. By 1998, DARE was operating in all fifty states and was used in 48 percent of American schools

(Manski et al., 2001). Its annual budget, subsidized by state and federal sources, was in excess of $700 million dollars. President Bill Clinton included praise for DARE in his 1996 State of the Union Message. Former president George Bush and Attorney General Janet Reno were enthusiastic supporters of the program. DARE was touted in a September 1995 Bureau of Justice Assistance Fact Sheet as "a validated, copyrighted, comprehensive drug and violence prevention education program."

The widespread dissemination and replication of DARE was well underway before any serious evaluation results were published. Many of the early evaluations, which DARE would later use to defend itself against its critics, were not very rigorous (Rosenbaum & Hanson, 1998). Most were "posttest only" designs, with survey instruments administered for the first time after students had participated in the program. An evaluation of DARE in Ohio (Donnermeyer, 1998) used posttest only interviews with 3,150 eleventh graders to classify self-reported DARE participants and nonparticipants under three risk categories, based on their self-reported involvement with drugs. In the high-risk category were 15 percent of the non-DARE students but only 10 percent of the DARE students. The results of this methodologically weak study were trumpeted around the state and the nation despite the fact that more rigorous studies of DARE had failed to find any significant impact on drug use (Clayton et al., 1991; Ennett et al., 1994).

Some early DARE evaluations failed to use a control group (Aniskoiewicz & Wysong, 1987; Carstens et al., 1989; Correll, 1990). Other studies required the respondents to recall whether they had received DARE (DeJong, 1987; Dukes et al., 1996), or they used nonequivalent control groups (McDonald et al., 1990). The effects that were most often touted by DARE reported changes in attitudes and knowledge, rather than changes in actual behavior. In the early 1990s, DARE America put together a forty-nine-page Evaluation Compendium that summarized a number of studies that appeared favorable to DARE. Most of the studies had very weak designs and showed improvements in attitudes and knowledge only. The Honolulu evaluation, first reported in 1986, found DARE students more proficient than controls in identifying risks and found more satisfaction with the program among students and parents. The Los Angeles evaluation, first reported in 1987 (posttest only), showed reduced substance use by DARE participants but suffered from severe attrition problems because a large number of students who only attended part of the DARE classes were dropped from the study. The Lexington study (Clayton, 1987) showed that out of thirty-four items relating to drug knowledge, DARE participants improved on twenty-five items compared with non-DARE students, who improved on only sixteen items.

It's not the case that the LAPD was unaware of the weaknesses in the evaluations they used to proclaim the program's effectiveness. There was a long series of correspondence between Dr. Mac Klein, a distinguished professor of criminology at USC, and Commander Eric Lillo, who was the Commanding Officer of Operations—Juvenile Group, LAPD. Klein was a nationally recognized expert on evaluation methods and Lillo was part of the LAPD hierarchy responsible for managing DARE. The correspondence began on August 26, 1996 with a letter from Lillo to Klein asking for his opinion about a group of DARE evaluations described in the previously mentioned Evaluation Compendium compiled by DARE, and a recently completed evaluation of DARE in Ohio. Klein responded on September 13 with a detailed critique of the studies in the Compendium and the Ohio study, finding serious deficiencies in them all. At one point, Klein wrote: "The survey studies in the Compendium, as your letter notes, are simplistic—they have little value for your purposes. The eight studies you refer to as scientific also fall far short of that for a variety of reasons."

Lillo wrote back to Klein several days later thanking him for his "helpful comments" and asking his opinion of the Kentucky evaluation (Clayton, 1987) that found no significant impacts of DARE in twenty-three of that state's elementary schools. On October 1, 1996, Klein responded to Lillo that the Kentucky evaluation was much sounder than any of the DARE evaluations he had been shown to date.

One month later Lillo again wrote to Klein requesting his opinion of yet another evaluation that purported to show positive effects from DARE. Once again Klein responded that the study was not methodologically rigorous enough that its findings could be trusted.

A number of quasi-experimental evaluations of DARE found fairly consistent short-term effects on mediating variables such as knowledge, attitudes, and social skills (Clayton, 1987; Faine & Bohlander, 1988), but provided little evidence to support the claim that DARE had positive impacts on drug-use behaviors (Rosenbaum & Hanson, 1998). Even the effects on mediating variables were found to be much more modest than in the methodologically weaker "posttest only" evaluations. The results of DARE evaluations with random assignment and sufficiently large samples began to appear in the early 1990s and consistently showed small or insignificant impacts on drug use (Clayton et al., 1991; Ringwalt et al., 1990, 1991; Rosenbaum et al., 1994; Ennet et al., 1994).

With the publication of an increasing number of high-quality evaluations showing no preventive impacts, the defensive tactics of DARE's supporters changed. Rather than attempt to refute the more rigorous evaluations with their own earlier but weaker studies, their response was to claim that the curriculum was being revised, and thus studies of the earlier curriculum no longer applied. They also worked to prevent publication of further damaging studies. When Research Triangle Institute (RTI) researchers presented preliminary findings from their evaluation, funded by the National Institute of Justice (NIJ), of DARE at a San Diego drug-education conference in 1993, they were immediately threatened with legal action and other challenges that interrupted the presentation of the study, which was not supportive of DARE (Glass, 1997). Herb Kleber, a Columbia University professor who headed DARE's Scientific Advisory Committee, and later went on to work in the White House as a presidential advisor on drug policy, called the RTI study flawed. DARE America arranged for supporters to flood the Justice Department and Congress with phone calls objecting to the study (Glass). RTI completed its final report in 1994, but NIJ refused to publish it after it had been publicly peer reviewed. Shortly thereafter, the study was accepted for publication by the *American Journal of Public Health*, a respected academic journal.

DARE America and its supporters reportedly used the same type of intimidation tactics to prevent unfavorable stories about DARE in the media as well. A major story on DARE and its critics was prepared to air on NBC's *Dateline* but was canceled when DARE executives complained to higher-ups in the network's executive management (Glass, 1997).

In 1998, Dennis Rosenbaum and Gordon Hanson published the most methodologically rigorous evaluation of DARE that had been made until that time. The Illinois DARE evaluation was conducted as a randomized field experiment with one pretest and multiple posttests. The researchers identified eighteen matched pairs of schools and randomly assigned one of each pair to receive DARE. The results showed that DARE had no long-term effects on a wide range of drug-use measures, nor did it show a lasting impact on hypothesized mediating variables.

After 1998, the road got a little bumpier for DARE. Under orders from Congress to start documenting program impacts, the Department of Education's Safe and Drug Free Schools Program used an expert advisory committee to compile a list of nine drug- and violence-prevention programs that they concluded had demonstrated their effectiveness, and thirty-three programs that could be considered promising. DARE was not listed in either category. Also, a number of local jurisdictions began opting out of DARE in favor of more proven school-based models for drug prevention, such as Botvin's Life Skills Training (Botvin et al., 1998) or Project ALERT (Ellickson et al., 1993). Both of these programs were developed and tested at the same time that DARE was launched, but both chose to abstain from heavy marketing or dissemination campaigns until they had been adequately tested. Large-scale dissemination for these two programs did not begin until the mid-1990s.

Under pressure from the U.S. Departments of Justice and Education, DARE officials eventually agreed to participate in several meetings with leading drug-prevention experts and to develop a list of evidence-based principles for school-based programs directed toward drug-prevention. The Robert Wood Johnson Foundation committed over $13 million toward the development and testing of a new DARE curriculum, to be carried out in partnership with the University of Akron (Miller, 2001).

There are a number of lessons to be drawn from the DARE experience. One is that it makes no sense to actively market or disseminate an unproven program model on a scale of nearly $500 million a year, except to those who stand to gain financially. Most of the money spent replicating an unproven program just ends up getting wasted. Another lesson is that even the most heavily marketed programs may eventually be vulnerable to evidence refuting its claims.

DARE didn't work when it came to reducing drug use. As indicated previously, the attempt to teach resistance skills did not use the most effective methods, and it came at a time in the lives of the targeted youth when they were not yet ready to consider such issues. The early success of DARE may be due to its coming along when conditions were ripe and having a great promotional campaign behind it. It also worked quite well as a vehicle for increasing support for the police, and fattening up the wallets of those who controlled it at the top. It was (and continues to be) a very long and good ride for this latter group indeed. DARE also provided a publicly visible way of demonstrating one's antipathy toward drugs. However, these relatively small public-relations contributions of DARE must be weighed against the damage caused by its diversion of attention away from much more effective programs, and the large number of adolescents who could have been helped to reduce all forms of substance abuse.

The only way to estimate the impact of particular drug-prevention programs in any sample of schools is to conduct some type of survey of the teachers or administrators responsible for that aspect of the curriculum. The only such national survey was conducted by Ringwalt et al. (2002) in

1998. That survey found DARE to be offered in 52.9 percent of public middle schools and 54.5 percent of private middle schools. Project ALERT and Life Skills Training were used in 19 percent and 12 percent of public schools, respectively, and 6 percent and 3 percent of private schools. Note that this survey was taken after the U.S. Department of Education had published its Principles of Effectiveness in 1998. The Principles specified that schools should implement prevention strategies that were supported by evaluative evidence of positive effects (U.S. Department of Education, 1998). In the survey by Ringwalt et al., there was little association between school characteristics and their choice of programs except that large urban schools were more likely to use evidence-based programs.

In 2004, under pressure to cut costs, the LAPD reassigned all of its DARE officers to regular patrol duties. The Los Angeles Unified School District adopted Project ALERT.

Boot Camps

The rapid spread of military-style boot camps for juvenile as well as adult offenders is another example of a popular delinquency-prevention strategy that developed without any sound evidentiary basis. Boot camps share some of the same popularity-enhancing characteristics as DARE, but they also exhibit some striking differences. Both DARE and the boot-camp strategy are relatively inexpensive programs that involve public safety or corrections officers working in nontraditional settings to help at-risk youth. Both make good media copy. Both use powerful cultural symbols of manhood and authority: the police and the military. Both generate enthusiasm and optimism among participants and the general public.

Unlike DARE, however, there was never a single organization promoting the boot-camp concept. The idea of using basic military training as a way of building discipline, social skills, and self-esteem appeared to spread first among enthusiastic correctional administrators and public officials. It was then reinforced and promoted by favorable coverage in the media. By the time it attracted important high-level political support, it had become a type of program that every state and large county was eager to experiment with.

Boot camps differ from traditional corrections programs in that they are highly structured, include military components of drill and physical training, are designed for nonserious, youthful offenders, and are short term (Cullen et al., 1996). The average length of stay for boot-camp participants is just under four and one-half months (Camp & Camp, 1993).

The first boot camps for adult offenders were started in Georgia and Oklahoma in 1983 (MacKenzie, 2002). That first generation of correctional boot camps, which proliferated through the late 1980s and early 1990s, were the closest copies of military models emphasizing military discipline, physical training, and hard work (Parent, 2003). Video footage of camp life always featured grizzled former army and marine drill instructors tongue-lashing one of the inmates, who stood at rigid attention. Pictures showing former delinquents doing pushups, marching in formation, or shining their shoes for inspection was a novelty that seemed to have an appeal across class and racial lines. The camps made corrections look more tough and demanding than the usual exercise-yard scene of inmates lounging around or playing games. During their involvement in the program, boot-camp participants appeared to be more uncomfortable and stressed out than regular prison or jail inmates, and they appeared more respectful and polite when they graduated. Some thirty such camps for juveniles had been established by 1995 (Parent, 2003).

Both the Office of Juvenile Justice and Delinquency Prevention (OJJDP) and the Bureau of Justice Assistance funded demonstration boot-camp programs, as did many state and county systems, before there was any evidence as to how well these programs actually worked. A so-called second generation of boot camps added more traditional treatment and rehabilitative components, such as substance-abuse treatment and training in social skills. Some of the more recent camps have substituted educational and vocational skills training for some of the military components (Parent, 2003).

It appears that boot camps were the beneficiary of a kind of agnosticism that seemed to have the correctional field in its grasp. With the exception of drug-treatment programs, very few corrections departments had done any serious experimenting with rehabilitative programs since Lipton, Martinson, and Wilks (1975) appeared to condemn the whole enterprise thirty years ago. There are few promising models in corrections. Very little other than cognitive-behavioral programs and drug treatment seem to make much of a difference. Boot camps, because of their shorter length of stay, are less expensive than regular prison sentences, if that is their true alternative, and they seem to be just as acceptable to the public. For these reasons alone, boot camps should be the budget-challenged correctional administrator's dream.

A multisite evaluation sponsored by NIJ found no difference in recidivism rates between adult boot-camp graduates and members of a comparison group, although those programs with more treatment services, longer programs, and intensive postrelease supervision appeared to do better (MacKenzie et al., 1995).

Table 5.1. Characteristics and outcomes of experimental boot camps

Program characteristics	Denver	Cleveland	Mobile
Number assigned to boot camp in study	124	182	187
Percent custody bound	56%	100%	27%
Percent of those assigned completing program	64.5%	93.4%	86.6%
Percent of those entering who completed	76%	95.5%	87%
Recidivism rate for those assigned to boot camp	39%	72%	28%
Recidivism rate for controls	36%	50%	31%
Cost for boot camp ($)	8,141 per youth	14,021 per youth	6,241 per youth
Cost for custody ($)	23,245 per youth	25,549 per youth	11,616 per youth
Cost for probation ($)	944 per youth	n.a.	515 per youth

Source: Aos et al., 1997.

Random assignment evaluations of three juvenile boot camps sponsored by OJJDP and one conducted by the California Youth authority found no positive impacts on recidivism (Peters et al., 1997; Zhang, 1999; Austin, 2000). By 1995, boot camps began to loose their luster and since then have seen their populations and numbers of camps decline by more than 30 percent.

Unlike DARE, boot camps have never had a body of evidence-based practice on which to build. They also have never enjoyed the support and backing of a strong advocacy organization like DARE America. The primary factors that appeared to promote their growth were media and public interest, lower costs compared with traditional placements, and flexibility. Each jurisdiction was able to design its own boot camp to meet its own unique needs.

In her review of evidence-based programs in corrections, Doris MacKenzie (2002) attributes the large decline in the use of boot camps to the clear and compelling evidence that they are not effective in reducing recidivism rates. However, a closer look at the evaluations of the three OJJDP-funded boot camps reveals that they might be effective in terms of cost effectiveness. All of the relevant figures are presented in table 5.1.

The first thing to notice is that the three sites differed significantly in the proportion of boot-camp participants who would have been placed in traditional custody if the boot camp were not available: 100 percent in Cleveland, 56 percent in Denver, and only 27 percent in Mobile. Boot camps represent a cheaper and less restrictive placement in Cleveland, but a more expensive placement and net widening in Mobile. Since the Mobile program at $6,241 per case costs considerably more than the traditional pattern of placements in that site ($.27 \times \$11,616 + .73 \times \$516 = \$3,513$ per case), without any significant improvement in recidivism rates, it is clearly not an effective alternative to probation.

In Cleveland, the boot-camp placements resulted in an immediate savings of $11,528, or 45 percent of the traditional costs of confinement. That short-term savings, however, must be balanced against the longer-term costs associated with youth having more time to offend in the community and a greater percentage of them re-offending and being returned to custody. The cost-effectiveness of this trade-off depends on the seriousness and frequency of boot-camp participants' subsequent crimes, the taxpayer cost associated with their subsequent sanctions, and the larger social costs associated with their increased offending. It is impossible to evaluate this trade-off without some method for projecting future offense and sanction patterns for the targeted youth, based on whatever recidivism data is available, and making some assumptions about the costs of various types of crime to the victims and the larger community. Given these findings, we can expect boot camps to remain popular as alternative sanctions in instances where low-rate/low-seriousness juvenile offenders have been traditionally placed in more secure custody. The central issue in assessing the effectiveness of boot camps is determining the likely alternative to boot-camp placement. To the extent that it is less restrictive and less costly, it need not reduce recidivism to be more cost effective.

Why don't boot camps work to reform delinquents, and yet appear to work fairly well in turning raw recruits into trained soldiers. There are two basic reasons. One is that military boot camps are fairly selective about who they accept, and screen out a fairly high percentage of those who seek to enter. With that kind of selectivity in an environment in which every graduate is assured an appropriate job, it is no wonder that military boot camps appear effective. Correctional boot camps cannot be as selective or guaranty their graduates a job, and often do not include the kind of therapeutic programming that has been shown to produce positive results. The boot-camp concept for corrections was based more on a hunch than on any hard evidence.

Scared Straight

The history of Scared Straight, a program that relies on prison inmates to educate young delinquents about the life-and-death perils of the criminal life-style, is almost as amazing as the story of DARE. The program was started in 1976 by a group of inmates in New Jersey's Rahway State Prison. Groups of girls and boys were brought into the prison where menacing inmates subjected them to threats, intimidation, emotional shock, and verbal bullying. The purpose of this program was literally to scare them out of delinquency. Although Scared Straight never reached the level of support and prevalence enjoyed by DARE, it has managed to reach thousands of youth, and still continues to be used in spite of the fact that it has been shown to make youth more likely to be delinquent rather than less.

The program was created by a small group of inmates at Rahway known as the Lifers' Group, who were serving sentences of twenty-five years or more. The group's initial goal was to counter the Hollywood stereotype of prison inmates as immoral and inhuman. An early activity of the group involved finding, repairing, and gift-wrapping Christmas toys for needy children. Another activity was the creation of a Juvenile Intervention Committee, the purpose of which was to try and keep at-risk kids from getting involved in crime. This committee was the brainchild of the president of the Lifers' Group, an inmate serving a double-life term for rape, kidnapping, and armed robbery, and whose own twelve-year-old son was starting to run afoul of the law (Finkenaur & Gavin, 1999).

The idea of bringing adolescents into prison for educational purposes was an outgrowth of tours of the prison that had been conducted for college students. If prison tours could be used to educate college students, the inmates reasoned, they could also be used to educate juvenile delinquents about what awaited them if they continued in crime. The Lifers convinced the superintendent of the prison, a local police chief, and a juvenile-court judge to give the Juvenile Awareness Project a try. In September of 1976, the first group of youngsters entered the prison, an event covered by the *Hackensack Record* in an article titled "Rahway Lifers Give Juveniles the Unvarnished Facts—Youths Get Lowdown on Jail." The plan initially called for admitting one group of youth to the prison per week, but by January 1977 the concept had become so popular that they were admitting two groups a day, five days a week (Finkenaur & Gavin, 1999).

The Juvenile Awareness Project started out fairly low key, with inmates conversing with the youth and conducting tours. When that approach did not seem to be getting through to the kids, however, the Lifers shifted their approach to a more intimidating form of shock therapy. Once inside the prison, youth were subjected to threats and intimidation as the inmates described the risk of assault, murder, rape, and suicide in the most graphic terms.

The program quickly caught the eye of public officials and the media. The initial coverage was generally favorable and portrayed the program as a great success. On March 17, 1977, the *Bergen Record* reported: "Since the program started seven months ago, the Lifers' Group has talked to six hundred juvenile ex-offenders. Only nine have been arrested following the talks, all on minor offenses." On April 17, 1977, the *Trenton Times Advertiser* reported: "Since last September, when the program began, fourteen hundred youths in trouble with the law have been through the program. . . . [O]nly fourteen youth who went through the two-hour shock treatment have gotten in trouble with the law, only five seriously." On July 30, 1977, the *Newark Star Ledger* reported that 2,921 juveniles had undergone the program and that a "preliminary survey shows that only 10 percent have been in trouble since their visits." The astounding but erroneous recidivism numbers reported in these articles were based on responses to follow-up form letters sent out by the inmates to the parents of visiting youth, many of whom had not had any problems with the law prior to their visit (Finkenaur & Gavin, 1999).

The most outspoken and vigorous supporter of the program was George Nicola, the juvenile-court judge who helped initiate the program. Nicola claimed the program was serving "revolving door delinquents" and that "less than 1 percent have gotten into trouble again" after visiting the prison. Judge Nicola claimed that he was receiving calls from all over the country about the program and that "New Jersey is becoming a model for the rest of the nation."

The amount of attention received by the project increased considerably with the publication of an article in the January 1978 *Readers Digest.* The article by Roul Tunley titled "Don't Let Them Take Me Back" presented a vivid portrayal of what the program looked like to the kids. One of the 30 million readers reached by the article was Arnold Shapiro, a producer at television station KTLA in Los Angeles. Shapiro secured the backing of his station to produce a documentary on the project. Filming of youth entering the prison, the actual session, and their stunned departure took place on May 1, 1978. Publicity material distributed with the documentary film claimed that "80–90% of the kids in THIS unique program are Scared Straight."

Scared Straight was aired on KTLA on November 2, 1978. The documentary became an immediate smash. The *Los Angeles Times* proclaimed it "One of the most unusual and powerful television programs ever broadcast." The public response was overwhelmingly supportive. On March 5, 1979, *Scared Straight* was shown in two hundred major cities from coast to coast, again with very strong and positive viewer reaction. The film was endorsed by such groups as the National Education Association and was awarded the Oscar in 1979 by the Academy of Motion Picture Arts and Sciences for Best Documentary Feature of the Year. The next year it won a prestigious Emmy award as well.

Unlike the enthusiastic public response, many criminologists were openly skeptical of the program. If the Juvenile Awareness Project has any effect on future offending it would be through deterrence—increasing the youths' perception of the severity of going to prison. However, previous research had demonstrated that deterrence effects are increased primarily by increasing the swiftness and certainty of punishment, not the severity.

The first serious evaluation of the program was conducted by James Finkenauer in 1979 using a quasi-experimental design. The study showed that program participants were not as seriously at risk as had been claimed, with 41 percent not having any prior delinquency records. It also found that those who visited Rahway State Prison and talked with the Lifers showed little change in their attitudes and were more likely to be arrested in the future than similar youth who were not exposed to the program. This was a far cry from the 80–90 percent success rate previously claimed for the program. Not surprisingly, Finkenaur's study was vigorously attacked by the Lifers' Group and their supporters.

Publication of a critical study did not end the program. An article in the *New York Times* on May 16, 1996 described a visit by a small group of youth to the Juvenile Awareness Project at the East Jersey (formerly Rahway) State Prison. The article described the program as being at the height of its popularity, hosting about ten groups a week, amounting to more than twelve thousand youth visitors a year. The article also claimed a success rate for the program of 51 percent and went on to describe the changes in attitude exhibited by the youth. Although the Lifers' Group claims to provide more factual data to the youth than formerly, stories about the nightmarish life in prison still play a central role in their presentations.

Programs like the Juvenile Awareness Project were subsequently developed in many other states and continue to this day. One such program in Ohio called Convicts against Prison Sentences was featured in a 1994 OJJDP publication titled "What Works: Promising Interventions in Juvenile Justice." Another similar program, known as the SQUIRES, has been operating in California's San Quentin prison for many years. A study (Lewis, 1983) evaluating that program found no differences in outcome between youth participating in the program and a control group that did not, yet the program still continues. A number of meta-analyses have included Scared Straight programs as a separate category or combined with "deterrence" or "confrontational" programs (Lipsey, 1992; Petrosino, 1997; Gendreau et al., 2000). None of these analyses found positive effects on recidivism and several found that, on average, these programs increase the likelihood of future delinquency.

Competition between Proven and Unproven Models in the Prenatal and Infancy Home-Visitation Market

One might expect that the kind of premature promotion and dissemination of unproven prevention programs that characterized the implementation of boot-camp programs and DARE would not occur in the field of health-care, which has a stronger scientific base than does criminal justice. Much of medical training is scientific and hence evidence based, whereas most criminal justice officials and practitioners have very little scientific training at all. But even in the health field, these same problems are found. One such struggle is currently taking place among the various models developed to improve the care of infants in low-income families through prenatal and infancy home visitation.

Early-childhood, home-visitation programs are those in which parents and children are visited in their home during the child's first two years of life by trained personnel who provide some combination of information, support, or training regarding child health, development, and care. Home visitation has been used for a wide variety of objectives, including improvement of the home environment, family development, and prevention of child abuse or child behavior problems (Hahn et al., 2003)

One of the most highly regarded models in this field is the Nurse Family Partnership (NFP), which is an outgrowth of the Prenatal/Early Infancy Project developed by Dr. David Olds. "Nurse Family Partnership" is also the name of a new nonprofit organization that was formed to support the operation and replication of Olds's model. The key elements of the NFP model, as was described earlier in chapter 4, include the following:

- The focus is on low-income, first-time mothers.
- The home visitors are nurses.
- Nurses begin making home visits during pregnancy.
- The nurses follow detailed program guidelines that focus on the mother's health, quality of caregiving for the child, and parents' own life-course development.
- A standardized information system is used to track progress.

The first randomized clinical trial (RCT) for the NFP model was conducted in Elmira, New York from 1978 to 1982. Experimental and control families were followed-up for fifteen years after their enrollment in the program (Olds et al., 1997, 1998). Subsequent RCTs, with shorter follow-up periods, have been conducted in Memphis (Kitzman et al., 2000) and Denver (Korfmacher et al., 1999). All of these trials have demonstrated that the NFP has positive effects on a wide range of child and maternal outcomes including substantiated child abuse, injuries, and hospitalizations. The Denver study also demonstrated that nurses were far more successful than paraprofessionals in implementing the program and producing the desired outcomes. NFP has been designated a "proven" program model by Blueprints and the Surgeon General's Report (see chapter 3), and by many other agencies that list what they consider to be proven models.

Dissemination and replication of NFP as a cost-effective prevention program was undertaken by the National Center for Children, Families and Communities (NCCFC) at the University of Colorado Health Sciences Center, beginning in 1998, after the U.S. Justice Department called for the NFP to be disseminated in six high-crime communities under its Weed and Seed initiative. After that, the program was promoted under the Blueprints for Violence Prevention initiative (Olds et al., 1998). Funding for local program operations has also been provided by states and localities out of public dollars.

At this point in time, NCCFC claims to be expanding NFP to new sites selectively, while still devoting considerable effort to sustaining high-quality programs at its existing sites. Statewide implementation efforts are focused on Pennsylvania, Oklahoma, Colorado, and Louisiana. Communities and states that are interested in becoming NFP sites must meet the following rather daunting list of conditions:

- Have firm commitment to implement the program with fidelity to its essential elements.
- Focus exclusively on low-income, first-time mothers.
- Begin the program before the twenty-eighth week of gestation and continue through child's first two years.
- Use only qualified nurses as visitors.
- Have nurses follow in-depth protocols for each visit.
- Have nurses follow a visit schedule keyed to the developmental stages of pregnancy and early childhood.
- Have nurse visitors involve the mother's support system, including other family members and friends.

- Have nurse visitors help participating families learn how to use other health or human services they may need.
- Limit caseloads to no more than twenty-five active families per nurse visitor.
- Provide a minimum of a half-time experienced supervisor for every four full-time nurses.
- Operate the program through a local organization known for being a successful provider of services for low-income families.
- Use the clinical information system designed for the program.
- Ensure that all nurses and supervisors in the program are trained in the model by clinical staff at the University of Colorado in Denver.
- Ensure that all nurses and supervisors in the program are trained in the method of assessing early-infant development and parent-child interaction titled the Nursing Child Assessment Satellite Training (NCAST) system.
- Agree to serve a minimum of one hundred families and establish ties with local sources of referral.
- Ensure a strong organizational commitment to the model by operating agency.
- Ensure that the operating agency has an established reputation for effective collaboration with other health and service providers serving low-income families.
- Ensure that the program is needed and does not duplicate services already available.
- Have capable, credible, and committed leaders within the jurisdiction publicly support the program.
- Put strategies in place to increase the proportion of nurses whose racial and ethnic backgrounds reflect those of the families to be served.
- Ensure that the organization provides working conditions, scheduled supervision, flextime, access to computers, adequate office space and supplies, and appropriate security conducive to effective professional practice by nurse visitors.
- Ensure that the site agrees to collaborate with the University of Colorado in providing and using data from the clinical information system or otherwise to help guide improvements in program operations.
- Make certain that the site can obtain three years of funding to implement the program through one complete cycle for participating families, with the first year of funding already committed before program staff begin their training. Ensure that there is also a clear and convincing strategy in place to secure sustainable funding beyond the first three years.

- Have program staff and leadership agree not to copy or distribute the written program protocols or the clinical information system. Both are copyrighted by the University of Colorado.
- The willingness of the sponsoring entity to enter into a contract with one of the universities certified to help them implement the program according to the above standards.

To some degree a competitor of NFP for state and local funding is Healthy Families America (HFA), an initiative developed by the National Committee to Prevent Child Abuse (since renamed Prevent Child Abuse America) that "seeks to expand the availability of high-quality intensive home visitation services" and other services that provide "a supportive atmosphere for all new parents." The HFA model, which is based somewhat on the popular Hawaii Healthy Start Program, assumes that effective prevention initiatives require universal availability, varied levels of support, flexible replication procedures, and greater integration across multiple service systems and economic sectors (Daro & Harding, 1999).

Unlike NFP, the HFA program-development strategy is not committed to a single monolithic approach but rather to a set of principles distilled from literature reviews (Daro & Harding, 1999). These principles cover the areas of service initiation, service content, and service-provider selection and training. HFA's specific principles include:

SERVICE INITIATION

- Services need to start prenatally or at birth.
- Programs need to implement standardized assessment to ensure efficient allocation of resources.
- Services need to be offered on a voluntary basis and use positive, persistent outreach.

SERVICE CONTENT

- Services for families facing the greatest challenges need to be intensive (at least once a week) with well-defined criteria for increasing or decreasing intensity.
- Services must be made available for an extended period of time (three to five years).
- Services should be culturally competent.
- Services should be comprehensive, supporting the parents as well as parent-child interactions.

- Families should be linked to a medical provider to ensure timely immunizations and well-child care. Depending on need they also may need to be linked to other services such as school-readiness programs, childcare, job training, and so forth.
- Staff should have limited caseloads to ensure that home visitors have adequate time to spend with each family.

SERVICE-PROVIDER SELECTION AND TRAINING

- Service providers must be selected on the basis of their ability to demonstrate a combination of requisite personal characteristics (e.g., compassion, ability to establish trusting relationship, and empathy), and knowledge base as represented by specific academic degrees or experience.
- All service providers must receive intensive didactic training specific to their roles as defined by the critical elements and related standards of best practice.
- Program staff should receive ongoing, effective supervision.

A comparison between these principles and the conditions required of NFP replication sites indicates that any site that qualifies for NFP replication would clearly satisfy most of the principles for HFA. The two principles or criteria in which HFA is more demanding than NFP are in the area of coverage and duration. HFA is designed to be a universal program, while NFP focuses exclusively on families at risk. HFA calls for a service period of three to five years, whereas NFP only lasts for two years. An economic analysis of NFP demonstrated that such programs are not cost-effective with lower risk families and there is no evidence that periods of service longer than two years increase long-term effects (Karoly et al., 1998).

In 1997, an estimated eighteen thousand families were enrolled in intensive home-visitation services offered in more than 270 HFA programs, in thirty-eight states and the District of Columbia (Daro & Harding, 1999). By November of 2003, the HFA web site at www. healthyfamiliesamerica.org heralded the existence of HFA programs "in over 420 communities in the United States and Canada."

Data from a 1997 HFA site survey indicated that nearly one-third of families offered intensive home visitation were enrolled prenatally. Forty-four percent of home visitors were college graduates and another 39 percent had some college attendance (Daro & Harding, 1999).

In addition to its principles and promotional activities, the HFA initiative includes a Research Network, which is a partnership among more than fifty researchers who are engaged in evaluating HFA programs, some with randomized trials and others with more modest quasi-experimental designs.

There have been two large randomized clinical trials of HFA conducted to date—one in Hawaii (Duggan et al., 1999) and the most recent in San Diego (Landsverk et al., 2002). Neither found a significant difference in child-abuse reports between experimental (HFA) and control groups. In the San Diego study, 488 families at high risk for child abuse and neglect were selected through a two-stage process at the time of the index child's birth and enrollment in the clinical trial (247 intervention families and 241 control families) from February 1996 through March 1997. Three years of services were provided for the 247 intervention families. Interviews and assessments were completed on the 488 clinical trial families (including the 241 control group families) for all three annual follow-up data points with retention rates of 89 percent, 83 percent, and 85 percent, respectively. The randomization was successful with no statistically significant differences (except for enrollment in managed care—Medicaid) observed between the intervention and control groups at baseline. Additionally, no differential attrition between the two groups were observed.

The intervention program provided services at a significantly higher rate than reported for the Hawaii Healthy Start Program. Over 10,500 home visits were completed over the thirty-six months, an average of forty-three per family. At the end of year one, more than 75 percent of intervention families were receiving home-visitation services as compared to 49 percent reported for Hawaii.

Over the full three years of outcome measurement, a few positive outcomes were observed in the areas of child preventive healthcare, maternal life course (school attendance, reproductive health), and psychological aggression by mother toward the index child. Over the first two years, but not for the third outcome year, positive outcomes were observed in the areas of maternal depressive symptoms and child-developmental functioning.

Significant differences between the two groups were not observed for the full three years in the following areas:

- Mother to child physical aggression.
- Neglect of child by mother.
- Mother-child interaction.
- Home learning environment.
- Parenting stress levels.

- Intimate-partner violence.
- Maternal substance use.
- Maternal life-course items (reproductive health, degree completion, employment, receipt of welfare) as reported by the mother of the index child.
- Use of social, mental-health, and substance-abuse services as reported by mother of the index child.
- Child-behavior problems at years two and three as reported by the mother.
- Use of safety measures in the home as reported by mother (Landsverk et al., 2002).

Taken together, these evaluations provide fairly conclusive evidence that the current HFA model is not effective in preventing child abuse.

An article in a special 1999 issue of the *Future of Children* (Daro & Harding) demonstrates how the results from some of these studies have been used to support continued expansion of the program. The strongest evidence from RCTs, which demonstrate no effect on abuse, are sandwiched between findings from less rigorous evaluations that do purport to demonstrate positive effects. On the positive side, it is reported that "thirteen of the non-RCT evaluations with data regarding child abuse and neglect rates report rates of subsequent maltreatment of less than 6 percent among program participants." It is then pointed out that while the national average rate for maltreatment reports is only 4.7 percent, studies suggest that the rate could be two to three times higher among the types of families enrolled in HFA. From these facts it is implied that HFA must be having an impact on the rate of child abuse.

Then, on the negative side, the article reports that neither of the two RCTs completed at that time found any significant effects on child abuse. Then again on the positive side, the article mentions an incomplete RCT in Hawaii that did find differences in reported child-abuse complaints in favor of the experimental group. In this style of presentation, the discouraging impact of the negative evidence is somewhat neutralized by its being surrounded by more optimistic findings, which themselves derive from weaker or incomplete studies.

NFP and HFA represent quite different approaches to the development and dissemination of programs for improving early-childhood and maternal outcomes for high-risk families. NFP was developed through a more traditional process of model development and testing by a single team of investigators. The model is very highly specified in terms of content, training, delivery, and supervision. Broad-scale replication efforts await the successful completion of appropriate RCTs. Potential replication sites are carefully screened and selected to ensure a high degree of fidelity to the model design. HFA was developed by a group of nonacademic planners on the basis of their review of the literature. The model is purposely very general. Considerable adaptation and flexibility is encouraged at replicating sites. National dissemination efforts were well underway before rigorous evidence was available on program effectiveness.

A recent report by the Centers for Disease Control, evaluating the effectiveness of home visitation in preventing violence, concluded that the basic strategy was effective, particularly in preventing child abuse. Compared with controls, the median effect size of home-visitation programs was a reduction of approximately 40 percent in child abuse or neglect. Programs delivered by professional visitors (nurses or mental health workers with either post-high-school education or experience in child development) produced larger effects (48 percent reduction) than those delivered by paraprofessionals (18 percent reduction) (Hahn et al., 2003).

Explanations for the Persistence of Programs That Have Been Shown Not to Work

There are a number of reasons why juvenile-prevention programs that have been demonstrated not to be effective continue to receive support and to be adopted by new sites. One reason is simply political momentum. A program like DARE, which has built a network of organizations and political supporters, is difficult for other less well-established programs to compete with. Our federal and state budgets are loaded with programs supported by particular constituencies for which there is little or no evidence that they accomplish their purported goals. This amounts to prevention as public relations.

Another reason has to with the fact that delinquency-prevention programs can serve a number of purposes in addition to just reducing crime. Providing services to high-risk children and families, providing resources to struggling community-based organization, providing employment for particular segments of the population, gaining support from particular segments of the voting public, and reinforcing other political values—all these and more can be part of the motivation for backing a particular program. Unfortunately a program's impact on crime is probably the most difficult of all these many potential impacts to measure.

Another factor that helps ensure replication of some prevention programs, in spite of evidence finding limited or even negative impacts, is that the science producing evidence of program effectiveness often goes unchallenged. Only when a study produces results that are contrary to what the general public have been led to expect is the science questioned. One contributing factor toward this perception is that "junk" science, paraded as valid by some public officials, usually goes unexposed. Take the case of the increased waiver of juveniles to adult courts and corrections. Virtually every state in the nation has passed legislation making it easier for prosecutors to file charges against serious juvenile offenders in adult courts, increasing the likelihood they will serve time in adult institutions. This in spite of reasonably good evidence that such treatment is counterproductive for the youth involved and for public safety (Bishop & Frazier, 2000).

Or take the further case of California's Three Strikes law, a draconian measure in which *any* felony could count as a third strike against someone with two prior convictions, and trigger a mandatory life term. The attorney general of California publicized analyses that claimed to demonstrate that the law was having large positive crime-prevention effects, when in fact the crime rate had been falling steadily before the law was passed (Lungren, 1998). Never mind that crime rates were falling in most other states at the same time as well. Never mind that the decline began many months before the law was passed. Never mind that the crime-rate decline was just as large in "liberal cities" where the law was invoked more sparingly (San Francisco and Oakland) as in those where it was invoked more frequently (Los Angeles and San Diego). Never mind that the percentage of all felony arrests accounted for by individuals who were eligible for prosecution under the law did not diminish after the law was passed (Zimring et al., 2001). The attorney general's evaluation would score only a 1 on the Maryland Evaluation Quality Scale. All of the later Level 3 and 4 evaluations showed little or no impacts whatsoever (Greenwood & Hawken, 2001). However, no one was able to get this point across to the media or the general public. Legislation narrowing the scope of Three Strikes is still taboo for most public officials in California, in spite of a growing budget gap that is due in part to escalating corrections costs.

When Glen Levant, the head of DARE, was interviewed for an article in *Time* about Richard Clayton's 1987 findings that DARE was not effective, he replied: "Just because someone publishes a paper and calls it a study does not really mean anything, particularly when your dealing with something as subjective as whether prevention works. Only in America do you get kicked for doing good work" (Biema, 1996).

If we consider the potential implications of these assorted factors acting in tandem, it's clear they pose a formidable obstacle to the widespread dissemination of the more proven delinquency-prevention programs.

First, the powerful constituencies required to help promote a program are likely to decide which programs to support on the basis of how well they line-up with their own agendas, rather than waiting for RCTs to see the impact they have on delinquency or substance abuse. The scientific evidence for a program's effectiveness is not available for at least four years or so after the program goes into the field, or possibly not at all. A program that has a five-year head start in marketing itself will have a good chance of staying ahead of its more evidence-based competitors if it has established the appropriate supportive relations with many of the affected parties. According to Laurie Robinson, who was the deputy assistant attorney general responsible for the U.S. Department of Justice's grant programs at the time when it became clear that DARE was not effective, dropping the program was never considered an option. It had too much support on Capital Hill and among the police (Boyle, 2001).

Even when more rigorous evaluations begin to show that another program is much more effective, the less effective program will likely be able to "spin" some of its own less rigorous evaluation outcomes to make it seem that the two programs are equally promising. Until there is an easy way for policymakers to determine which programs appear to be most effective, on the basis of the most reliable information available, unscrupulous and misinformed promoters of delinquency-prevention programs will continue to hold a significant share of the market, in spite of their unjustified and unsubstantiated claims.

Yet despite these obstacles, the potential of evidence-based programs to continue making headway is not as bad as it may sound. When public officials continue to fund and support programs that have been shown not to work, the evaluations discount any crime-prevention claims made for the program and force its proponents to develop other justifications for its use. Evaluation studies have led many public agencies to stop funding DARE, have forced juvenile courts to find alternative placements to boot camps, and have even persuaded many prosecutors to use the California Three Strikes law with considerable restraint.

Three Lessons from This Chapter

Three basic lessons can be drawn from this chapter, which has focused on the continuation of delinquency-prevention programs even after they have been proven ineffective: the complementary role of both manifest and latent functions in promoting the program; the calculus of comparative advantage; and the importance of a culture of accountability.

The Influence of Latent Functions

The first lesson concerns the important influence of latent functions in mobilizing support for particular programs. Each of the programs we reviewed serves several functions for particular constituencies, in addition to the primary function articulated by its promoters. The benefits of these latent functions may be much easier to assess than the primary ones the program was originally designed to achieve. The primary function of DARE at its inception was to reduce student drug use. However, more than ten years elapsed between the introduction of the program and an accurate assessment of its impact on drug use, which turned out to be insignificant. But beyond the question of its capacity to affect the rates of juvenile use of drugs, DARE also provided a terrific public-relations vehicle for the police at a time when the demands of community policing required a more friendly and accessible view of law-enforcement officers in the field. DARE was quite successful in improving the image of the police among both students and parents. It also provided community members with a highly visible opportunity to take a stand against drug use, and it provided the officers who delivered the DARE curriculum in the classroom with an unusual opportunity to serve their communities, which many found to be a boost to their morale.

With boot camps the primary goal is rehabilitation, but the camps also appear to serve some constituency's desire for tougher-looking punishment, particularly among those who do not believe that time served should be the sole measure of sanction severity. Because of this "tougher" appearance, boot camps have become a way for corrections agencies to save money, by allowing them to reduce the average length of stay per case. In many sites, if they were to simply grant early releases to those in custody, without adding the boot-camp format, the public would probably not stand for it.

In addition to its primary goal of preventing child abuse, the HFA universal home-visitation initiative seeks to expand the resources and political clout of the primary sponsoring agency—Prevent Child Abuse America. Unlike the Nurse Family Partnership which is restricted to first births of high-risk mothers, and much more demanding in what it requires of participating sites, the less restrictive, more inclusive HFA initiative is more compatible with building a large political constituency, rather than ensuring the quality and cost effectiveness of individual programs. Because the outcomes of most delinquency-prevention programs are difficult and time consuming to measure, most constituencies will in part base their decisions whether to support a particular program on what they perceive its latent functions to be.

The Calculus of Comparative Advantage

The second lesson deals with the calculus of comparative advantage. An old Henny Youngman joke began with someone asking him "How's your wife?" Henny's response was the punchline: "Compared to what?" The same response can be given to the question regarding the effectiveness for a particular prevention program: compared to what? Boot camps are not cost effective when the alternative is regular probation. But for less serious offenders, they may be very cost effective compared to traditional custodial placements.

If we did not have other school-based programs for preventing drug use, which are far more effective, the DARE program might look pretty good, particularly when we add in the public relations benefits as well. However, the availability of a superior alternative should greatly reduce the attractiveness of a program whose impacts are found to be marginal. These observations apply as well to home-visitation programs. Yes, the meta-analyses conducted to date support the general strategy of home visitation. But when one particular model consistently achieves significantly better outcomes than another, the meta-analysis should not continue to be used in support of the weaker program.

The most cost effective of the Blueprints programs described in chapter 4 is Multidimensional Treatment Foster Care (MTFC), a single-family residential alternative to more traditional group homes and institutional placements. Out of concerns for both public and youth safety, the juveniles placed in MTFC would have wound up in some other residential setting if MTFC were not available. The cost-effectiveness estimates developed by the Washington State Institute of Public Policy compare MTFC to these alternative placements, which are fairly expensive in themselves, but not to the alternative of no placement at all.

The Need for a Culture of Accountability

The third lesson of this chapter concerns the importance of developing a "culture of accountability" within the delinquency-prevention field. For many years, the lack of proven, evidence-based prevention methods and the presence of limited evaluation efforts produced more a culture of creativity, in which novelty was rewarded and replication disdained. If most people are making judgments about the value of a program on the basis of its description, rather than on valid evidence of its effectiveness, then its success with funders will depend on its promotional efforts and salesmanship, rather than on how well it achieves its primary goals. The development of a culture of accountability in which every program is expected to offer proof of its impacts is an essential step in avoiding the "flavor of the month" phenomenon, which conjures up new and supposedly promising programs on the strength of their novelty rather than proven track record. Accountability is the process that keeps everyone honest and allows for fair comparisons between competing approaches and programs.

Part 2

Prevention and Policy

Chapter 6

The Uses and Limits of Cost Effectiveness in Allocating Crime-Prevention Resources

The previous chapters reviewed how the effectiveness of delinquency-prevention programs has been evaluated in the past, how they could be evaluated in the future, and how currently available programs rate on various measures. In chapter 3, I argued that the most appropriate measure by which to compare programs is cost effectiveness. For any specified level of funding, a more cost-effective program directed toward delinquency prevention will prevent a greater number of crimes than a less cost-effective program. We also saw how most social-service programs, of which delinquency prevention is one particular type, invariably confer a variety of collateral benefits on their various constituencies, which are difficult to quantify but nevertheless influential. This chapter reviews how these competitive perspectives can be expected to interact, along with several other challenging issues regarding the use of cost-effectiveness methodology that must be dealt with in contexts of delinquency prevention.

I begin with a review of what cost effectiveness is all about, followed by a few examples of its implementation. Particular attention is given to two critical issues that are of special interest in criminal justice. One issue involves differences in the timing of outcomes. It takes five years or more after the implementation of a delinquency-prevention program for that program to yield positive and measurable results. The impacts of increased enforcement or incarceration, however, are almost immediate. Political preferences appear to favor the more immediate payoffs.

The other issue involves the apparent public bias in favor of some types of prevention over others. We are a society that appears to favor enforcement and punishment over assistance, deterrence over treatment, and immediate and direct action over programs that work more slowly and indirectly. How can these preferences be factored in with cost-effectiveness considerations?

Subsequent sections of this chapter consider the questions of whose perspective should be adopted in cost-effectiveness studies—the funding agency, tax payers, or society in general—and how to handle situations in which individual risk levels are directly related to potential individual benefits, making the most troublesome youth the biggest beneficiaries of a program.

I conclude this chapter by considering who has the authority to make choices among delinquency-prevention programs, and how their position should influence their choice of the "best" decision criteria to use.

Origins and Evolution of Cost-Effectiveness Analysis

Cost-effectiveness analysis is designed to assess the comparative impacts of expenditures on alternative interventions that all have the same basic goals. The methods utilized are derived from the fields of economics, decision analysis, and operations research. "Cost effectiveness" was first introduced in the U.S. Department of Defense (DOD) by a group of economists brought into the department under Robert McNamara during the Kennedy years. This group was charged with developing better ways of comparing alternative weapon and support systems. One of the leaders of this group, Charles Hitch, the DOD comptroller, had been developing such concepts while heading up the Economics Department at RAND. Hitch went on to become president of the University of California in 1968.

The technique quickly spread to other governmental departments as part of the program budgeting reforms of the 1960s. Within a decade, it was put into practice by state and local governments as well. Since then, cost-effectiveness techniques have been widely adopted for the allocation of resources in such diverse fields as environmental quality, transportation, and health. Many of the methodological problems that currently appear to limit its use in crime prevention have already been resolved in these other fields.

How Is a Cost-Effectiveness Analysis Conducted?

Cost-effectiveness analysis (CEA) is designed to assess the comparative impacts of expenditures on different types of interventions that share the same goals. It is based on the premise that for any given level of resources, society wishes to achieve the intended goal (in our case, preventing juvenile crime) using as little resources as possible (Gold et al., 1996). In a military context, the goal might be the capability to withstand a particular type of attack or to be victorious in certain types of military campaigns. In the public health context, it is the aggregate health benefits conferred (Gold et al.).

The primary outcome measure used in CEA is the cost-effectiveness ratio. In comparing two alternatives, the ratio is the difference in their costs divided by the difference in their effectiveness, or C/E. The C/E ratio represents the incremental price of obtaining a unit crime-prevention effect (such as in dollars per crime) using a particular crime-prevention program compared with the use of an alternative program. If an intervention is both less costly and more effective than the alternative, it is said to *dominate* the alternative, and no CEA needs to be carried out. In the more typical case, however, an intervention under study is more costly than the alternative, but also more effective. A low C/E ratio represents a low price for achieving a desired unit of outcome. Adopting all interventions with C/E ratios below some specified threshold will be an optimal decision rule in two respects: (1) the resulting set of interventions will maximize the amount of crime prevention achievable by the resources expended, and (2) the resulting crime-prevention effect will have been achieved at the lowest possible cost (Gold et al., 1996).

A cost-benefit analysis of the alternative interventions directed toward crime prevention involves the following six basic steps:

1. Identify the primary outcome of interest, usually reductions in crimes of a particular type.
2. Assess all additional costs attributable to the intervention.
3. Estimate outcome effects attributable to the intervention, projecting them into the future where appropriate.
4. Discount all future costs and benefits back to their present value.
5. Conduct sensitivity analysis of key assumptions over their plausible range of values.
6. Calculate range of C/E ratios resulting from the sensitivity-analysis results.

The first two steps are fairly straightforward. The primary outcome of interest is the one you are attempting to maximize. The additional costs attributable to the intervention are the appropriately prorated fixed and direct costs that will have to be borne by anyone replicating the intervention.

The third step is typically the most difficult to achieve. Usually the outcome of some experimental intervention is presented in terms of its effect on recidivism rate or some area specific crime rate. That estimate is frequently made at some specified period after the intervention has begun or ended. If the difference in recidivism rates for participants in two different programs during the first year after their release is 20 percent, what is it projected to be five or ten years down the road? If some difference can be expected to remain, then there will be benefits to be counted during each year they continue to exist. Taking a conservative approach, and only including those effects that are documented by an evaluation, puts effective preventive interventions at an extreme disadvantage. We may anticipate that the effects of many interventions will continue over a significant period in the life of the participants, while most evaluations trace impacts for less than a year or two.

There have been enough long-term, follow-up studies of prevention programs to demonstrate that treatment effects can persist for a considerable period into the future. One such study of the Perry Preschool and Nurse Home Visitation Project found significant treatment effects among subjects fifteen to eighteen years after their participation in the program (Karoly et al., 1998). On the other hand, we have examples of programs for which treatment effects that appeared significant shortly after program completion were no longer evident several years later (Ellickson et al., 1993).

This variation in the persistence of treatment effects requires cost-effectiveness analysts to develop rules for handling long-term effects in the absence of data that is specific to the program they are evaluating. The two techniques that have been used most frequently are the specification of some decay factor and truncating all impacts after a specified period. The decay factor is used to reduce projected impacts gradually over time, and can be varied in the sensitivity analysis. The truncation method has been used by the Washington State Institute for Public Policy (WSIPP) to cut off all projected benefits beyond age thirty, after giving full credit for all observed effects up until that age (Aos et al., 2001).

In addition to estimating the long-term, crime-reduction effects of an intervention, CEA must also estimate the savings in criminal-justice resources resulting from this reduction in crime. This is accomplished by one of two means. One is by estimating the probabilities of arrest and conviction for each type of offense, and the expected sentence, adding up the totals, and then applying cost factors to each expense category. The other involves building a computer model to simulate the behavior of the offender population and their interactions with the criminal-justice system.

Once the potential savings in costs and crimes have been estimated for individual years, out to the time horizon of the study, the next step involves determining their total present value by discounting all those results back to the present time of the study. Costs divided by crimes prevented then becomes the C/E ratio.

The methods used to estimate changes in the rates of future offending, and the responses of the criminal-justice system, invariably require simplifying assumptions and very rough estimates of parameters for which better estimates are not available. For instance, the only evidence available from a small pilot program might show an effect size of 0.30 on a baseline recidivism rate of 50 percent, two years after the intervention is completed. A CEA might assume an impact only half as large (0.15) in a full-scale program, with that effect lasting as long as ten years after the intervention.

Sensitivity analysis involves altering these assumptions and estimates over a reasonable range of values to determine how the C/E ratio is affected. In the example above, this might include varying the effect size between 0.10 and 0.30 and varying the effect duration from two to ten years. A finding or conclusion that holds up over a wide range of values for all of the assumptions and parameter estimates is said to be "robust." One that does not is contingent on the untested assumption or parameter values whose variation causes a change in the conclusions of the analysis.

Examples of Cost-Effectiveness Analysis

The first study I review was conducted in the early 1990s; it attempted to compare the cost effectiveness of alternative strategies for reducing cocaine consumption in the United States. The alternatives included crop eradication, increased enforcement, and expanded drug treatment for heavy users. This controversial study was subjected to a detailed review and critique by a special panel convened by the National Research Council (NRC) at the request of the federal government.

The next two studies reviewed in this chapter estimated the cost effectiveness of California's Three Strikes law as a crime-prevention measure compared with the most promising programs for delinquency prevention in use at the time. The final two studies to be considered utilized similar methods for estimating the monetary value of outcomes, so that different types of outcomes can be directly compared. One of these studies assessed the costs and benefits of early-childhood interventions. The other evaluated many of the crime-prevention alternatives funded or considered for funding by the State of Washington.

Controlling Cocaine

One of the first CEAs that attempted to compare alternative criminal-justice policies was the Controlling Cocaine study. RAND analysts Peter Rydell and Susan Everingham (1994) built a computer model to estimate the impacts that alternative changes in the supply and demand of cocaine would have on its use in the United States. The study was undertaken with support from the Office of National Drug Control Policy and the U.S. Army at a time when the total consumption of cocaine in the United States had remained at peak levels for almost a decade, despite a 20 percent decline in the number of users. The four policy alternatives analyzed in the study were the following:

- *Source-country control:* coca leaf eradication; seizures of coca base, cocaine paste, and the final cocaine product in the source countries (primarily Peru, Bolivia, and Columbia).
- *Interdiction:* seizures of cocaine and other drug-supply assets (manufacturing equipment, boats, planes, etc.) by the U.S. Customs Service, the U.S. Coast Guard, the U.S. Army, and the Immigration and Naturalization Service.
- *Domestic enforcement:* seizures of cocaine and other drug-marketing assets (cars, houses, etc.) and arrests of drug dealers and their agents by federal, state, and local law enforcement; imprisonment of convicted drug dealers.
- *Treatment of heavy users:* utilizing outpatient and residential-treatment programs.

The first three alternatives emphasize control of supply insofar as they raise the cost to dealers of supplying cocaine. The fourth alternative is a demand-reduction program that focuses on reducing demand for cocaine by heavy users, who were estimated to consume cocaine at eight times the rate on average of light users.

Although time-consuming in practice, the process of determining annual expenditures on these four programs at the time of the study was fairly straightforward. The total was estimated to be approximately $13 billion with 73 percent going for domestic enforcement, 13 percent for interdiction, 7 percent for source-country control, and 7 percent for treatment (see figure 6.1).

Measuring the benefits of the alternative programs was much more difficult because each had such disparate impacts. The common measure of effectiveness adopted for the analysis was the cost of a given reduction

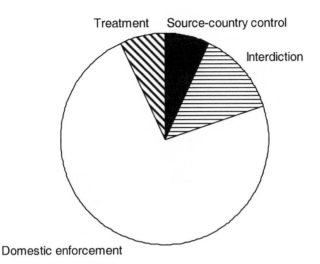

Fig. 6.1. Distribution of annual expenditures on cocaine control in 1992 (Rydell & Everingham, 1994, fig. 5.2)

in U.S. consumption of cocaine. The analytical goal of the model was "to make the discounted sum of cocaine reductions over 15 years equal to 1 percent of current annual consumption" (Rydell & Everingham, 1994). The most cost-effective program would be the one that achieved the specified goal for the least additional expenditure in the first projection year.

Figure 6.2 shows the required spending for each alternative: $783 million for source-country control, $366 million for interdiction, $246 million for domestic enforcement, and $34 million for treatment. The least costly supply-reduction alternative (domestic enforcement) was estimated to cost seven times as much as treatment of heavy users to achieve the same effect.

Additional funding for supply-reduction efforts increases the costs to producers of supplying the cocaine, because they must replace seized assets and compensate those working in the supply chain for the additional risk of arrest. These added costs are passed along to consumers as higher prices for the drug, which in turn reduce demand. The final results obtained by the analysis were based on the assumption that "the percentage decrease in consumption caused by a price increase is half the percentage price increase" (Rydell & Everingham, 1994). Some of the decrease in consumption was estimated to occur immediately after the price increase, while some took place only later as a limiting effect on the entry of new users into the market.

The reductions in use caused by additional expenditures on treatment included both those attributable to most users staying off drugs while in

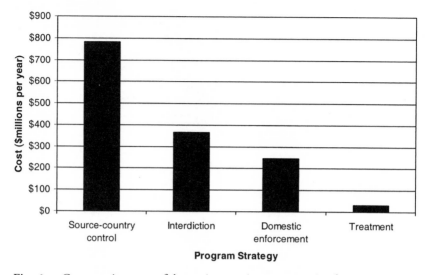

Fig. 6.2. Comparative costs of decreasing cocaine consumption by 1 percent (Rydell & Everingham, 1994, table 3.2)

treatment, and some small percentage (13 percent) who continued to stay off drugs after treatment. Even if all heavy users returned to drug use after treatment, the reduction in use that occurs while they are participating in treatment was still large enough to make treatment much more cost effective than any form of supply reduction. The RAND Controlling Cocaine study concluded that the relative cost effectiveness of the four alternatives remained the same for a variety of outcome measures, including the number of users or societal costs of crime and lost productivity due to cocaine use.

Given the disproportionate allocation of funding among these alternatives at the time the study was published, the Controlling Cocaine study became both controversial and influential almost immediately. Its findings were cited favorably in congressional hearings at the same time as they were vigorously attacked by supporters of supply-side interventions.

In a 1995 statement to the Subcommittee on National Security, International Affairs, and Criminal Justice, under the aegis of the Committee on Government Reform and Oversight, U.S. House of Representatives, Lee Brown, then director of the Office of National Drug Control Policy (ONDCP), remarked:

Let me now talk about what we know about what works in addressing the drug problem. There is compelling evidence that treatment is cost-effective and provides significant benefits to public safety. In June 1994, a RAND Corporation study concluded that drug treatment is the most cost-effective drug control intervention. (Manski et al., 1999)

In response to the RAND study, another think tank, the Institute for Defense Analysis (IDA), undertook a reanalysis of the RAND study data, which produced opposite conclusions:

> A rough estimate of cost-effectiveness indicates that the cost of decreasing cocaine use by one percent through the use of source-zone interdiction efforts is on the order of a few tens of millions of dollars per year and not on the order of a billion dollars as reported in previous research [the RAND study]. The differences are primarily attributed to a failure in the earlier research to account for the major costs imposed on traffickers by interdiction operations and overestimation of the costs of conducting interdiction operations. (Crane et al., 1997)

At the request of ONDCP, a special subcommittee of the National Research Council was formed to review both studies. Its findings were as follows:

> The RAND study is best thought of as conceptual research offering a coherent way to think about the cocaine problem. The study documents a significant effort to identify and model important elements of the market for cocaine. . . . However, the RAND study does not yield usable empirical findings on the relative cost-effectiveness of alternative polices in reducing cocaine consumption. The study makes many unsubstantiated assumptions about the process through which cocaine is produced, distributed, and consumed. Plausible changes in these assumptions can change not only the quantitative findings reported, but the also the main qualitative conclusions of the study. (Manski et al., 1999)

The subcommittee's report particularly criticized the RAND study on several counts:

- The studies it relied on to estimate treatment outcomes.
- The way it interpreted those studies.

- Its assumption of a downward-sloping cocaine industry average-cost curve.
- Its assumption that control activities affected production costs in an additive fashion.
- Its assumption that the market for cocaine equilibrates by price alone.
- Its lack of attempt to check the predictions of the model against the historical record.

The subcommittee also found much to criticize in the IDA study. It identified the centerpiece of that analysis as the comparison of time-series data on cocaine street prices with the timing of eight major drug-interdiction events identified by the historian of the U.S. Army's Southern Command. After acknowledging the wealth of information developed by the IDA study, the subcommittee's assessment of that study concluded:

> These positive features notwithstanding, the IDA study makes many questionable inferences about the effects of interdiction on the cocaine market in the United States. The primary shortcomings of the study are the conclusions drawn using the statistics presented. There are many plausible alternative interpretations of the price fluctuations found by the IDA study. . . . With the exception of the 1989 interruption, none of the price changes that the IDA study attributes to interdiction events was large, and none of the price changes lasted longer than approximately 1 year. Thus, even if one accepts IDA's interpretation of the data, the effects of interdiction are small and temporary. (Manski et al., 1999)

Each of the subcommittee's key criticisms of the RAND study was vigorously refuted by Jon Caulkins in a paper published by RAND (2000). In the preface to that work, the codirectors of RAND's Drug Policy Research Center, Martin Iguchi and Audrey Burnam, responded to the failure of the committee to offer any recommendations or advice on how cocaine-control funding should be allocated:

> Meanwhile, current policies are sustained, new ones introduced. We believe policy should be informed by the best methods and information available—that considering the results of analysis representing the current state of the art, imperfect though it might be, is better than relying on no analysis. Policymaking cannot afford to let "better" become the enemy of "good enough." (Caulkins, 2000)

Iguchi and Burnam's defense of the Controlling Cocaine study uses the same logic that is used to justify any cost-effectiveness study that must rely on untested assumptions. Jon Caulkins used an updated version of the Controlling Cocaine model to show that mandatory sentences for convicted drug dealers was less cost-effective than traditional enforcement or treatment of heavy users (Caulkins et al., 1997).

In addition to laying out the conceptual framework it is credited with by the NRC, the RAND Controlling Cocaine study appears to have reinforced the views of those who were skeptical of supply-reduction efforts and instead favored more treatment, but it did not finally resolve the debate. When another respected institution can produce contradictory conclusions, and a neutral panel of experts called in to referee the debate cannot declare either side as superior, the results are probably better seen as a draw.

Many of the same issues that limited the impact of the RAND Controlling Cocaine study appear in later attempts to apply CEA to delinquency prevention. However, proponents of more traditional methods of crime control have not yet had to defend their turf as vigorously as did those in favor of drug-supply-reduction strategies. The superiority of effective delinquency-prevention programs as a strategy for controlling crime has yet to penetrate the public consciousness or the policymaking community on a large scale.

The crux of the controversy surrounding the drug-treatment versus enforcement cost-effectiveness debate was uncertainty regarding both benefit calculations and their cost components. RAND estimated a unit of cocaine prevention cost seven times as much to achieve through domestic enforcement as through treatment, and argued that "foreign source" prevention was fourteen times as expensive as treatment per unit of prevention. The RAND critics alleged that it had overestimated costs by a factor of more than twenty. "The cost of decreasing cocaine use by one percent . . . is on the order of a few tens of millions of dollars per year and not on the order of a billion dollars" (Crane et al., 1997). We are thus put on notice that the margins of error for cost estimates, at least in the adversarial discourse of drug-enforcement debates, is vast. It would be hard to imagine relative cost advantages that are not vulnerable to estimation errors that large if fourteen-to-one differences can be discounted.

Three Strikes

Some of the same RAND analysts involved in the Controlling Cocaine study also participated in a subsequent analysis that compared the cost effectiveness of California's Three Strikes law with several other mandatory-sentencing alternatives that were being considered at the same time. The study was conducted during the seven-month period between the time the California legislature passed its Three Strikes law, and the appearance of a proposition on the November 1994 general election ballot that was a duplicate of the legislative version. At that time no one was quite sure of the consequences of passing a law both by legislation and ballot, but it was assumed that doing so would make the law extremely difficult to modify or repeal.

The general characteristic shared by all Three Strikes laws is that three convictions for qualifying offenses (each one considered a "strike") triggers a mandatory life sentence in prison. The distinguishing characteristic of the California law is that even second-strike sentences can be pretty rough:

- Convictions as juveniles and those from other states could be counted as strikes.
- Multiple counts in previous convictions could be counted individually as strikes.
- Sentences were increased considerably after a defendant had one strike on his or her record.
- Once an offender had accumulated two strikes, any new felony conviction could be counted as a third strike, making the defendant eligible for a life sentence.

It was obvious that future downstream costs of the law would be quite large, but how large was difficult to say. When the law was passed no one knew what fraction of defendants would qualify under the various provisions of the law. No one knew how the law would be utilized by prosecutors or how it would change the plea-negotiation process by which the majority of cases are settled.

The legislative version of Three Strikes was passed almost unanimously in March of 1994 without any serious attempt to estimate its impacts on crime or costs, illustrating one of the political advantages of new mandatory sentences over prevention programs for youth. A mandatory-sentencing law such as Three Strikes has no immediate financial consequences for the state. The first consequences to appear were court delays and overcrowding in local jails as defendants refused to plead guilty to offenses that could be counted as a strike against them. The legislature did not concern itself with this issue until the counties began complaining about the added costs and the impacts of the delays on their civil calendars. Although felons with Three-Strike enhancements began showing up in prison reception centers

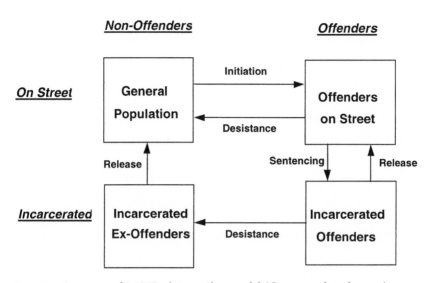

Fig. 6.3. Structure of RAND three-strikes model (Greenwood et al., 1994)

within a few months of passage of the law, significant increases in the prison population due to Three Strikes would not occur until the affected inmates served beyond what would have been their completed sentences before Three Strikes was passed. Thus the costs became something the next legislative session might have to deal with.

The model developed by Peter Rydell for analyzing Three Strikes contained many of the same creative estimation methods and complexities that were included in the Controlling Cocaine model. Current crime rates and prison population data were combined with inmate self-reported offense data, as shown in figure 6.3, to estimate the size of the offender population "on the streets" and its rate of change. Year by year, the model calculated the number of active offenders by estimating the number of new offenders initiating their criminal careers, the number quitting or desisting from crime, and the number sent to prison.

The number of offenders in prison was increased each year by the difference between the new admissions and those who were released. Release and admission rates were determined by parole and sentencing policies, all fairly easy to describe but difficult to estimate accurately.

Because no one knew what fraction of offenders would qualify for second- or third-strike status under the new law, these and other characteristics of the offender population, both those in prison and those on the streets, had to be estimated by the model. Parameters were modified over a number of runs until the outcomes converged on values that were similar to those being experienced at the time the new law went into affect.

The RAND Three Strikes model distinguished between high-rate and low-rate offenders, just as the cocaine model had distinguished between heavy and light drug users. Previous research, much of it done at RAND (Chaiken & Chaiken, 1982; Greenwood & Abrahamse, 1982; Blumstein et al., 1986), had shown individual offense rates to be highly skewed toward the low end. Therefore, the RAND model divided the offender population into two distinct groups, those with high rates of offending and those with lower rates. This distinction was deemed necessary because high-rate offenders, while accounting for a disproportionate amount of crime, are much more likely to be arrested, convicted, and sentenced to prison during any specified time period.

The RAND Three Strikes study concluded:

> If fully implemented as written, the new law will reduce serious felonies committed by adults in California between 22 and 34 percent below what would have occurred had the previous law remained in effect. [Juvenile offenders were not affected by the law. They now account for about one-sixth of all arrests for violent crimes.] . . . This reduction in crime will be bought at a cost of an extra $4.5 billion to $6.5 billion per year in current dollars, compared to what would have been spent had the previous law remained in effect. The intent of the three-strikes law is, of course, to lock up repeat offenders longer, and that requires the construction and operation of more prisons. Some police and court costs may be saved in not having to deal so often with such offenders once they are locked up, but greater prison costs overwhelm such savings.

Figure 6.4 shows the trend in the number of serious crimes predicted by the model to be prevented. The number prevented increases steadily during the first six or seven years, as the number of repeat offenders incarcerated in prison continues to grow; and then levels out as the prison population was predicted to do as shown in figure 6.5.

The plot in figure 6.4 depicts Three Strikes as an effective crime-control plan—an intervention that will prevent three hundred thousand to four hundred thousand serious crimes a year. But what about that extra $4.5 to $6.5 billion per year in additional criminal-justice costs to support the growth in prison population? That trend is shown in figure 6.5.

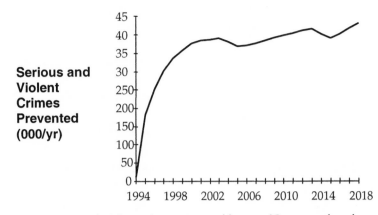

Serious and Violent Crimes Prevented (000/yr)

Fig. 6.4. Serious and violent crimes prevented by year (Greenwood et al., 1994)

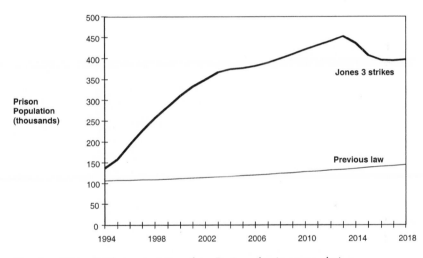

Prison Population (thousands)

Jones 3 strikes

Previous law

Fig. 6.5. Three Strikes vs. previous law: Projected prison populations (Greenwood et al., 1994)

At the time of the study, it was estimated to cost about $21,000 per year to keep one inmate in prison. A sentence of twenty-five years to life incurred an obligation of $500,000 to $1 million to pay the corrections costs. No wonder the Correctional Peace Officers Association, the guards union, strongly supported the bill. It meant a giant boost in their membership. No wonder their political-action committee (PAC) is the most generous donor to political campaigns in California. But I digress.

For this particular study, there was no question what the effectiveness measure should be. Three Strikes was advertised and passed as a measure to prevent "serious" crimes, so *cost per serious crime prevented* was the appropriate measure of effectiveness. "Serious crimes" are defined in the Three Strikes law as those that can trigger first and second strikes. They include most violent crimes, residential burglaries, and certain drug offenses. The only remaining questions were the stringency with which it would be applied and its probable efficiency (or cost effectiveness). The RAND study punted on the first question but developed a best estimate for the second—the C/E ratio for Three Strikes was ultimately computed to be $16,300 per serious crime prevented.

Obviously this estimate had a wide margin of error. In order to test the sensitivity of the results to errors in some of the key assumptions, the RAND analysts varied the ratio of crime rates for high- and low-rate offenders, and the rate of desistance for those with one strike by plus or minus 25 percent. Under the changes most favorable to the new law, the number of crimes prevented would be 6 percent larger while the increase in prison population would be 7 percent smaller, changes that would reduce the C/E ratio to $14,301 per serious crime prevented.

The same model and set of assumptions that were used for the analysis of Three Strikes were also used to compare it with several other mandatory-sentencing alternatives that had been recently considered by the legislature or suggested by the RAND analysts:

- Keeping the second-strike enhancements but eliminating the third-strike provisions.
- Limiting strikes to include only violent felonies.
- Adopting the provisions of a bill proposed by former Assemblyman Rainey, which would have been harsher on violent felons and more lenient on others.
- Eliminating the concept of "strikes" altogether and adopting a measure that sends all those convicted of a serious felony to prison, eliminates "good time" for all such felons, and shifts some minor felons from prison to probation.

None of the alternatives would have prevented as much crime as Three Strikes, as shown in figure 6.6, but all of them cost less, as shown in figure 6.7, and were more cost effective than Three Strikes.

The C/E ratio for each of these alternatives, as illustrated in figure 6.8, was found to be lower than that for Three Strikes. The C/E ratio for the second alternative, in which only violent felonies qualified as strikes, was $11,800 or 28 percent less than Three Strikes. The authors of the study

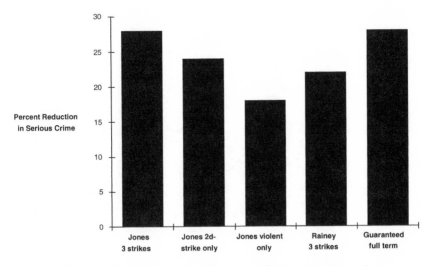

Fig. 6.6. Three Strikes vs. alternatives: Percent reduction in serious crime (Greenwood et al., 1994)

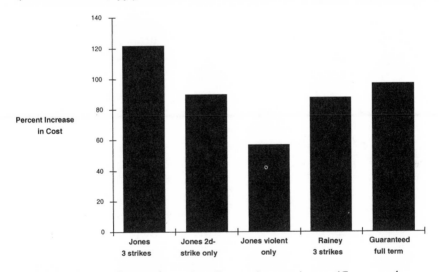

Fig. 6.7. Three Strikes vs. alternatives: Percent increase in cost (Greenwood et al., 1994)

concluded that the Three Strikes law would probably not be fully applied in practice because the additional resources required to carry it out were not being provided. Full implementation of Three Strike was estimated to require a 122 percent increase in the prisons budget. The only source for such funds were the budgets for higher education or transportation.

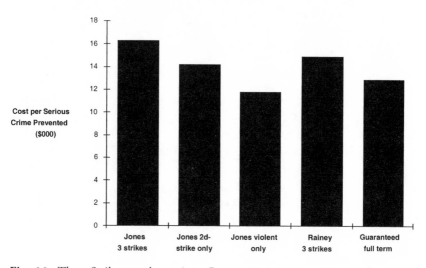

Fig. 6.8. Three Strikes vs. alternatives: Cost per serious crime prevented (Greenwood et al., 1994)

The RAND report concluded by raising a series of questions about the cost effectiveness of alternatives that might produce similar or even greater impacts—for example, additional and better trained and motivated police, and programs aimed at high-risk kids.

> In recent years, law enforcement officials have stressed that they can make only so much headway against crime if the root causes are not addressed. The reasons for this are clear: Our analysis suggests that there may be as many as 1 million felons on the street in California. At some point, these individuals will stop committing crimes and will be replaced by another million felons. The typical criminal career lasts roughly a decade. This implies that something on the order of 1 million California children under the age of 10 will become felons. The Three Strikes law does little or nothing to change that prospect. . . . It works by transferring felons from the street to prison; it does not act to shut off the supply.
>
> The root causes of much serious crime are well known: broken families, dysfunctional families, poverty, sociopathic inclinations, the drug culture. Can money spent combating these causes be as effective as the Three Strikes law? To do so, $5.5 billion would have to persuade 28,000 children who would have become felons not to take up a criminal career. The question can thus be rephrased. Can

$5.5 million be targeted to environments in which children have a high propensity for crime in such a way as to keep 28 children who would otherwise have become criminals from doing so?

These cost-effectiveness arguments about Three Strikes appeared to be favorably received by a wide variety of audiences ranging from academics (at American Society of Criminology [ASC] panels and other such forums) to members of the legislature and other opinion leaders. No one refuted them.

It is difficult to determine the impact the RAND study had on the Three Strikes law. There have been other studies that have identified flaws in the design of the law. Most notable is an assessment by Zimring, Kamin, and Hawkins (1999) that used samples of arrestees, from before and after the law was passed, to demonstrate how selectively the law is applied and its impact on sentences. The arrest samples showed that only about 11 percent of all adult felony defendants were eligible for enhanced sentencing under Three Strikes, a much lower percentage than had been estimated by the RAND model. Furthermore the analysis demonstrated that, even in the early years after passage of the law, second-strike enhancements were applied in less than 60 percent of the eligible cases, and third-strike enhancements applied in only 10–20 percent of those cases eligible.

The law itself has not been changed. The appellate courts have granted judges additional discretion to nullify the law by setting aside strikes "in the interests of justice." In 2004, the Ninth Circuit reversed a third-strike sentence of twenty-five years to life in a case of petty theft, a sentence the court appellate court characterized as cruel and unusual punishment. The attorney general elected not to appeal. Many prosecutors have established written filing and case-settlement policies that have narrowed the application of the law to something like the RAND second alternative of only counting serious violence as strikes (Greenwood & Hawken, 2001). Although a number of states have enacted their own Three Strikes laws, most were narrowly targeted to affect only a small number of repeat violent offenders; none of them was as inclusive as the California law. Eventually the California legislature appropriated hundreds of millions of dollars to support new and innovative delinquency-prevention programs.

In retrospect, criticism of the California Three Strikes law on the basis of its cost effectiveness did not have as much impact as might have been expected. As Zimring, Hawkins, and Kamin (2001) reported in their analysis of the political decisions that produced the law, Three Strikes was more a symbolic means of demonstrating support and sympathy for crime victims than a serious effort to deal with crime. Arguments for and against the law had more to do with politics than with the merits of the law itself. The law was passed at a time when the economy was not in trouble and Sacramento had recovered from the recession of the early 1990s. Crime was the number one problem on the electorate's mind in 1994, not the economy. It was virtually impossible at that time to find an elected official willing to raise the issue concerning how the state would be able to pay the downstream costs of keeping a growing population of "lifers" in prison. Clearly, passage of the Three Strikes law and many other sentencing enhancements in the boom times of the 1990s has contributed to the financial crisis that California faces today. The governor (Davis) who vetoed almost every parole of a "lifer" recommended by the Parole Board was ousted in a recall election and replaced by one who promised to solve the budget crisis.

The Three Strikes impact estimates RAND developed turned out to be too high by a wide margin on both the costs and effectiveness of the new law, both for the same reason. Nothing approaching even 50 percent enforcement of the mandatory twenty-five-years-to-life provisions occurred in California. Only 10 percent of the three-strikes eligible felony arrests received that penalty (Zimring et al., 2001). By 1999, the use of the third-strike provision had declined almost by half again. The good news was lower prison populations and costs. The bad news was much less crime prevention.

Juvenile-Delinquency Prevention

The next public application of CEA in the field of criminal justice was its use in comparing two very different strategies: delinquency-prevention programs on the one hand and, on the other, harsher sentencing. This RAND study, titled "Diverting Children from a Life of Crime" (Greenwood et al., 1996), was an outgrowth of the Three Strikes analysis that had estimated a C/E ratio of $16,300 in criminal-justice costs for every serious crime prevented through harsher sentencing. The RAND analysts identified four delinquency-prevention strategies that appeared to be the most promising at the time: home visits and day care for infants; parent training; graduation incentives for at-risk youth; and special monitoring and supervision of delinquents in the community. The researchers assumed that the impacts that would be achieved by implementing these programs on a large scale would be smaller than those achieved in their original pilot studies due to losses in effectiveness associated with the performance of large-public agencies. They also assumed that there would

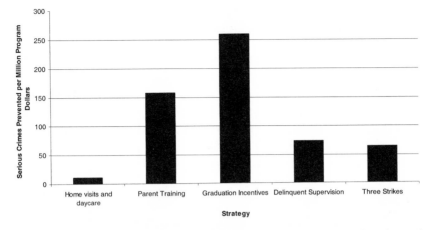

Fig. 6.9. Serious crimes prevented per $million invested (Greenwood et al., 1998)

be a gradual decay in their effects on individuals over time. For these reasons, the impact sizes reported for these interventions in experimental studies were adjusted downward, both initially and over time to account for anticipated losses.

Data from the control groups in the experimental studies were used to estimate the "targeting ratio," which is the offense rate for the targeted group divided by the offense rate of all youth in general. The targeting ratio for an experimental intervention provides analysts both with a way to calculate the risk level of the targeted group, as well as with a means of projecting the impacts of that intervention onto a larger population.

The final results of the Diverting Children cost-effectiveness analysis are displayed in figure 6.9. These results show that some of the interventions, even after conservative adjustments downward, were several times more cost effective in preventing crime than the imposition of longer sentences mandated by Three Strikes. The findings were widely reported and proved pivotal in arguments for increased prevention efforts. Where the cost-effectiveness analysis of Three Strikes had made little headway toward reforming that law, the CEA of prevention programs helped justify substantial increases in prevention funding, possibly because they came at a time when state revenues were increasing each year. Policymakers could increase funding for both prevention and prisons without being forced into making trade-offs.

The crime-prevention analysis had two consequences. First, discussions of the study at a national workshop encouraged officials from Deschutes County, Oregon to develop their Community Youth Investment Program

(CYIP), a program that shifted funding from "backend" residential placements, by reducing the length of youth placements, to "frontend" prevention programs. The program was sold to the community as a cost-effective, crime-prevention strategy by the head of the Deschutes County Community Justice Agency, and proved very popular locally (Greenwood et al., 2003). Second, at the request of their legislature, the Washington State Institute for Public Policy (WSIPP) began systematically estimating the costs and benefits of a wide variety of programs then being utilized by the state or recommended as promising in the prevention literature.

Several factors appear to be at work in the failure of the Controlling Cocaine and Three Strikes studies to have more of an impact on public policy. One is that cocaine interdiction, drug law enforcement, prison construction, and prison operations are all huge, well-organized enterprises, with large and influential constituencies. Their heroic exploits are mythologized in motion pictures and on television. And their more cost-effective alternatives, which stress the advantages of treatment and prevention, do not have anywhere near the same level of organizational clout and backing. There is no strong lobby that supports them.

Another factor is the U.S. preference for combatlike forcefulness in solving social ills, rather than selective diplomacy and the use of incentives and positive reinforcement. American policymakers on balance appear to believe that enough force and enough punishment will eventually effect behavioral changes—whether in Iraq, among the cocoa growers in Colombia, or on the part of juvenile delinquents in the United States. What they either overlook or choose not to acknowledge is one of the most well-established tenants of psychology: positive reinforcement and incentives are much more effective in changing behavior than punishment and fear.

A third factor may be a much higher political discounting rate than we typically want to acknowledge. A high discount rate greatly reduces the value of benefits to be received in the future, while increasing the value of benefits that accrue immediately. Public concerns about crime and drug use ebb and flow in cycles that are not always driven by objective facts. Rather, when an issue like crime gets promoted to the top of the public's list of social ills, quick, simplistic, bumper-sticker solutions usually win out over those that are more complex and take longer to achieve. Interdiction and enforcement are perceived to have immediate impacts. Law-enforcement officials are often shown posing with the big stash of drugs and weapons their operations have seized. High-profile traffickers are covered by the media as they are arrested, tried, and imprisoned.

Treatment and prevention, on the other hand, have impacts that extend well into the future. Even though the aggregate of these benefits in the long run exceeds the benefits from enforcement and imprisonment, policy-makers and the public at large tend to be drawn to what is politically expedient in the here and now. One method of expressing the public's preference for measures that seem to offer immediate results is to talk of a high discount for crimes avoided in the future, a calculation that would include only a fraction of the future savings in the "present value" of a prevention effort. But this may misstate the psychology that influences the prevention choice. If a prevention effort does not have any immediate impact on crime (say its subjects are preschool students, twelve years removed from possibly being a criminal threat), the public may not consider this "future only" intervention as real competition for any immediate crime countermeasure. The public demand may be such that a policy must address current crime fears before it is seriously considered. On the other hand, policies with *some* immediate impact—for example, twenty-five-year sentences that start now but deliver the majority of their prevention more than ten years down the line—may not be discounted because they appear to have immediate effect, even though this appearance is false.

The comparison of delinquency prevention programs with programs like Three Strikes raises one further possibility to be considered when different prevention approaches compete for resources. It may be that an angry and vengeful public prefers to inflict punishment on offenders, even if nonpunitive measures have the same effect and cost less. If punishment itself is regarded as a public benefit, then punitive alternatives will always be favored in spite of their higher costs.

The demand for immediate responses to the control of crime and the preference for punishment are both limits to the strict cost-effectiveness standard wherever they exist. It may not be prudent to assume that the public is indifferent to the means used to prevent crime or to the timing of crime prevention. Instead, it may be that the study of cost effectiveness in crime and punishment must involve both psychology and political science, as well as economics.

Cost-Benefit Analysis and Funding among Alternative Programs

Cost-benefit analysis (CBA) takes the economic approach to evaluating outcomes one important and controversial step further than CEA by converting all outcomes of interest into monetary terms. The kind of cost-effectiveness analysis described above works fine so long as all of the alternatives can be compared on one single outcome measure, such as thefts avoided or cocaine consumption prevented. It does not work, however, when the alternatives being compared produce different kinds of outcomes. Such is the case when comparing delinquency-prevention programs with programs designed to improve education or health outcomes for youth, or comparing a program designed to prevent drug abuse against one designed to reduce violence. The same holds when comparing programs expected to produce positive gains in several outcome domains, such as improved educational performance, reduced dependence on welfare, and reduced offending. Some common metric is needed to aggregate outcomes across the various domains. This is where CBA comes into play, as analysts attempt to convert all relevant outcomes into a monetary terms.

If this conversion of outcomes into dollar amounts is successful, one of the most critical features of cost-benefit analysis is that it provides a rational means of deciding which, among a variety of opportunities, to invest in. Cost-effectiveness analysis can tell you which of several alternatives is the most efficient in achieving a particular outcome, but it cannot tell you if an investment in achieving a particular outcome is "better" than an investment in achieving some other outcome. Cost-benefit analysis can help inform such decisions.

Let's start with the challenge of combining all of the benefits a delinquency-prevention program might produce into one single outcome measure. As I reported in chapter 4, long-term, follow-up studies of the Nurse Home Visitation Project in Elmira, New York (Olds et al., 1997) found a number of positive outcomes when the high-risk group of experimental families were compared with similar control families:

- Fewer reported acts of child abuse and neglect.
- Less time on welfare.
- Less criminal activity on the part of mothers and children.
- Lower health-care costs for the child.
- Fewer subsequent pregnancies for mother and longer intervals between pregnancies.
- Increased income and taxes paid by the mother.

Many of these outcomes translate into direct savings for particular government programs. A cost-benefit analysis of the Elmira program by RAND (Karoly et al., 1998) estimated that the participation of high-risk families in that program produced total savings to government of roughly four times the program's $6,000 cost. Savings in criminal costs accounted for just 20 percent of the total savings.

Table 6.1. Lower and upper range of net program benefits estimated by WSIPP*

	Net direct cost per participant	Net taxpayer benefits per participant	Net benefits per participant to taxpayers and victims
Nurse home visiting	7,733	−2,067	15,918
BBBS Mentoring	1,054	225	4,524
FFT	2,161	14,149	59,067
MST	4,743	31,661	131,918
MTFC	2,052	21,835	87,622
Diversion with services	−127	1,470	5,679

Source: Aos et al., 2001.

*All monetary values are in Year 2002 dollars.

Of course, programs that prevent crime produce saving or benefits for entities other than just the government. Potential crime victims (and their relatives and friends) are spared the pain and suffering that often result from being victimized, along with the out-of-pocket costs of replacing stolen property and medical expenses.

Many of these outcomes are difficult to measure, the pain and suffering of crime victims especially so. As I indicated in chapter 3, Cohen (1988) developed a method for estimating these costs by combining jury awards for pain, suffering, and reduced quality of life with income differentials for occupations involving risks of injury that are similar to those involved in crimes. This method was used in research commissioned by the National Academy of Sciences (Cohen et al., 1994) and in subsequent research funded by the National Institute of Justice (Miller et al., 1996).

The Washinton State Institute for Public Policy (WSIPP) has used these estimated victim costs to calculate the net benefits (total benefits less costs) produced by alternative corrections and prevention programs (Aos et al., 2001), as shown in table 6.1. The WSIPP model first estimates the number of crimes that will be prevented by a particular program based on its effect size and target population. The number of crimes prevented is multiplied by a cost factor reflecting the likelihood of arrest and conviction, the likely sentence, and the costs of each. In the WSIPP approach, this figure, less the program cost, is considered the "lower-end" estimate of net benefits; it includes only benefits to taxpayers. The "upper-end" estimate of net benefits includes the expected savings to potential crime victims, which is calculated by multiplying the number of crimes prevented by the crime-cost estimates of Miller et al. (1996).

The estimated benefits shown in table 6.1 include only those savings associated with crime prevention. They do not include the many other benefits produced by programs such as Nurse Home Visitation. The program does not appear to yield positive benefits when only taxpayer savings are considered. When the savings to crime victims are factored in, however, the net benefits from Nurse Home Visitation clearly are positive. Also notice that the net direct cost of diversion from regular Juvenile Court processing is negative. Diversion is cheaper than taking the youth to court.

The use of such cost-of-crime data for analyzing the costs and benefits of criminal-justice policies was severely criticized by Zimring and Hawkins (1995) on several grounds. Some of their criticisms concerned the opportunistic use of the jury-award and wage-rate differential studies, which they claimed were adopted simply on the basis of their availability. Zimring and Hawkins further argued that jury awards for pain and suffering are widely acknowledged to be arbitrary and highly inflated. Presumably the more recent cost-of-crime data obtained through the use of contingent-valuation methods, described below, silences that particular objection insofar as it has a stronger theoretical basis in welfare economics.

Zimring and Hawkins, however, used another argument to show that the estimated $2 million cost for each homicide, as determined by Cohen et al. (1994), was too high. They argue that if the average cost of homicide is $2 million, the 2.16 million deaths experienced in the United States in 1990 generated an aggregate cost of $4.32 trillion dollars, approximately 5 percent more than the $4.12 trillion gross national product (GNP). To those who would respond that applying the $2 million average cost figure to every death fails to take into account the differences in ages, health conditions, and levels of economic activity for the persons who died, Zimring and Hawkins pointed out that the same objection applies to the use of such average cost-of-death data for determining the cost of homicides.

Zimring and Hawkins's final arguments against the simplistic use of aggregate-cost data was that it blurred the distinction between public and private costs, and ignored the presence of less costly alternatives. If the theft of a $40,000 automobile could be prevented by the installation of a $200 security devise, why should the theft of cars without such devises be considered a $40,000 social loss?

There is an approach economists use to estimate the monetary value of outcomes similar to those used in crime-prevention analyses. It gauges the level of the public's "willingness to pay" (WTP) to reach some desired

Table 6.2. Comparison of estimated cost of individual crimes ($)

	Miller et al. estimate	WTP low estimate	WTP high estimate
Burglary	3,360	21,000	30,000
Armed robbery	31,800	174,000	314,000
Serious assault	35,600	57,000	86,000
Rape and sexual assault	114,000	185,000	313,000
Murder	3.9 million	8.5 million	11 million

Sources: Figures in Miller et al. column from Miller et al., 1996; figures in WTP columns from Cohen et al., 2004.

end—how much, for example is the public willing to pay to achieve a specified level of crime reduction? Economists estimate WTP using "contingent valuation" (CV). A sample of the population for whom the analysis is being performed is asked about their willingness to pay specified amounts, for instance by having their taxes raised, in order to achieve specific outcomes, such as a 10 percent reduction in violent crime.

CV has mostly been used to place dollar values on such nonmarket goods and improvements as air quality and saving endangered species (Cohen et al., 2004). Cook and Ludwig (2000) used this method to estimate the amount a U.S. household would be willing to pay to reduce gun violence by adult and juvenile offenders. Cohen et al. adopted CV in order to measure the public's WTP to prevent the crimes of burglary, armed robbery, assault, rape or sexual assault, and murder.

In general, the studies that used CV found the costs of crime to be considerably higher (sometimes orders of magnitude higher) than previous estimates. Table 6.2 compares the total social cost of specific crimes as estimated by Miller et al. (1996) from jury awards with those estimated by Cohen et al. (2004) using WTP. The WTP method produces a probability range bounded by low and high estimates. The new low or conservative estimate for the cost (or society's willingness to pay) to prevent a burglary is $21,000, for rape it is $185,000, and for murder it is $8.5 million.

It is difficult to sort out exactly what these new estimates mean. Since they are far larger than Miller et al.'s earlier estimates, they are even more subject to the criticisms by Zimring and Hawkins (1995). In comparing alternative crime-prevention strategies, the estimates would not have much impact because they would increase or inflate the value of all crime-prevention effects proportionally. But when it comes to comparing crime-prevention efforts with other governmental activities, the new WTP estimates suggest that crime prevention is of much more value to our citizens than had been previously thought.

Moreover, since this data were derived without considering other potential investment opportunities for taxpayers, it is not clear that taxpayers would still want their taxes raised 10 percent to prevent crime if similar increases would produce significant gains in other areas of government as well.

The advantage of cost-benefit analysis is that it reduces different types of outcomes—crimes, educational achievements, welfare savings—into dollar values so that the most valuable mix of outcomes can be selected to receive scarce governmental resources. A cost-benefit analysis can also tell us if a particular program produces value beyond its cost. The problems with such conversions to dollar terms, however, are the uncertainties and assumptions that must be made to construct a dollar value. The problems of figuring cost that we encountered in the attempt to reduce cocaine use—did supply-country interdiction cost $1 billion or less than one-twentieth that amount?—are multiplied when different types of public and private outcomes must be transformed into a single dollar standard. And the money measurement—$200 million of costs avoided—tends to hide the mix of heroic assumptions behind any such estimate.

It can be argued that to date there are no successful and uncontroversial cost-benefit analyses using competing forms of crime reduction, and that at present, CBA is a hope rather than an achieved methodology in crime-prevention analysis. However, several recent studies suggest that it is gaining some traction in crime-prevention policy circles. Since 1999, WSIPP has published a series of evaluations and CBAs for a wide range of interventions being used or being considered for use in Washington State for juvenile and adult offenders (Aos et al., 1999, 2001; Barnowski, 2002). The large net benefits reported for some of the most promising pilot programs, including projected benefits to potential victims, convinced the Washington legislature to fund and evaluate several large field trials of those programs statewide (Barnowski). The 1998 RAND cost-benefit analysis of early-childhood programs described earlier was used by advocates of California's Proposition 20 in 1998 to help win passage of a new tobacco tax that provides approximately $500 million a year to expand programs at the local level. Since their first publication in 1999, the WSIPP cost-benefit figures have been routinely cited by Blueprints founder Del Elliot to support adoption of the Blueprint model program (Mihalic et al., 2002). So long as those programs that are identified as having the highest benefit-to-cost ratio, when potential victim costs are included, also have the highest benefit-to-cost ratio when victim losses are not included, we have no way of knowing how the estimated victim savings enters into decisions about whether to adopt the program.

Cost Effectiveness and Appropriate Criteria for Allocating Delinquency- and Crime-Prevention Resources

This final section of the chapter begins with asking who is in a position to allocate prevention resources among competing programs. Local public officials are clearly in such a position. The local probation chief or juvenile court judge usually has considerable discretion regarding which programs are funded, as do those responsible for local programs serving children and families. Members of the city council and those who sit as county commissioners or supervisors also deal with line items in their budgets affecting specific programs. These officials often make the crucial decisions regarding which programs are funded and which ones are cut. Agencies that operate individual programs themselves must often determine which among several competing program models they will adopt and incorporate into their repertoire of offerings, which need to be modified, and which will be dropped. We could even imagine a situation in which an individual parent, guardian, or just an advocate for a particular youth is seeking the most cost-effective intervention, given the risk and protective factors that pertain to that youth. Should such persons use cost effectiveness or other criteria to make budgetary and spending decisions?

In almost all of these situations we can assume that we are dealing with individuals who have limited budgets, making it impossible to fund all of the programs that the population they are responsible for assisting could benefit from or would like to have. All such individuals, even those within the juvenile justice system, must consider other direct investments for the revenues they control beyond delinquency prevention. For example, in addition to public safety and prevention programs, county commissioners must also administer programs intended to improve public health, education, services for seniors, and road repairs, to name just a few. The chief probation officer must allocate funds between programs that may reduce delinquency in the future and those that monitor and hold accountable currently delinquent youth. In order for many of these policymakers to make rational and efficient budget allocations among delinquency-prevention programs and those that serve other purposes, the effectiveness of these programs and their alternatives must be measured using some common metric. There is no other alternative.

Without a common measure of effectiveness, it is impossible to compare resource allocation decisions except on a political or subjective basis. Political allocations usually favor the status quo or the program with the greatest political clout. The case histories of the DARE and Scared Straight programs presented in chapter 5 should be argument enough against such an approach. I present another example of how the political approach works (or fails to do so) in chapter 7, with a brief look at how prevention programs faired in President Clinton's 1994 anticrime legislation, and with the Republican Congress that followed its passage.

Consider the alternatives if we do not use cost effectiveness as the standard measure of performance. The goal of any program is to have an impact on one or more specific outcomes. The standard measure widely adopted by the scholarly community for evaluating and reporting the impact of any program is the effect size—, that is, the mean difference in outcomes between the experimental and comparison group, divided by their combined standard deviation. It is usually the case that larger impacts and effect sizes are preferred over smaller ones.

Recognizing the economic postulate that less expensive ways of achieving a particular result are preferred over more expensive alternatives, cost-effectiveness and cost-benefit analysis take the effect-size measurement one step further by including resource requirements in the equation. Combining just effect sizes and offense rates can only help you estimate how many crimes you prevent for each participant in a particular program. Including the cost of treating each individual subject can tell you the cost-per-crime prevented.

So cost-effectiveness measures definitely trump effect size when it comes to selecting among programs to accomplish a particular goal. The cost effectiveness of any candidate program can be estimated if you know the program's cost and the size of its effect, and the expected future offending pattern of its prospective subjects.

If you want to compare the benefits achieved by delinquency-prevention efforts with the benefits that could be derived from other types of government programs, then cost-benefit analysis is required. Cost-benefit analysis takes cost-effectiveness analysis one step further by assigning a value to program outcomes. If the data are available and can be trusted, cost-benefit analysis can indicate the relative rate of return from investing in different types of programs.

An alternative approach used by many communities for making program-allocation decisions is based on "need." The decisionmakers arrange for a community "needs assessment" to be conducted, which identifies the risk factors that must be addressed, and often the types of services required to address them. The decisionmakers then fund those programs that appear to meet the most pressing needs. This approach may work well if the needs of a community are apparent—food, clothing, or shelter—needs that can usually be readily satisfied. But if juvenile-crime rates are high, particularly gun violence by juveniles, what then is the need? Pull together a group of community leaders and they are likely to recommend better schools, recreation, job opportunities, and an end to racism. Gun control advocates will urge more restrictions on gun possession and ownership. Residents of the most impacted neighborhoods will probably ask for more police and more aggressive enforcement. Increased investments in proven delinquency-prevention programs are usually not the first choice.

Needs assessments come in all shapes and sizes. Some are derived on the basis of collective brainstorming as to what are currently unmet needs. Others are based on detailed analyses of demographic data, school and arrest records, and current program offerings. In some sense, all communities have the same basic needs for prevention. They just vary in the degree to which each is needed. But priorities for funding must still be established because it is usually not possible to secure the small amounts of each of the programs that will be needed, except in very large metropolitan areas. Economies of scale and administrative realities usually require that only one or two new programs be added to the local mix at a time. The usual question to be faced, therefore, is where are funds needed most.

But here's the rub: this kind of deductive reasoning, starting from identified needs, does not take into account the effectiveness of programs that might serve these particular needs. If a community determines that its primary need in the delinquency-prevention area is improved afterschool recreational activities and programs to keep youth from joining gangs, a frequent finding, then they have reached a kind of dead end. Many programs offer afterschool activities and antigang programming, but none of them have been shown to be effective in reducing delinquency. Picking programs just on the basis of needs ignores the very real limitations on what programs can actually accomplish.

This is the kind of strategy that was adopted by eighteen community coalitions that were provided with five-year community-action grants by the California Wellness Foundation as part of its youth-focused Violence Prevention Initiative. None of these efforts was able to demonstrate an impact on youth violence (Greenwood et al., 2001).

An alternative approach is to start with a list of programs that have been proven effective—the Blueprints list or the Surgeon General's Report (see chapter 4) are both good choices. Starting with the programs that are most effective, the optimal choices for a community to make are how much of each of these programs they require to meet their needs.

Table 6.3. Proven and promising programs ranked by effect size

	Targeted age range (yrs)	Effect size	Taxpayer benefits/costs
MTFC	12 to 17	−0.37	11.6
MST	12 to 17	−0.31	7.7
Quantum Opportunity	15 to 18	−0.31	0.5
Nurse Home Visit	0 to 2	−0.29	4.1
FFT	12 to 17	−0.25	7.5
Seattle Social Development	7 to 12	−0.13	0.9
Perry Preschool	3 to 4	−0.1	2.1
BBBS Mentoring	11 to 16	−0.04	1.2
Intensive Probation	12 to 17	−0.05	1.1

Source: Aos et al., 2001.

This approach brings us back to the issue of how programs should be rated: by effect size, by category and then effect size, or by their cost effectiveness alone?

If we look at the data in table 6.3, some of the problems are apparent by considering effect size alone. Table 6.3 contains a subset of the information presented in table 4.5: program name, age-range targeted, effect size, and taxpayer benefits/costs. Unlike table 4.5, however, which ordered programs by the age of the targeted youth, in table 6.3 the programs are ordered by effect size. The larger the negative effects on recidivism the better.

As I explained in chapter 3, effect size is usually measured as the difference in experimental and control mean-value of recidivism, divided by their pooled standard deviation. An effect size of .12 is equivalent to the difference between a 44 percent recidivism for the treatment group and a 50 percent recidivism rate for the control group.

The largest effect size shown in table 6.3 is achieved by Multidimensional Treatment Foster Care (MTFC), a program that places individual youth with specially trained foster parents as an alternative to placement in a traditional group home. These youth are usually older, fairly serious offenders who require some type of placement. Tied for second place in the effect-size competition are Multisystemic Therapy (MST) and Quantum Opportunities Program (QOP). Although QOP has been delisted by Blueprints as a result of poor results reported in some recent replications, we can still use the numbers developed from its first pilot programs to make a point. A large effect size does not guarantee a high benefit to cost ratio. MST returns $7.70 for every dollar invested whereas QOP returns only 50 cents on the dollar.

The fourth highest effect size in table 6.3 is achieved by the Nurse Family Partnership (NFP), which targets high-risk, first-time mothers. It is unlikely that any one agency or individual will find themselves having to choose between funding services for high-risk mothers, treatment foster care, or family therapy. A county commissioner or supervisor might. In the latter case, the political supporters and advocates for the two different target groups are likely to have more of an influence over the allocation funding than their relative effect sizes.

So what's wrong with using effect size as the standardized measure of outcomes when choosing among programs? Two problems in particular make the point. The first problem is that effect size alone tells you nothing about the size of the expected impacts on the outcomes we value. Outcomes of prevention programs are usually measured in terms of recidivism rates or rates of future offending. It is possible to derive an approximate estimate of one of these measures from the other (Greenwood et al., 2003). If recidivism is the outcome of interest, then effect size tells you nothing about the size of the impacts you care about unless you know what the base recidivism rate is. Once you know the base recidivism rate and the effect size, you can estimate what changes in recidivism and offense rates the program will produce.

The second problem has to do with resources. If one program requires four times the resources of another to achieve similar impacts, on the same type of population, would we not prefer the program that accomplished our goals at one-quarter the costs? Clearly this is the case. Cost per unit of outcomes is the outcome measure that cost effectiveness provides. Cost effectiveness is clearly the appropriate criteria for selecting among programs to achieve a specific goal such as delinquency prevention. Cost-benefit analysis can clearly play a useful advisory role in determining the amount of resources to devote to pursuing different types of outcomes, but political value judgments and constituency politics will continue to be key factors in such decisions. The role of CBA in instances where program allocations are less than optimal is to identify the costs of the opportunities forgone.

Summary

Cost-effectiveness analysis is the most appropriate criteria to use in selecting programs or allocating resources across programs in order to maximize the amount of outcomes achieved for a given level of resources. Cost-benefit analysis has a wider potential use but raises more problems in implementation and interpretation.

CEA is often preferred over CBA because it does not require the controversial step of converting outcomes into monetary terms. Critics of CBA will argue that it is impossible to put a value on human life, the pain and suffering incurred by a rape victim, or the safety of our food supply. Proponents of CBA respond that many of our resource allocation decisions already imply such values and that the best estimates of these values can be determined by appropriate "willingness-to-pay" methodologies. CEA can only be used to compare alternatives on a single outcome measure, as in comparing apples to apples or oranges to oranges. CBA can handle multiple outcomes (comparing apples and oranges).

The acceptability and influence of CEA or CBA depends on the complexity and transparency of the models used to estimate outcomes and on the number and nature of the assumptions they require. Innovative models and reasonable assumptions become powerful ammunition in the hands of critics, despite the best efforts of the analysts to test the sensitivity of their assumptions. This was clearly the case with the NRC panel's review of the RAND Controlling Cocaine study. Since different assumptions could lead to different outcomes, the panel determined that the RAND model did not provide any outcomes that could be used for policymaking purposes

The appropriate outcome measure for any CEA of alternative crime-prevention strategies is cost per crime of a particular type (serious, felony, violent, etc.) prevented. Because delinquency-prevention programs are intended to have effects on their participants well into the future, most CEAs of delinquency-prevention programs require the analyst to project long-term effects (five to twenty years) from those that are measured in the near term.

A large proportion of the benefits produced by effective delinquency-prevention programs are in the form of savings to taxpayers, who are responsible for footing the costs of future law enforcement, court, and correctional needs. These benefits are easily estimated in monetary terms, but still require a number of simplifying assumptions. A few delinquency-prevention programs are clearly so cost effective that they pay for themselves several times over in future taxpayer savings.

The beneficiaries who reap the greatest rewards from effective delinquency-prevention programs are the potential victims of serious crimes of violence. Using the most appropriate methods to estimate the social costs of serious crimes to the public produces estimates that are several times greater than just the criminal-justice processing costs. The inclusion of these social cost savings in CBAs for delinquency-prevention programs will greatly increase the number of programs that are able to demonstrate more benefits than they cost.

The findings from CBAs of effective programs geared toward delinquency prevention will begin to have more influence on public policy when the following steps in these analyses become standardized across studies, as has been done in the fields of health and medicine (Gold et al., 1996):

- Making a downward adjustment in any effect size that is produced from an experimental or pilot study to account for the anticipated degradation in program fidelity associated with going to scale. Large-scale field trials of model programs have not found them to achieve the same level of effectiveness they did in small clinical trials.
- Discounting or truncating the estimated effects of an intervention over time. We usually do not expect effects observed in childhood or adolescence to persist throughout the life course, but we do not yet have enough long-term, follow-up studies to determine exactly how effects decay.
- Projecting future crime rates as a function of control-group offense or recidivism patterns and treatment-group risk factors. The amount of crimes prevented by a program depends both on its effect size, and what would have been the crime rate in the absence of the intervention.
- Estimating future criminal justice cost savings as a function of future crime-rate reduction. Many jurisdictions do not have the appropriate data on hand to estimate the probability of arrest, conviction, and expected sentence length for different types of crime. Since variations in processing costs across sites can be expected to be less than many of the other sources of variance in these types of studies, it would make studies more comparable if all analysts used the same projected probabilities of arrest, conviction, and various sentencing outcomes, unless they were known to be very different from the national average.
- Discounting future crimes, costs, and savings to determine their present value.

The influence of CEAs or CBAs on policymakers declines as you move from comparing delinquency-prevention programs for specific age and risk-level groups, to multiple age and risk-level groups, to other crime-prevention strategies, and to other government programs. This loss in influence is due to constituency politics and differing values placed on latent benefits other than crime reduction. Cost-effective delinquency prevention may have a strong cost-benefit case but it has a very weak constituency base, and politics is still the name of the resource allocation game.

Chapter 7

Politics, Government, and Prevention

Effective delinquency-prevention programs take many forms. Teaching young, at-risk mothers about infant healthcare and development; working with families to improve communication and problemsolving skills; training foster parents to deal with troubled kids; helping students learn the social skills to resist using drugs—all are effective strategies.

This chapter explores the issue regarding where in the American system of government crime prevention in general and delinquency prevention in particular should be located. There are actually two sets of questions we must ask. One concerns the appropriate *level of government*, whether it is the federal government, the fifty state jurisdictions, or government at the local level. While I do address the issue in part in this and the next chapter, level of government questions are not central to this analysis. Funding and ideology can come from federal and state governments, but service delivery for prevention programs is primarily a local matter.

The second set of questions mentioned above has to do with the *branches of government*, and is the more critical for present purposes. The concern is not so much the division among the executive, judicial, and legislative branches of government. With the exception of programs administered by the judiciary, a topic considered in chapter 8, the units of government principally involved in prevention are located in the executive branch of local, state and federal government. The more pressing question asks which departments of the executive branch should budget and administer prevention programs: those most concerned with youth policy (education, social services, and health) or those most concerned with public safety and the administration of justice. At the state and federal levels this is a choice between the Department of Justice, with all its crime specialists, and the Departments of Health, Education and Human or Social Services.

The path I take to address this set of questions is anything but direct. The first section of this chapter is about the politics of crime prevention at the national level during the mid-1990s, a time in which the responsibilities of the various departments of government was not an issue. This provides a helpful perspective for the encounter with two problems that affect crime-prevention decisions at all levels of government: the American penchant for punishment and the demand for quick solutions in dealing with crime.

The second section of the chapter addresses some of the problems with locating prevention services in crime-control departments of government. The third section seeks to develop guidelines for the placement of prevention activities within the proper unit of government.

The Political Economy of Crime Control at the National Level

There is no more detailed source of information on the politics of crime control at the national level than the record provided by the passage and implementation of the 1994 Federal Crime Act. Here were the two major political parties (and critical factions within each) struggling to achieve what they and their supporters considered to be critical goals, while at the same time posturing for maximum political advantage. Democrats from financially strapped and high-crime-rate, inner-city districts faced off against Republicans, backed by the powerful National Rifle Association (NRA) over gun control. Congressional Black Caucus members, concerned about racial disparities in the outcomes of death-penalty cases, vied against Republicans pushing for more prison construction and tougher sentencing policies. Advocates pressing for the expansion of recreational and employment opportunities for inner-city youth had to contend with fiscal conservatives trying to rein in the $30 billion cost of the bill. There was a tag-team match among those advocating stricter gun control, community policing, increased use of imprisonment, equality of justice in use of the death penalty, expansion in the number of federal crimes punishable by death, and social programs for youth. When the dust finally settled, only a few of these objectives had been achieved. The process that produced the eventual winners and losers in this, the first omnibus crime control bill in a quarter century, is a cautionary tale of considerable importance to advocates of more effective crime-prevention policies.

When the voting public becomes concerned about rising crime rates, most politicians feel compelled to support stricter policies, which generally translate into more police and tougher sentences. Even when crime rates are no longer rising, as was the case in the latter years of the 1990s, many elected officials tend to believe that there is still political capital to be made in passing tougher sentencing laws. Unlike most other government programs, tougher sentencing laws appear to achieve their primary purposes before any additional funds must be spent. Criminals are simply put on notice that the penalties have gone up and those who helped enact the new laws can claim them to their credit.

The bill for these tougher sentencing laws only comes due when the number of inmates in custody begins to swell. By passing tougher sentencing laws that require offenders to serve longer terms, this day of financial reckoning is postponed for the length of time that prisoners would have served before the new laws were passed. Additionally, if the prosecutors and courts only use the new laws selectively, or if the parole board increases the amount of good time earned by those serving sentences, the financial bill for tougher sentencing laws may never come due at all. This is not the case when it comes to hiring more police officers and certainly not the case when it comes to expanding delinquency-prevention programs. Investments in delinquency prevention must be made up front in hopes that they will reduce crime rates some time in the future.

Given these basic political facts of life, it should come as no surprise that the increasing crime rates of the late 1980s produced an avalanche of mandatory sentencing laws, overcrowded prisons, and increasing disparities between sentence lengths imposed and terms actually served. By 1993, the typical state-prison inmate committed for a violent crime was serving only about 25 percent of his actual sentence length (Turner et al., 2002).

The 1994 Federal Crime Bill

Responsibility for responding to violent crime is primarily a state matter. Ninety-three percent of all prison inmates are held in state facilities (Zimring & Hawkins, 1995). Only in those rare circumstances when crimes involve federal property or activities of the federal government does federal law-enforcement have a role to play. The history of recent federal crime legislation is a record of the federal government's attempts to expand its modest role in crime control, or at least appear to take some decisive action.

Efforts by Congress to respond to citizens concerns about increasing crime rates began with the Armed Career Criminal Act of 1984 (Windlesham, 1998).

Under this law, if a person was found in possession of a firearm and had three prior convictions for robbery or burglary, the minimum sentence could be enhanced from ten years to not less than fifteen years to life without the eligibility for parole. During the next congressional session, the qualifying offenses for invoking the statute were widened to include any violent or serious drug offense.

In 1986, Congress passed the Anti-Drug Abuse Act of 1986, which linked the mandatory minimum sentence for drug offenses to the amount of drugs involved, rather than the offenders role or culpability. Two years later, responding to concerns about the epidemic of crack cocaine use, Congress passed the Anti-Drug Abuse Act of 1988, which imposed a mandatory minimum sentence of five years for simple possession of more than five grams of crack cocaine.

During his first presidential campaign, Bill Clinton decided that one of the priorities of his administration would be a crime bill that combined support for long-neglected crime-prevention efforts with stronger penalties and more effective law enforcement. The starting points for this - effort were the compromises reached in the Conference Report on the Bush administration's crime bill, which had been blocked in the Senate in its final stages (Windlesham, 1998). In his run for the presidency, Clinton pledged to put one hundred thousand additional police officers on the streets. These additional officers would be added to local police departments, with initial funding provided by the federal government—a strategy that had much in common with a no-down-payment car loan.

Following his election, Clinton launched his administration's crime initiative at a press conference in the White House Rose Garden on August 11, 1993. The President was flanked by the attorney general, members of Congress from both parties, and representatives from several national organizations representing prosecutors and police. Key elements of the proposed program were:

- The availability of 3.4 billion dollars in funding for a new community policing initiative.
- Several measures designed to restrict the availability of assault weapons to the general public.
- Measures restricting the availability of all guns to those with criminal records or indications of mentally instability (Windlesham, 1998).

The remainder of the crime initiative was to be developed by Congress.

At that time, some of the specific programs being supported by the Republican leadership included:

- Increased federal aid for local law enforcement.
- A "three strikes and you're out" law for defendants in federal courts.
- Mandatory minimum sentences for crimes by gang members.
- Support for construction of additional state prison capacity.
- Restrictions on the recourse to habeas corpus petitions by death row inmates.

The Republican proposals made no mention of gun control.

In order to speed up the legislative process, the Democratic leadership in the House and Senate introduced parallel bills. Each bill authorized expenditures that would enable states and local governments to employ fifty thousand additional police officers and develop local education and training programs to prevent crime, violence, and drug abuse in schools. Both bills would also phase in drug treatment in federal prisons and allow the Drug Enforcement Administration to hire additional agents and staff. Both measures provided for funding to help states expand their prison capacities and the Senate version encouraged states to develop military-style boot camps as alternatives to state prison for younger nonviolent offenders. Both measures extended the number of federal crimes punishable by death and restricted the right of federal habeas corpus to a single petition. When it became apparent that no agreement could be reached on the omnibus bill before the House of Representative, the individual measures were broken out into a number of separate bills, each to proceed at its own pace.

Despite the pressure from the White House for swift passage, the crime bills in the House became bogged down by two primary factors: liberal dissatisfaction with the direction the bills were taking and obstruction by the Congressional Black Caucus (CBC). The more liberal penal reformers in the House had been encouraged by the pro-prevention stance adopted by Clinton's attorney general, Janet Reno, and the generally positive public reaction with which it was met. It seemed that the political climate was right for the consideration of alternative policies to the ever-harsher penalties and reliance on increased incarceration being pushed by the majority (Windlesham, 1998).

The CBC had been developing its own crime bill (H.R. 3315) in response to special electoral pressures that were not being felt by other representatives. Between 1983 and 1993, the number of incarcerated drug offenders increased by 510 percent, the majority of whom were low-income African Americans (Windlesham, 1998). In 1990, one out of four African American males between the ages of twenty and twenty-nine was under some form of criminal-justice supervision. In that same time period, firearm-related injuries were found to be the leading cause of death among young black males. The CBC bill placed more emphasis on prevention, drug treatment, and gun control than those put forward by the Democratic leadership. It also sought to remedy the sentencing disparities between those convicted of using crack and powder cocaine. The CBC bill attracted twenty-four sponsors and was well received by the press. The most significant impact of the CBC effort was that it was able to sustain a much greater level of funding devoted to prevention throughout the period that the anticrime legislation was before the 103d Congress.

One of the single House bills (H.R. 3355), which provided federal funds for community policing, had the backing of both parties in Congress, and eventually became the vehicle for the comprehensive legislation that was enacted at the end of the session. The major problem with the community-policing bill lay in developing a way to pay for its significant costs, which were expected to be $9.6 billion over five years (Windlesham, 1998). The solution eventually worked out was to set up a trust fund that would be supported by the anticipated savings resulting from the administration's plan to reduce the federal workforce.

Once a method of funding was established, other parts of the omnibus crime bill began to fall into place. The politically popular Three Strikes law was included but the qualifying conditions were sufficiently restrictive that it was not expected to affect many cases. A provision strongly supported by the CBC that would allow death-penalty cases to be overturned, where race was a contributing factor, was dropped from the bill when it became clear that it would greatly reduce support among prosecutors and southern congressman. Despite this setback, some members of the CBC continued to support H.R. 3355, primarily because of the funding it was meant to provide for prevention programs.

Unlike the issues of community policing and tougher sentences, on which there was a fair amount of support within both parties, Republicans and Democrats differed considerably in their views on crime-prevention programs. Conservatives were generally suspicious of crime-prevention efforts, which they looked on as just one more branch of an ineffective and flabby system aimed at social welfare. Democrats, on the other hand, looked favorably on innovative prevention programs that were devoted to providing at-risk youth with employment, education, and recreation as alternatives to crime and violence (Windlesham, 1998).

One of the House bills dealing with prevention, H.R. 4092, would have authorized expenditures of $7 billion in federal grants to fund a variety of programs aimed at cutting crime, including summer and afterschool programs, mentoring and tutoring programs, substance-abuse treatment, and job placement. The bill would have established an "Ounce of Prevention" Council, involving several cabinet-level officers and other officials to oversee the programs. The council would have also advised communities on how such programs could be developed and integrated with other services. The program was designed to build on the positive experiences that had resulted from a program, passed by Congress in 1978, to help distressed urban areas develop improved recreation facilities. The grants would be targeted toward rehabilitating and expanding recreation facilities in urban areas with high rates of crime. Testimony by police officials, park directors, and organizers of Boys and Girls Clubs spoke to the value of recreation programs as effective crime-prevention measures. The Minnesota Democrat who sponsored the bill claimed to have the backing of more than fifty national organizations for such an effort.

Unfortunately, no matter how well intentioned, the expenditure of federal funds in only selected localities confers political advantage on those politicians who can claim credit for securing the grants. Naturally, their political opponents are opposed to such targeted efforts and find it easy to raise the often-invoked charge of "pork-barrel politics" to challenge such uses of federal funds. In opposing the targeted prevention bill, Representative Jim Bunning from Kentucky voiced his concerns as follows:

> The bill before us is still too soft and full of pork. In fact, it is so full of pork I am surprised that it did not squeal and run out of the Chamber when it was brought to the floor. Once again, Members with pet projects that could not pass on their own have larded on the pork in a bill that they are certain will pass because it carries the "crime bill" label.

Bunning urged the House to defeat the bill and come back with one that would let the people know that "we are on their side, not the criminals" (Windlesham, 1998). One of the primary organizations lobbying to defeat the bill was the NRA. In addition to its opposition to the proposed ban on assault weapons, the NRA was also opposed to the bill's prevention programs. Their lobbyist was quoted as saying: "We want prisons, not pork; police, not empty promises; crime fighters, not social workers."

The House crime-prevention proposals were accepted in the Conference Report, at an estimated cost of $7.6 billion. The overall cost of the bill had by then grown to $33.5 billion, larger than the estimated costs for either the House or Senate versions at $28 billion and $22.3, billion respectively. However, the Democrats could not muster enough votes to bring the bill to the House floor. After defeating the administration attempts to reform the nation's healthcare system, it had now become a matter of national Republican strategy to deny Clinton whatever political capital he might gain from signing a crime bill.

Intense negotiations and lobbying efforts were immediately underway. Clinton used an appearance at the National Association of Police Organizations to show the American people that law enforcement was solidly behind the bill. The president was joined on the convention podium by a number of big-city mayors from both political parties. Rather than attacking the goals of the bill directly, Republicans attacked its high cost. They demanded a 10 percent or $3.3 billion cut. The original plan brokered by the administration was an across-the-board cut of 10 percent for all of the programs in the bill. However the more hard-line Republicans succeeded in requiring that $2.5 billion of the cut be made in the prevention programs, with only $800 million coming from the prison-construction grants (Windlesham, 1998).

The 1994 Act representing a federal investment in excess of $30 billion over six years was the largest federal anticrime legislation ever passed. With the exception of the prevention measures, as Congress debated the bill there was little display of concern for the traditional American values of fairness, economic efficiency, or the social consequences of governmental action. The new law represented a series of political compromises played out against a background of partisan politics. On the issue of prevention programs, the administration won the battle, but Republicans were to win the war. The 103d Congress adjourned soon after passing the Crime Act, to be replaced by the Republican-led 104th.

The victorious Republicans returned to Washington after the midterm elections proclaiming a new "Contract with America." The Contract, which had been signed by more than three hundred Republican candidates, contained a set of reform proposals aimed at "restoring the faith and trust of the American people in their government." The goal of the Republicans, now led by Representative Newt Gingrich from Georgia, was to produce new legislation implementing the Contract within one hundred days of taking office. Of the ten proposed bills in the Contract, one was an anticrime package that would increase funding for prison construction, repeal the funding allocated for prevention, and convert the funding for one hundred thousand new police officers into unrestricted block grants that states and communities could use as they wished. When it became clear to Republican strategists that a broad frontal attack on the anticrime legislation passed by the previous Congress would produce an outbreak of trench warfare between congressional rivals, the individual elements in the Contract's anticrime package were broken down into six individual bills:

- H.R. 665 required mandatory victim restitution.
- H.R. 667 provided an additional $2.5 billion for state prison construction for those states whose violent offenders serve at least 85 percent of their sentence.
- H.R. 728 eliminated the social spending (prevention programs) in the Democrats' bill and provided block grants to states and localities to use the for "genuine law-enforcement programs," such as putting more cops on the street.
- H.R. 666 provided a "good faith exception" to the exclusionary rule.
- H.R. 729 limited the time for filing death-penalty appeals.
- H.R. 668 facilitated the deportation of criminal aliens.

All but the prison-construction and block-grant provisions were acted on swiftly by both houses and incorporated in an antiterrorism bill, which was passed in the wake of the Oklahoma City bombing and signed into law in June of 1995. The funding provisions for new prison construction and block grants had significant budgetary implications and became part of the struggle between the Clinton administration and the Republican Congress over the next twelve months (Windlesham, 1998).

Funding for the prison construction favored by Republicans and for the prevention programs favored by Democrats were tied together insofar as both had to be paid out of the Violent Crime Reduction Trust Fund, which was established by the 1994 anticrime legislation. H.R. 728, which would have eliminated all the prevention funding, was not passed by the Senate but its main thrust was incorporated in a broader attack on the administration anticrime crime legislation, S. 3, which would have converted both the prevention and community funding programs to block grants. In addition to allowing states and localities to spend their anticrime money any way they wished, this action would also have the effect of preventing Clinton from fulfilling his pledge to put one hundred thousand more police officers on the street. Clinton vetoed this package as part of the battle over the budget in December of 1995.

Throughout the battle over the block grants, funding for prevention programs continued to be pruned from the package. Republican antipathy to such spending appeared to be based on two primary factors: cynicism about the effectiveness of social interventions in reducing crime, and the fact that those interventions were directed primarily to urban areas represented by Democrats. Congressman Bob Barr of Georgia summarized one Republican line of reasoning during a hearing on H.R. 3, the original Contract with America bill, as follows.

> I will pose the following scientific evidence: that if you have a wife beater who is in prison, if you have a child abuser who is in prison, beyond any scientific doubt, that wife abuser will not be abusing his spouse, that child abuser will not be abusing a child while in jail, so I think building prisons is effective prevention. . . . I have talked within the last few days with folks in my district, and they have some very innovative programs, and they weren't funded specifically through the 1994 bill. They are using them. They are effective because they are based on the views of, for example, a U.S. Attorney, a local District Attorney, a police chief.
>
> They know they work and they are going to continue to implement those because they do work, regardless of whether there is a line item in this bill or any other bill that specifically funds them. And I think that it is in the marketplace of ideas in the local community where these decisions are best made, with regard to whether a particular program works. (Windlesham, 1998)

Republican skepticism was supported by conservative criminologists such as John DiIulio, who testified that none of the scholarly literature enabled criminologists to specify precisely the conditions under which given types of interventions prevent crime, nor could they be replicated widely (Windlesham, 1998). Furthermore, anyone familiar with the wide variety of delinquency-prevention efforts currently being funded by the Office of Juvenile Justice and Delinquency Prevention (OJJDP) was aware that few if any of those efforts had rigorous scientific evidence to back them up. A few years later, lack of credible evaluations was found to be the Achilles' heel of recent crime-prevention efforts (Sherman et al., 1997).

In support of arguments for greater prevention funding, there were a number of prevention strategies that had shown promise. These included the sort of early-childhood-education programs such as the Perry Preschool and David Olds's Nurse Home Visitation project (see chapter 4); the kind of family-focused intervention being developed by Jerry Patterson and his colleagues at the Oregon Social Learning Center and by Jim Alexander and Don Gordon at the University of Utah; and Gill Botvin's work on a school-based, drug-prevention curriculum (see chapter 4). Yet all of these prevention strategies still had a way to go before they could be considered proven.

One could make the argument that most prevention funds would not be invested in replicating and refining the most promising models, but frittered away on a variety of ill conceived and poorly managed efforts that sprang from the interests of local providers. Then again, it could also be argued that most of the mandatory sentencing laws being passed were not locking up the wife beaters and child abusers, as Congressman Barr assuredly promised. Rather, they were often released back into the community after very little time served, because the jails and prisons were full of low-level drug dealers and older offenders who were serving long mandatory terms. In other words, the superiority of longer sentences over the most promising prevention programs as a crime-reduction strategy was not as certain as Congressman Bar implied. In fact, a 1996 study showed that several proven prevention approaches were three to four times more effective than longer prison terms (Greenwood et al., 1996).

The Midnight Basketball program became a favorite target for Republican attacks on Democratic efforts to fund prevention in the federal crime bill. Republican Speaker Lamar Smith of Texas lumped Midnight Basketball together with arts and crafts when ridiculing their insertion into the anticrime bill "on the theory that the person who stole your car, robbed your house, and assaulted your family was no more than a disgruntled artist or would be NBA star." In fact, the right to participate in Washington, D.C.'s widely acclaimed Midnight Basketball leagues reflected a carefully thought out incentive to keep young men involved in arduous physical-training programs. The project also included mentoring and tutoring programs designed to increase these youths' motivation to stay in school. Only a few years earlier, President George Bush Sr. had recognized Midnight Basketball as one of his "thousand points of light."

The Appropriations Act for fiscal year 1996, which ended in September of that year, was not signed until April, four months after the president had vetoed the first version. Figure 7.1 shows the differences in funding between the original 1994 bill and the appropriations of 1996 that amended it. Between the Community Oriented Policing Services (COPS) program and the Law Enforcement Grants program, the plan to subsidize the hiring of an additional one hundred thousand police officers was left intact and fully funded, at about $13 billion. Funding for new prison construction was

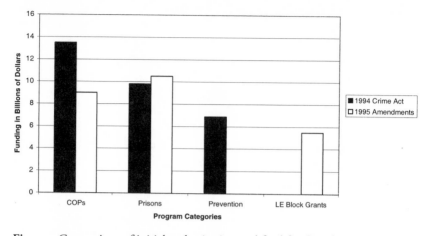

Fig. 7.1. Comparison of initial authorization and final funding for programs in the Omnibus Crime Bill of 1994

Notes: Amounts authorized and prevention appropriations from Windlesham, 1998. Appropriation for community policing from J. A. Roth & J. F. Ryan, *The COPS Program after 4 Years—National Evaluation* (Washington, D.C.: U.S. Department of Justice, 2000). Appropriation for violent offender incarceration and truth in sentencing from S. Turner, T. Fain, P. W. Greenwood, E. Chin & J. R. Chiesa, *National Evaluation of the Violent Offender Incarceration/Truth-in-Sentencing Incentive Grant Program* (Santa Monica: RAND, 2001). Appropriation for delinquency prevention and block grants from Windlesham, 1998.

actually increased with the amendments of 1996. Gone almost completely were most of the individual prevention programs, replaced by additional block grants to local law-enforcement agencies.

So there we have it. The most important piece of anticrime legislation to be passed by Congress did nothing to advance the cause of prevention. Rather, at a time when crime rates were actually declining, states and local governments were encouraged to build additional prison facilities, which they would need to cut back on in just a few years, and to hire additional police officers, whom that they would soon need to lay off. In the end, the only real contribution of the 1994 anticrime legislation to prevention was to demonstrate its liabilities as a political cause. Several years later, after the peak of the Republican tide had ebbed, Congress demonstrated a somewhat more thoughtful approach to the issue when it mandated that the Department of Justice's National Institute of Justice conduct a rigorous review of what worked in crime prevention (Sherman et al., 1997). OJJDP, which up until that time had a fairly poor record as a supporter of evidence-based prevention efforts, redeemed itself somewhat when it became a supporter of the Blueprints project at the University of Colorado, described in chapter 3. But these were both administrative efforts well removed from the give and take of representative politics. When it came to obtaining a place at the federal funding trough, crime prevention had flunked its most important political test to date.

Two Political Liabilities of Prevention

The battle over the 1994 crime bill illustrates two of the primary liabilities of delinquency prevention in its competition for resources with police and prisons: lack of a punitive dimension and delayed impacts. As for the first of these, not only do most prevention programs not feature any punitive components, but in addition to their educational and skill-building elements they often include rewards and other benefits as incentives for positive behavior. This bias toward rewards and avoidance of punishment is not merely a reflection of liberal softhearted bias. A long line of research has clearly demonstrated that positive reinforcement is much more effective than punishment in shaping behavior. Punitive interventions have been found to have the least impact on recidivism of any intervention method (Lipsey & Wilson, 1998).

The American public by and large appears to want its troublesome youth to be punished for their misbehavior. The old adage "Spare the rod and spoil the child" is apparently alive and well. This penchant for punishment is why Scared Straight and boot-camp programs described in chapter 5 are still popular, in spite of their demonstrated ineffectiveness. Thus, the absence of a punitive component may be one of the many reasons that prevention programs often take a back seat to law-enforcement and prison-construction efforts, crime-control measures that in part are characterized by their punitive nature. On the other hand, the addition of a punitive or at least retributive component to a prevention program can improve its public image. In 1998, on the basis of cost-effectiveness arguments, officials in Deschutes County, Oregon adopted a policy of decreasing the length of their residential placements for juvenile offenders and investing the savings in early prevention and intensive aftercare. This is the sort of policy shift to which "tough on crime" advocates might be expected to object. However, Deschutes County blunted these objections by incorporating in the program strict restitution and community-service requirements, and undertaking a public-service ad campaign to let the public know of their presence. As a result, the program appeared to be very favorably received by members of the public, despite some objections by victims groups (Greenwood et al., 2003).

The other liability of delinquency-prevention programs is the delay in their impacts. Particularly in the wake of a highly publicized criminal act, citizens out of fear or outrage want immediate action and assurances that the problem has been taken care of. Increased police patrols or enhanced enforcement of particular ordinances can have such an immediate effect. So can a quick arrest, trial, and sentencing of the offender. The benefits of delinquency-prevention efforts, on the other hand, usually take longer to be realized. The clientele of such programs do not ordinarily pose an immediate risk to the community. Moreover, the crimes that are prevented one or two years after a youth's participation in a program are crimes that the public is never aware of. For these reasons, the positive impacts of effective delinquency-prevention programs can be characterized as both slow in materializing and invisible as well.

Of course, the impact of the extra law-enforcement effort dissipates as soon as the extra efforts are withdrawn. The prison inmate after release often reenters society as a greater threat to the public than when he went in. But in a world in which only the immediate impacts are counted, police and prisons represent security while prevention is a somewhat suspect activity pursued for nebulous goals.

Two Issues of Implementation

Having briefly canvassed the political liabilities of programs directed toward juvenile-delinquency prevention, I now turn to some awkward problems concerning how and where in government crime prevention could and should be lodged. This chapter on the political science of prevention is meant to be both specific and complex—specific insofar as it goes beyond the usual political science of policing and building prisons, and complex in that it must deal with a multitude of agencies and contexts and its results are more difficult to monitor than other types of crime-control programs. This section considers two persistent problems posed by prevention programs designed for at-risk youth; the section following this one takes up the question regarding which branches of government are best suited for administering delinquency-prevention efforts.

The Paradox of Perverse Rewards

Any program that produces concrete benefits for youthful offenders must face the problem of appearing to reward the undeserving. Effective delinquency-prevention programs may benefit participating youth and other members of their family, as well as potential crime victims, by increasing their educational and vocational skills, income, or quality of life. These often-unmeasured benefits may create, at least in the minds of some, perverse incentives or rewards for youth who are the most delinquent. When these programs achieve their goals, the largest rewards are reaped by the youth that are most at risk. This perverse incentive feature, in which prevention programs appear to bestow the greatest benefits on those who are not only the most at risk but also the most troublesome, may be another factor that makes prevention such a hard sell to some audiences.

The first response to this concern is that high-risk individuals have long been the recipients of disproportionate government programs and services. Special education, social services, and mental health are all areas where this has taken place. It can be argued that juveniles are more deserving beneficiaries of prevention services than adults because the factors that place them at risk are less under their control. It would be foolish for taxpayers to forgo the clearly demonstrated benefits of effective delinquency-prevention programs just because the targeted youth and their families might benefit as well.

The Problem of Deviant Labeling

Criminologists have long argued that official interventions could have negative impacts on youth behavior by helping develop delinquent careers through a process called "deviant labeling" (Becker, 1963; Lemert, 1967; Bernburg & Krohn, 2003). It is argued that deviant labeling might increase delinquency by altering the individual's self-concept, or by hindering his or her access to the kind of structured opportunities and conventional peers associated with positive social development.

The theory languished for a while when early attempts to test its validity failed to find supporting evidence (Hirschi, 1980; Title, 1980). Most of these early studies suffered from a number of methodological limitations, including (1) being limited only to individuals who had been subject to arrest, (2) using cross-sectional data with very limited follow-up periods, and (3) lacking data on intervening processes that might help explain the causal relationship with delinquency (Paternoster & Iovanni, 1989).

More recent efforts at testing the theory have solidified claims of its validity (Bernburg & Krohn, 2003). Sampson and Laub (1993) have described how official intervention during adolescence may negatively affect future life chances and therefore increase the likelihood of later involvement in delinquency and deviance. A key component of these findings is that the deviant labeling of a disadvantaged youth during a critical life stage may lead to further marginalization from conventional structured activities, particularly education and employment. From this perspective, disadvantage has a cumulative or snowballing effect. The deviant labeling associated with official intervention simply adds to the accumulated disadvantage already caused by the offender's circumstances, behavior, and other social or family factors. Seen in this light, nondisadvantaged youth are less affected by deviant labeling because they have more resources to resist or counter its impacts.

More specifically, it is argued that official intervention may negatively affect educational attainment by triggering various forms of stigma or exclusion from school. Research has demonstrated that youth identified as having a "delinquent character" by school officials are subject to harsher disciplinary procedures such as suspension, transfer to another school, or expulsion (Bodwitch, 1993).

Bernburg and Krohn (2003) used longitudinal panel data from the Rochester Youth Development Study to show that both police arrest and involvement in the juvenile-justice system interfered with normal social development. Not only did these contacts reduce the likelihood of graduation from school, but they narrowed the prospects for later employment while increasing the probability of criminal activity in young adulthood, particularly for the more disadvantaged youth and African Americans.

Increasingly, research findings show that police and juvenile-justice interventions in the lives of delinquent youth produce negative impacts on educational attainment, crime, and employment. The better response, however, is not to expand the boundaries of our current delinquency-prevention efforts by asking the police or juvenile-justice system to cast a wider net across those children identified as being at risk. Rather, we should hold to the position, long advocated by some, that wherever possible troubled youth should be treated in natural settings, and not by police or probation officers, but by trained professionals familiar with the healthy development and social welfare of youth.

This finding in regard to deviant labeling may help explain Lipsey and Wilson's (1998) meta-analysis findings that, all other things being equal, programs that take place in the community are more effective than similar programs in institutions, and programs delivered by mental health professionals are more effective than those delivered by justice professionals. Mentoring and skill-building efforts may help kids stay on the straight and narrow, but they do a better job if they are not labeled as delinquency-prevention efforts and not run by staff affiliated with the justice system.

To the extent that negative labels impede the effectiveness of programs, naming or describing the subjects of prevention programs using such negative labels as "offenders," "delinquents," or "school failures" may be self-defeating. Thus, eliminating these negative categories from those factors that are considered when assessing program eligibility may simultaneously eliminate the perceived injustice of rewarding bad behavior and improve the chances for the program's having a positive impact on treated youth.

Branches of Government

We now come to the problem concerning where in government to vest the primary responsibility for developing, implementing, and operating delinquency-prevention programs. The three primary contenders in this particular version of musical chairs are the Departments of Justice, of Health and Human Services (HHS), and of Education. Justice is a contender because it has been in the prevention business for a long time, and crime and criminals are its primary business. But there are problems with choosing that department—it brings several liabilities to the table, including the negative effects of deviant label, a generally authoritarian approach, and a penchant for punishment as the primary means of correcting behavior. Just look at how the police handle their own internal affairs.

HHS is in the running for primary provider of prevention programs because the kinds of programs that are effective for delinquency prevention also produce other beneficial outcomes in HHS's domain as well. Furthermore, many of the basic methods used in prevention approaches have also been developed and utilized in HHS contexts. Also in its favor is that HHS staff appear to outperform similar programs using Justice staff, and HHS has a much better record of monitoring outcomes.

Finally, the Department of Education is in the running because the majority of at-risk youth are enrolled in school, which provides an efficient method for delivering delinquency-prevention programs and services, particularly those that are designed to reach all children of specified age.

Of course not all delinquency-prevention programs have to be operated by a single agency. Programs that deal with the families of very young children might be best placed within HHS, while programs that deal with older, more serious delinquents might belong in Justice. This section looks more closely at those programs that could be placed in one of several domains of government – like the ones that deal with older delinquents with serious mental health issues, or the ones that deal with young children whose parents are under the supervision of the criminal-justice system.

There turn out to be many programs that share this ambiguity. What is necessary as a first step is to identify those characteristics among the various departments of executive-branch government that are of most importance in deciding where to vest responsibility for assorted program types.

Organizational Missions, Capabilities, and Constituents

An agency's "mission" is its primary purpose, its chief reason for existence. Its "capabilities" are the means at its disposal for carrying out its mission. The "constituents" of the agency are those groups or individuals who are its clients or its primary supporters—the people who give it clout. Law-enforcement and correctional agencies generally identify "public safety" as their primary mission. For instance, the goal of the Los Angeles Police Department is to "protect and serve." The criminal-justice version of public safety means safe from criminal harm. The primary means by which the police protect the public are by deterring crime by their presence, and by contributing to the deterrent and incapacitation effects of the criminal-justice system by identifying, apprehending, and punishing offenders. The more progressive law-enforcement agencies also attempt to prevent crime by educating and working with the public to reduce their risk of victimization.

The focus of the criminal-justice system's mission is on certain high-risk locations, situations, and individuals. When threats to public safety are plentiful, as they are in many metropolitan areas, the attention of the criminal-justice system is more strictly directed at the most immediate and most severe threats at that moment—serious crimes that may take place over the next few days or weeks. Because of the immediacy of their concerns, the focus is on the people and situations that pose the threats, rather than the individuals who are threatened, unless they have some special knowledge about an offender targeting a particular person.

The mission of health and human service agencies is to promote and support the health and well-being of all citizens. As such, they take a more expansive view of their clients' welfare—health and well-being are on-going concerns. There are many different threats to the health and well-being of the population that are posed by particular circumstances that carry unique dangers. Of course, in disadvantaged neighborhoods, the demands on the public-health and social-service systems far exceed their capacity to respond, so that emergency response to acute conditions consumes most of the available resources, and preventive care for families and youth are disproportionately underfunded.

The primary mission shared by school systems generally is to prepare their students to be responsible and productive adults. The principal way schools pursue this goal is through a formalized process of ability testing and grouping, and classroom instruction that follows a standardized curriculum. In many school systems, particularly those in disadvantaged neighborhoods with overcrowded and underfunded classrooms, new students enter with so many previous educational and social deficits that the primary purpose of the system becomes to maximize the number of students who can meet some specified minimum academic standards. In such systems, special attention to the nonacademic needs of at-risk youth is left to the initiative and voluntary efforts of overburdened staff.

In summary, the primary focus of the criminal-justice system is on controlling threats to public safety. Immediate threats take priority over those that are more remote, and the primary indicator of threat used by the system is past behavior. Therefore, those individuals with the most serious criminal record usually get the most attention—usually in the form of control. The primary goals of the agencies concerned with public health, social service, and education are to educate, train, and assist individuals in learning how to deal with their special needs and attendant risks while pursuing their own welfare and well-being. However, because of chronic underfunding, emergency and strictly mandated services consume the bulk of the available resources, leaving very little for preventive programs.

The primary capabilities and tool of those professionals concerned with criminal justice (CJ) are risk assessment, monitoring, and control. More effective risk assessment is measured by better identifying where crimes are likely to occur and/or who will commit them; this can lead to a more effective deployment of resources and countermeasures. Effective monitoring means reducing time lags between increases in risks and their detection. Effective control means bringing risk levels down to acceptable levels as swiftly as possible. The combination of a short-term perspective, an emphasis on control, and the element of personal danger generally lead to an authoritarian approach in the way most public-safety functions are carried out. The troublesome individuals with which the system must deal are viewed as potentially dangerous and at least partially culpable for their actions.

The primary capabilities of health and human service (HHS) agencies lie in assessing and prioritizing individual risks and needs, developing service plans for ameliorating high-priority risks and needs, and ensuring that those plans are carried out to the extent permitted by available resources. The principal differences between CJ and HHS programs are the following:

- CJ programs are focused almost exclusively on immediate risks associated with criminal behavior, while the programs of HHS agencies are concerned with a wider variety of longer-term risks to health and welfare.
- The preventive efforts of CJ programs are largely focused on short-term efforts addressing identifiable situations, locations, and individuals, while HHS preventive efforts are based on theories of health and social development involving much longer time frames.
- Law enforcement and other criminal justice agencies typically seek cooperation or change in behavior through persuasion, the direct use of authority, or physical force, while health and social service programs are more likely to rely on voluntary engagement and use education and training as the primary means to alter behavior.
- Criminal justice agencies rarely evaluate the effectiveness of their programs or activities, whereas HHS programs are more often evidence-based and subject to evaluation. In chapter 4 we saw that the most effective model delinquency-prevention programs were developed through HHS channels rather than within criminal justice.

Given these fundamental differences between CJ and HHS programs, we might expect substantial differences in the way each responds when charged with enhancing delinquency prevention. In all likelihood, CJ agencies would respond by widening the scope of their intake criteria to cover those juveniles who had been diverted from or ignored by the system. First-time offenders diverted from the CJ system by being placed on informal probation would be the likely targets. Their engagement would probably involve coercive or mandatory components and would likely include the use of graduated sanctions, all techniques that have consistently failed to work with more serious populations.

New CJ programs in response to the above mandate would probably not be based on the most current developmental theories and probably not be subjected to rigorous impact evaluations. DARE, afterschool activities run by the police, and Scared Straight are all examples of such efforts from the recent past. In fact, over the past decade, criminal-justice agencies were provided with ample opportunities and funding to develop prevention programs through the federal Office of Justice Programs and the COPS program established by the 1994 Crime bill. Very few of the programs attempted have been identified as promising, and not one is considered proven. The Boston Gun Project and Project EXILE are two of the better-known models to be developed with Justice Department discretionary funding. Neither one has been effectively replicated or demonstrated to have a convincing impact (Raphael & Ludwig, 2003; Kennedy et al., 2001). Both of these programs rely primarily on deterrence, which they seek to enhance using tougher prosecution and sentencing, and educating high-risk populations about their likely sentences if they are caught. The latest incarnation of this approach, Project Safe Neighborhoods, was heavily promoted by former attorney general John Ashcroft over the past five years and was granted more than $1 billion in funding from the Office of Justice Programs (www.psn.gov). The key elements of the program are partnerships among federal, state, and local law enforcement and prosecutors that are meant to help identify high-risk individuals and ensure that they receive the maximum sentence possible. But recall from chapter 4 that there is abundant evidence that deterrence-based approaches to delinquency prevention do not work.

In all likelihood, faced with the same mandate to enhance prevention of juvenile delinquency, HHS agencies would develop and test programs that focused more broadly on populations comprising those at lower risk. In the terminology of the public-health profession, HHS programs would most likely represent primary and secondary prevention efforts, whereas CJ programs would involve secondary and tertiary prevention. The HHS predilection for relying on voluntary participation would probably result in the nonparticipation of many high-risk individuals. Examples of the HHS approach to delinquency and violence prevention are provided by the many community-action and public-advocacy projects funded by the California Wellness Foundation as part of its youth-oriented Violence Prevention Initiative. These programs share two basic strategies: delivery of services such as afterschool programs to at-risk youth, and advocacy of policy changes at the local and state level. None of the programs pursued strategies for identifying and targeting very high-risk youth (Greenwood et al., 2001).

In addition to differences between their missions and capabilities, CJ and HHS agencies differ significantly in terms of their constituency. The primary constituents of CJ agencies are those organizations and members of the public who share a heightened concern for public safety. Victims groups, homeowner and business associations, and political leaders who are held accountable for public safety make up the primary core. There is a very small group of individuals and organizations concerned with the rights and welfare of offenders being processed by the criminal-justice system, but they are considered more as adversaries to the system rather than its constituents.

The primary constituents of HHS agencies are their clients—those whom the agencies are seeking to serve—and the families of those clients. Closely aligned with this group are those agencies and organizations that turn to HHS agencies for assistance in dealing with their own clientele. This group includes many organizations that are also part of the HHS service-delivery system such as schools, healthcare providers, family therapists, and drug-treatment providers.

The CJ system is organized vertically, with each level being administered by just one agency, which handles all the various cases that reach that particular level. In contrast, the HHS system is organized horizontally, so that each agency or service provider is responsible for treating a particular problem or type of case. This difference in organization allows HHS organizations to work collaboratively, coordinating one agency's services with those of another. CJ agencies, on the other hand, are much more used to having total responsibility for a case until they pass it off to the next responsible agency up the line. Coordination and collaboration as in the Boston Gun Project are still novelties in CJ while they are fairly routine in HHS.

Principles for Assigning Responsibility for Prevention

With this broad sketch of the CJ and HHS systems in mind, I now want to turn to the issue of how various responsibilities for developing and operating delinquency-prevention programs should be assigned to ensure their most likely success. It must be stressed at the outset that both CJ and HHS systems are needed. Neither the police nor probation officers will be very effective in working with infants or high-risk mothers to improve their health and child-rearing skills. HHS agencies, on the other hand, will not be very successful working with juvenile offenders who resist every attempt by adults to intervene in their lives.

A second point is that the allocation of prevention responsibilities between CJ and HHS should be based to some degree on the risk level of the individuals involved. Youth at high risk of delinquent activity generally should be handled within the CJ system for reasons of accountability and public safety. This is not to say that some of the services they receive, like individual and family counseling, cannot be provided by agencies that are part of HHS.

Young children who do not yet pose a significant danger to the community should be handled by HHS. This does not mean that CJ agencies will not play a role in identifying such youth, and urging or even ordering their parents to cooperate with the intervention. However, HHS should ultimately be responsible for the service delivery. Effective intervention programs for young children at risk are likely to have multiple benefits that cut across government service sectors. Assigning final responsibility for young children to HSS ensures that these multiple benefits are more likely to be considered in budget deliberations.

Let's move to the middle range and consider the ten- or eleven-year-old child who is becoming a problem at school because of his or her negative conduct in the classroom and aggressiveness toward peers. At this level of behavior, we might hope that the school would take the initiative in identifying and dealing with the problem, which may require some special programming and the involvement of parents. Any other approach would not be cost effective and potentially disruptive to the student's progress.

Now suppose that our eleven year old is caught doing damage to the school, carrying a weapon, or assaulting another youth—all activities that in many jurisdictions might be reported to the police. Is this the stage at which the responsibility for prevention programming should be turned over to probation or law-enforcement officials? At this point, there does not appear to be much that the CJ system can do, other than complete a report and refer the child to some type of service provider. The school, if it were to come up with a satisfactory response on its own, could handle the issue internally. If someone is needed to work with the parents or child outside of the school, then some other HHS agency may need to take the lead.

The point here is that, at this juncture, some assessment is called for and some intervention may be indicated. But unless there is some overriding public-safety concern, the assessment and intervention should both be performed in the most effective manner possible, with the least possible stigma to the youth. This is where deviant labeling and deviant peer contagion can have serious negative effects (Lipsey, in press). It is also where the engagement of the parents may be critical. The only statement less plausible than the old punch line "I'm from the government and I'm here to help" is probably "I'm from the attorney general's office (or the LAPD) and I'm here to help your kid."

Let's bump it up one more notch to consider a fourteen year old who is about to be suspended from school for assaulting another youth in the classroom. A police report has been filed and there have been several previous complaints filed as well. The youth has already participated in programs designed to improve his behavior, but without noticeable results. His parents report that he is just as much trouble at home.

This is a case that could easily end up with a petition in juvenile court. The adolescent will likely be seen by the constituents of the CJ system as a threat to public safety who must be dealt with. The question is where best should the court be able to turn to for service. The case at hand looks like one that might be appropriate for either Functional Family Therapy (FFT) or Multisystemic Therapy (MST), two forms of family therapy I described in chapter 4 that send trained clinicians into the home. MST is the more costly of the two but provides a more comprehensive range of services, including availability around the clock. These programs could be run within a probation department but are usually operated by an outside service provider.

Based on the agency characteristics reviewed above, it appears that the most-effective intervention with minimum stigma to the youth would be if the MST or FFT services were provided by a private provider, preferably under the monitoring of HHS. The provision of services is usually not part of the primary mission of probation nor is it one of its core competencies, where for the provider it is. Therefore, there is a greater chance that the services provided will be effective. Furthermore, the service provider will be more accustomed to dealing with youth and families as clients, creating a better chance of voluntary engagement and participation by all family members.

Not until the point is reached that a youth must be removed from his home, because of either the seriousness of their behavior or ineffectiveness of their parents, is it clear that he or she needs to be in a program operated by the CJ system. Even here, Multidimensional Treatment Foster Care (MTFC), described in chapter 4, offers a family-based alternative to traditional group homes that is significantly more effective in reducing recidivism. MTFC programs are usually run by private providers under the supervision of probation and/or DSS officials.

It should be clear that the primary responsibility for developing and operating an appropriate portfolio of prevention programs for at-risk youth should be assigned to HHS, not to the CJ system. Moreover, the responsibilities for prevention and punishment should not be shared, lest the proper boundaries separating preventive and punitive measures become blurred. The juvenile-justice system may in fact become a primary client of HHS programs, along with the schools and family counselors. As a client, it may be required to pay for the services received by those it refers, and it certainly should be involved in monitoring the quality of the services HHS provides.

Based on the foregoing considerations in this section, the basic principle for assigning responsibility for delinquency-prevention programs can be summarily articulated as follows: *Primary responsibility for developing and operating delinquency-prevention programs should be assigned to an appropriate agency in HHS unless immediate public protection is an overriding concern.* This principal applies to programs designed for youth already involved in the juvenile-justice system as well as for those not yet involved. It is critically important for programs involving the youth's family or other members of the community.

This principle is based on the observations that (1) the mission, capabilities, and constituencies of HHS agencies are more closely aligned with those appropriate for support and operation of delinquency-prevention programs; (2) such services will achieve more voluntary participation when offered by HHS rather than CJ agencies; and (3) assignment to HHS will minimize the likelihood of harmful labeling of the youth involved. The problems of deviant labeling are at their apex when a CJ agency is in charge.

Adhering to this fundamental principle is not always easy. While HHS programs have a better and more natural fit within branches of government that have broad mandates for helping delinquent and troubled youth, the political mandates for these branches often do not include crime prevention or public safety. Under such circumstances, the HSS part of government may be tempted to pursue its more traditional goals while leaving delinquency prevention to others. The response of the public-health community to the recent epidemic of gun violence among youth is instructive: although public-health experts played a key role in educating the public about the nature of the gun-violence problem, as well as challenging some of the traditional approaches to resolving it, they did not bring many resources or any proven programs to the table. Nor did they have much of an immediate effect on public policy. Of course, experts in criminal-justice policy did not have much impact either. Violence prevention, like drug-use prevention, remains a highly politicized topic in which open discussions of the positives and negatives of the various approaches are rare. The full impact of the Surgeon General's Report regarding prevention of youth violence remains to be seen (U.S. Department of Health and Human Services, 2001; see especially chapter 4). It could become the basis for a number of evidence-based reforms in how delinquency-prevention funds are allocated.

The atrocious state of foster care in many large U.S. cities offers another example of where delinquency prevention might be headed even if it is adequately funded. Foster care is run by HHS, with responsibility for funding and operations often divided between state and local government.

In some jurisdictions, however, there is no one person accountable for the administration of the program, with disastrous results. A significant fraction of kids that are taken into foster care languish there for a number of years without ever experiencing a stable home life. A startling number of youth are abused by their foster parents, and many emancipate directly into homelessness. Could we fail them any worse? Will at-risk youth be more fortunate in how the system works for them?

The sad history of foster-care administration in state and local government is not an argument for relieving HHS of its responsibility in this area but rather a lesson in the logic of political organization for youth services. Identifying the most appropriate area of government to administer prevention programs is no guarantee of those programs' quality, but it is nonetheless a necessary condition for effective programs.

Levels of Government

Historically, both law enforcement and youth welfare were local responsibilities. Education was a local matter as well. Since the 1960s, however, there has been a movement to position leadership and standards pertaining to law enforcement and education at the state and federal levels of government, but not always the responsibility for administering them. The Civil Rights Act, the War on Poverty, the Law Enforcement Assistance Administration that grew out of President Johnson's Crime Commission, the creation of a cabinet-level Office of Education, the anticrime legislation of 1994—all are examples of this movement.

The following developments have also created movement in this direction:

- For any number of reasons including incompetence, dwindling resources, or a dramatic increase in the number of more challenged and challenging clients, many large urban systems fail large numbers of youth.
- Public satisfaction and commercial interest in the areas affected goes down when crime rates go up.
- Outside experts debate about how best to rescue the system.
- It becomes a state political issue because the major metropolitan areas in the state, including often the capital, are affected.
- Local elected officials seek state financial help, making the problem even a bigger political issue.
- Many crime control issues become polarized into a zero-sum game in which every proposed reform is seen as a vote cast in favor of either

victims or criminals (Zimring et al., 2001). Recall how the voting went on the 1994 crime bill and the appropriations legislation that followed.

- The natural outcome of the federal political interest in these issues is a gradual increase in federal expertise. Ambitious staff members become acquainted with the research that has been done in the field. The discrepancies they discover between research findings and most local practice lead to calls for various types of federal action such as demonstration programs, technical assistance, and the education of policymakers.
- It is often the case that the science gets passed through a political filter before it is repackaged for public consumption.

Notwithstanding the inevitability of this movement toward state and federal jurisdictions, the evidence has shown that it is more effective to pursue operational policies and responsibilities on as local a level as possible. Charter schools, community policing, community justice, and community corrections are all examples of such efforts. Money and minimal standards can flow down from above, but any effort to serve troubled youth on a retail basis should be an organized part of the community in which those youth live. Decisionmakers at any other level cannot appreciate the many nuances that define local conditions, nor can they effectively calculate the potential benefits and costs delinquency-prevention programs might have.

Will we eventually get it right? Evidence from evaluations of therapeutic interventions for youth in the State of Washington suggests that only about half of the therapists trained to deliver proven programs did so in a competent manner. Outcomes were directly related to therapist competence. Those deemed incompetent sometimes even heightened the likelihood youths' future criminal behavior (Barnowski, 2002). The success of the evidence-based movement in delinquency prevention depends on service providers being able to identify and retrain or remove the incompetent staff.

The Future of Delinquency Prevention

Some communities remain unaware of the possibilities for increasing the effectiveness of their delinquency-prevention efforts, and reducing future expenses to taxpayers as well. Others may be aware of the possibilities but do not know how to capitalize on them. What is needed is a wake-up call of the sort Steve Aos et al. (2001) have provided in Washington State.

Eventually communities will wake up on their own, as the movement to evidence-based practice grows stronger. This doesn't ensure, however, that they will get it right. There is a long tradition in this field, particularly in the public sector, of freely manipulating successful models to fit local requirements and capabilities. The evidence now shows that failure to implement proven programs with a high degree of fidelity to the original model leads to significantly reduced outcomes. Delays in adopting proven programs will only cause additional victimization of citizens and unnecessarily compromise the future of additional youth. Inappropriate implementation will have the same effect.

We can hope that there will be much more research and experimentation on the role that families can play in preventing delinquency and other problem behaviors on the part of adolescents. Among all the proven programs, by far the most cost effective are the ones that work with families. Although school systems offer an alternative channel for delinquency-prevention efforts, they struggle to give such efforts the sustained attention they require. The temptation is great for schools to solve behavioral problems by expelling the troublemakers. Most parents do not find it quite so easy to escape the consequences of their child's negative behaviors.

We can hope that all programs will increase their use of standardized risk-assessment instruments, as they have in the State of Washington (Barnoski, 2004). Use of such instruments can improve the ability of practitioners to assess the effect of changes in their programs, independent of changes in the characteristics of their clientele. Likewise, the wider use of statistical-assessment techniques can help authorities do a better job in assigning youth to programs that meet their needs.

We can hope that those responsible for purchasing or approving programs and services for at-risk youth will require more evidence-based programming from their service providers or in-house programs.

We can hope that those responsible for allocating delinquency-prevention resources will use cost effectiveness as the primary criterion in determining at what level each program should be funded. Given the very high cost that citizens appear to associate with any victimization in their community, it would be foolish to put money into a crime-prevention effort that did not maximize the size of the crime-prevention effect.

Chapter 8

Programming in the Modern Juvenile Court

This final chapter addresses the current role of programming in the U.S. juvenile-court system. As the juvenile court enters its second century, philosophies of juvenile justice have changed markedly from those that were proclaimed with the optimistic rhetoric of intervention in the early years of the court. The modern court recognizes there are serious costs to intervening in the lives of young offenders and restricts its offices to cases of demonstrated seriousness. The modern juvenile court is also only one among many agencies that have evolved to serve youth and is not necessarily the agency of first resort for all children at risk. But the juvenile court of 2005 is still a powerful institution with a clear mandate to adjudicate and dispose of serious offenders in early and middle adolescence.

Earlier chapters have argued that health, education, and human-service agencies are better suited to deliver most prevention services than a court system confined to the already misbehaving and burdened with the stigma associated with delinquency and its control. Nevertheless, I argue in this chapter that extensive programming should be an important component in our society's responses to most serious delinquents—that is to say, that programming still has a central role to play within the juvenile-court system. The attempt to provide programmatic support to the juvenile courts' high-risk offenders is a critical part of the government's approach to providing services for the young.

Mission and Morale in Modern Juvenile Justice

The political complaints about juvenile courts have been loud and effective since the early 1990s. The typical complaint is that the juvenile court is soft on young criminals. In the hyperbole of the *Wall Street Journal*, "the current system is essentially a license to kill. No matter how awful the crime, violent youngsters rarely get more than a suspension or a year or two in jail." (*Wall Street Journal*, 1998). Throughout the 1990s, this assertion of the undue leniency of juvenile courts primarily was based on a comparison between what juvenile courts did with their charges and the increasingly harsh sanctions of the criminal courts, which reflected major policy changes over the last three decades of the twentieth century.

Figure 8.1 shows trends in incarceration for juveniles (under eighteen) and young adults over the period 1971–95. It also illustrates a plausible explanation for legislative efforts to put more punitive bite in the policies of American juvenile courts during the 1990s. The first trend is the huge increase in rates of imprisonment in criminal courts for young adults after 1975. Incarceration rates more than doubled in twenty years and in twenty-five years they almost tripled. The second trend is relative stability in juvenile-court incarceration policy. Over twenty-five years, the gross incarceration rate increased by 40 percent, with half of that increase coming in the five years after 1991. That would be a significant increase when compared to most institutional trends, but it is less than a quarter of the growth rate in incarceration for young adults. So there has been a large and growing gap between criminal-court and juvenile-court punishment trends, which explains some of the hostility toward juvenile courts in the early 1990s. Given the wide gap in policy between juvenile and criminal courts, the minimal political damage to juvenile justice is quite remarkable.

There has certainly been some "mission creep" in juvenile courts owing to such innovations as sentencing guidelines and mandatory sentences (Feld, 1988). But the major story in juvenile justice is continuity rather than change, and consistency in mission and programmatic preferences. And business has been brisk. All fifty U.S. states have retained the juvenile court as the primary agency for adjudicating adolescent crime, and only one state lowered its maximum jurisdictional age (Wisconsin, from eighteenth to seventeenth birthday). Figure 8.2 provides some data on both the volume of juvenile arrests and the mix of offenses for which juveniles are arrested. The figure uses age eighteen as the cutoff point because that is the age threshold in two-thirds of the states; a minority of states use criminal courts to adjudicate seventeen year olds and in a few cases sixteen-year-old defendants.

The volume of youth arrests has been relatively stable while the volume of arrests for "index" offenses has declined since the mid-1990s. Figure 8.3 shows the approximate volume of juvenile justice cases in 1999 at every

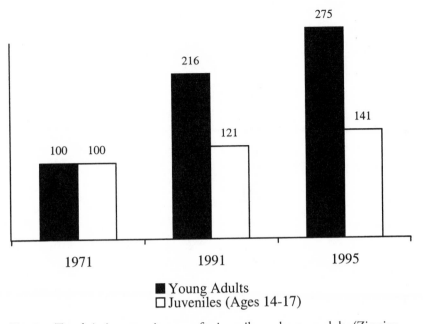

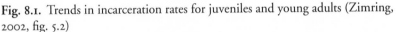

Fig. 8.1. Trends in incarceration rates for juveniles and young adults (Zimring, 2002, fig. 5.2)

Notes: Data on trends in incarceration for juveniles (ages 14–17; 100=393 per 100,000) and young adults (age 18–24; 100=508 per 100,000) from U.S. Department of Justice, Bureau of Justice Statistics, in the following: *Correctional Populations in the United States* 21 (1995), *Bulletin,* Aug. 1996; *Special Report,* April 1998 and Feb. 2000; fax from Allen J. Beck to Frank Zimring, Oct. 26, 2000; from U.S. Department of Justice, Criminal Justice Resource Center, *Sourcebook of Criminal Justice Statistics* (1973, 353; 1976, 644–45; 1997, 607; 1999, 484, 503); from D. K. Gilliard & A. J. Beck, *Prison and Jail Inmates* (Washington, D.C.: U.S. Department of Justice, 1995); C. W. Harlow, *Profile of Jail Inmates* (Washington, D.C.: U.S. Department of Justice, 1996); K. J. Strom, *Profile of State Prisoners under Age Eighteen* (Washington, D.C.: U.S. Department of Justice, 1985–97); from U.S. Department of Commerce, Bureau of the Census, fax to author, Oct. 24, 2000. See also J. Moone, *Children in Custody 1991: Private Facilities,* in 2 and 5 *Office of Juvenile Justice and Delinquency Prevention Fact Sheet,* Apr. and Sept. 1993; and J. Moone, *States at a Glance: Juveniles in Public Facilities, 1995,* in 69 *Office of Juvenile Justice and Delinquency Prevention Fact Sheet,* Nov. 1997.

critical stage of relevance to the design of programs. Again, as in figure 8.2, there is a separate counting of index and non-index offense cases.

While the overall number of youth processed at each step of the American juvenile justice may seem rather large, the most striking characteristic of the system is the steep drop from point to point along the way. The front door of the juvenile court receives about 1.5 million referrals each year, mainly from the police. But petitions beginning the formal adjudicatory process

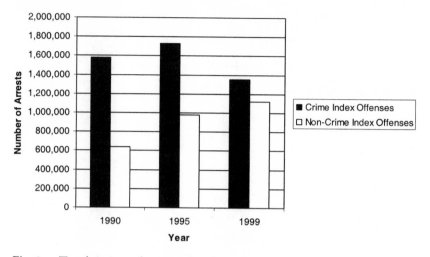

Fig. 8.2. Trends in juvenile arrests (Snyder, 2000)

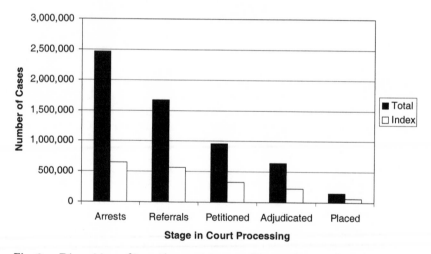

Fig. 8.3. Disposition of juvenile arrests in 1999 (Puzzanchera et al., 2003)

are filed in just over half of these cases. This rejection of hundreds of thousands of cases at what is called "intake screening" is based on a judgment that many cases do not require forceful interventions, that normal processes of maturity in community settings may be a preferable outcome. There is also, even amid the stricter climate characterizing juvenile courts of recent years, no strong preference for formal over informal methods of disposing of cases.

Each of the major stages of decisionmaking in the juvenile court can be a basis for formal or informal linkage to treatment programs in community settings. Often juveniles are screened away from petitions because of explicit or implicit agreements to enter drug-, alcohol-, or psychological-counseling programs. Even after petitions are filed, charges are often suspended or dropped when the juvenile offers to enter treatment. And if a youth is adjudicated delinquent, treatment programs are frequently an element of the probationary supervision that is the disposition for a majority of formally processed youth.

The 10 percent or so of juveniles referred to court by arrest and subsequently placed in secure postadjudication institutions cannot be involved in community-based programs while in secure confinement. For these youth, the choice is between programs that operate within the institution or no programming until the confinement period ends. The traditional preference in youth corrections is to tailor treatment programs to institutional environments, even if the setting compromised the efficacy of many treatment programs.

The danger of institution-based treatment is that the combination of poor quality, low visibility, and a coercive environment may cause a given program to be more harmful than nonintervention. Remember from chapter 4 that even proven programs delivered by incompetent therapists can be harmful, increasing recidivism. Incompetent staff are much more likely to be found in institutional programs than proven models because both expectations and accountability are lower in institutional settings.

Nevertheless, the failure to provide treatment to the most disadvantaged of all juvenile populations would undercut the legitimacy of the entire juvenile-justice system. Since institutional populations include heavy concentrations of disadvantaged minorities and also of the emotionally disturbed (Grisso, 2004), the system must remain committed to serving youth in secure confinement. But substantial resources must also be invested in quality control or the potential for positive program impacts will never really exist.

The Impact of Security and Punishment Objectives on Programming Opportunities in Juvenile Court

A new recruit at a monastery was surprised to see one of the regular members of the order smoking a cigarette while he was kneeling in prayer. "Are we allowed to smoke while we pray," he asked the brother when he got a chance. "I don't know," replied the brother, "but I asked the Monsignor if it was all right to pray while I smoked."

In the previous chapter, I argued that prevention programs should not be run by the same people who are responsible for enforcing sanctions. It is to easy to get the two functions mixed up. Prevention programs, by their very nature, are more effective when they are voluntary. They need to focus on positive reinforcement rather than the negative sanctions. However, just because a youth must be removed from his home and placed in stricter custodial settings because of the seriousness of his offense, there is no reason to give up on efforts to reduce the youth's future offending.

Secure confinement is never an optimal environment for multiphase programming, but any decent custodial setting can accommodate programming for a wide variety of goals such as drug and alcohol prevention, remedial education, anger management, social skills training, and the like. Meta-analyses of custodial programs for juvenile offenders have shown that some types of programs are more effective than others in reducing subsequent recidivism. General program characteristics were found to be more important than the specific type of treatment provided. The following characteristics were found to be associated with greater effectiveness (Lipsey & Wilson, 1998):

- The integrity with which the treatment model is implemented.
- Longer duration of treatment produces better results.
- Well-established programs perform better than brand new programs.
- Treatment administered by mental health professionals is more effective.
- Emphasis on interpersonal skills training.
- Use of the teaching family home methods.

A meta-analysis that looked at custodial programs for both juveniles and adults (Andrews et al., 1990) identified the following factors as being associated with the more effective programs:

- Focusing intervention efforts on higher-risk youth.
- Focusing on dynamic risk factors associated with criminal behavior.
- Using treatment methods appropriate to the individual.
- Using proven methods.

The research on custodial programs cited above has demonstrated that such programs can be effective in reducing recidivism, as well as in providing higher levels of public protection and accountability. Furthermore, the most effective of these programs have a number of characteristics in common.

The same meta-analysis that identified the characteristics of effective custodial programs also shows that programs implemented in community settings are more effective than similar programs in custodial settings (Lipsey & Wilson, 1998). Furthermore, participation in some community-based programs that are usually voluntary can be coerced by the juvenile court and still be effective. This finding holds true for compulsory education and drug treatment as well. There are limits, however, to the effectiveness of a coercive approach. Eventually, the targets of the intervention must choose whether to accept and act on the information and guidance provided by the intervention, or to just go through the motions without any real interest or intent of making the necessary changes in their behavior.

The juvenile court is situated in the overlap of societal interests for both preventive interventions and punishment. In many of its dispositions, the juvenile court must recognize the community's need for protection and accountability as well as the offender's need for therapeutic intervention. In fact, there is often a strong correlation between the requirements of punishment or accountability and intervention. A serious criminal act is both a threat to the community and a sign that some significant intervention may be required. Among youth aged six to eleven, participation in general offenses is the most important risk factor for serious delinquency (Lipsey & Derzon, 1998). It is the juvenile court's function to balance these two conflicting demands.

For much of its history, placement in a training school or other institution was seen as the most severe sanction the juvenile court could deliver. However, as reformers have attempted to improve the conditions and the quality of programs within these institutions, they may have lost some of their more punitive aspects. In some states and communities the use of "balanced and restorative justice" (BARJ) incorporating restitution and community service have become the preferred modes of punishment, providing the offender an opportunity to repair the harm he or she may have caused to the community and the victim (Braithwaite, 1998).

None of the proven programs described in chapter 4 make satisfactory sanctions for those citizens or public officials who demand more punitive approaches. Home visitation, assistance in school, mentoring, having the assistance of a trained therapist to help solve family problems—none of these sound very punitive. Even placement in a therapeutic foster home is usually more benign than placement in a traditional group home.

In many ways, the improved scientific basis for identifying the characteristics of effective prevention programs has made it easier for the court to distinguish between sanctions and treatment—a situation with both positive and negative aspects. On the one hand, the court has less opportunity to place youth in programs that are supposed to be both punitive and preventive, because there aren't any. On the other hand, the court is denied the luxury of resolving a case with a single disposition, and playing up its punitive aspects to victims, while emphasizing its preventive aspects to the youth and his or her family. No more talking out of both sides of the judicial mouth.

For less serious cases, in terms of public safety, the balance should be more toward programming and less toward sanctions. For more serious cases, sanctions will play a bigger role. It is here that the BARJ approach can be used to ensure that the sanctions serve a productive purpose by repairing some of the harm done to the victim and community by the juvenile's offenses.

But even though security conditions and institutional contexts inhibit the effectiveness of treatment programs, the problems associated with treatment during custody are not a conclusive argument against programmatic effort. Effective programming is difficult in institutions, but the evidence in current literature does not demonstrate that it is impossible. The best combination for any youth is a community setting and an effective program. But an institutional setting with programming may still be superior to an institutional setting without it.

The question is not whether youths should be incarcerated while participating in a program; that is the equivalent to the question about smoking while praying in the opening to this chapter. Rather, the question is whether programs should also be available for those youth who must be subjected to secure confinement.

Three Lessons for Juvenile Courts

A number of lessons can be drawn from our review of delinquency-prevention efforts. Three have particular significance for treatment programs in juvenile courts. Two of these lessons identify problems for the court in its pursuit of delinquency-prevention goals. The third identifies a special opportunity. I first consider the problems.

The formal jurisdiction of the juvenile court is rarely a first strike for its subjects. The court stands at the end of a long series of possible interventions in the lives of most troubled youth. Pediatricians, preschools, parents, teachers, school counselors, coaches and other recreational specialists, clergy, and child and family therapists all usually have the chance to help a young person gain control of problem behaviors before resort is made to juvenile court. It is extremely rare for a youth who commits an offense that lands him or her in juvenile court not to have a history of problem behaviors. For so-called chronic or life-course persistent (Moffit et al., 2001) offenders, it will be a long history. For the "adolescent-limited offenders," who do not exhibit problem behaviors until after puberty, the history may be relatively short, but it will still be there. Delinquency begins with small acts of misbehavior and progresses to the more severe. The youth's appearance in juvenile court is a clear indication that the previous efforts at intervention failed, or at least did not accomplish all that was hoped. This is one of the problems the juvenile court must take account of.

It might be hoped that the impact of a sequence of intervention efforts would be cumulative, that each successive effort would add to the gains achieved by the previous efforts until the appropriate level was reached to prevent further recidivism. Unfortunately this is ordinarily not the case. Given the state of current practice, many of the interventions that may be tried may prove to be ineffective or inappropriate for the particular situation. Thus few if any positive impacts are achieved. In fact, the cumulative effect of previous efforts to intervene with troubled youth may be negative in that they exacerbate existing problems, reinforce negative labeling, and reduce expectations of help from additional intervention.

Failure to respond positively to an intervention that is touted as appropriate for a given situation produces negative expectations for the youth, their families, and the community in which they reside. The youth becomes more skeptical about the consequences of intervention, experienced in manipulating the interventionists or in avoiding the therapeutic thrust of their efforts, and more convinced of his or her own identity as a troubled youth. The family typically becomes more annoyed or angry at the youth or the intervening party, and more pessimistic about the potential for positive change. The system typically blames the failure of the intervention on the youth and not on the intervention program. The entry made in the juvenile's record is "failure to adjust."

So its relatively late position in the delinquency-prevention chain of interventions puts the juvenile court at a disadvantage. In addition to all of the other risks and problems that youths will face, by the time that they arrive in the juvenile court they will bear the additional stigma as one who does not respond positively to programs nor take advantage of help when it is offered.

This leads to the second problem facing juvenile courts: the negative labeling that any involvement in court-based programming involves. Youth involved with the juvenile court will be seen as more at risk than other adolescents. Being placed under the jurisdiction of the juvenile court only adds to the cumulative negative-labeling process that may have characterized all previous attempts at intervention. This process affects not only the youth involved but parents and interventionists as well. It is a significant disadvantage indeed, and one reason that diversion from formal processing has retained its attractiveness.

If the filtering-out of less serious cases has been done correctly, the juvenile court comes up to bat with two strikes against it: negative expectations on the part of youth and their families regarding attempts at successful intervention, and the potential that the youth will experience additional negative labeling from any intervention it attempts. But it also comes up to bat with the bases loaded. The juvenile court's unique advantage over every other potential venue for prevention programming is the high level of risk represented by its subjects. School-based or community-based programs for delinquency prevention may involve considerably less stigma, but they also must deal with youth from a much lower risk pool. Because they deal with youth in the highest risk categories, prevention programs sponsored by the juvenile court can afford to expend significantly more funding on each individual case, and still expect the potential benefits to exceed those costs. According to the cost-benefit analyses conducted by the Washington State Institute for Public Policy (Aos et al., 2001), this is clearly the case for such programs as Functional Family Therapy, Multisystemic Therapy, Multidimensional Treatment Foster Care, and Aggression Replacement Training.

From Prevention to Programs: The Role of Juvenile Courts

Primary prevention addresses risk factors that apply to the population in general—for example, the use of alcohol, tobacco, or other illegal drugs. Secondary prevention addresses populations identified as being at a higher risk level than the general population, but not yet involved in delinquency. From the description of the programs and the arguments presented in the previous chapters, it should be clear that operational responsibility for primary and secondary delinquency-prevention programs belongs outside the justice system in institutions dedicated to issues of education, health, and human services. These agencies are better suited to deliver the types of services these programs require, and are able to do so without the negative-labeling effects associated with the juvenile court.

But just because many programs should be carried out apart from justice-system involvement, it is an error to suppose that no prevention programming should be vested in juvenile courts. Programs can be cost effective even working with previous program failures. Furthermore, a juvenile-justice system with a diversified portfolio of tertiary prevention programs is far superior to a court without treatment resources. Indeed, indications of program effectiveness in any domain should argue for more rather than less emphasis on programming throughout the system.

There is no level of custody that does not warrant some programming. The greater the level of custody probably the greater the need for programs. Even though the often-cited Lipsey and Wilson (1998) meta-analysis does show that community-based interventions are more effective, it also shows that custodial programs can also have positive impacts. If a custodial facility does not provide therapeutic programming, then that facility does not belong under the jurisdiction of the juvenile court.

The specific responsibilities that juvenile courts need to assume in order to ensure appropriate programs are deployed effectively include the following: awareness of the current evidence base; diversion of cases that can be handled informally outside the system; disposition of cases to appropriate programs; and quality control. I consider these responsibilities in turn.

Awareness of Current Evidence Base

Just because the juvenile courts are not responsible for every delinquency-prevention program does not mean they shouldn't stay abreast of the latest research and developments in the delinquency-prevention field. It is the court that in the end must hold the rest of the system accountable. Health and education institutions are likely to miss some new developments in delinquency prevention because their attention is directed mainly to new research in their own primary fields. The juvenile court has a role to play in ensuring that such information does not slip through the cracks.

Diversion

Intervention at the level of the juvenile court is an expensive proposition. Most programs are far from cheap, and the findings in regard to negative labeling and deviant peer contagion suggest that some can do more harm than good. The juvenile court is in the best position to distinguish between those cases that can be handled informally by diversion to appropriate services and those that require more formal proceedings.

Disposition

The juvenile court should consider programming needs as well as sanctions as part of the disposition of any case. It must to develop an empirical basis for determining which programs work best for particular types of juvenile offenders, and for deciding when a youth needs to be removed from a particular program and placed in another. The availability of standardized assessment instruments (Grisso & Underwood, 2004) and more evidence-based programs can take some of the guesswork out of what has tradition-ally been a hit-or-miss process.

Quality Control

The juvenile court is in an excellent position to identify gaps in the current program mix and identify programs that are not performing up to their true potential. The court is in a good positions from which it can observe the failures of other agencies. The records of individual cases that come before the court provide informative case studies of how well the system is currently performing and where there are screening, assessment, or programming gaps.

References

Achenback, T. (1991). The child behavior checklist: Manual for the teachers report. Burlington, VT: Department of Psychiatry, University of Vermont.

Alexander, J. F. (1988). Phases of family therapy process: A framework for clinicians and researchers. In L. Wynne (Ed.), *The state of the art in family therapy research*. New York: Family Process Press.

Alexander, J., Barton, C., Gordon, D., Grotpeter, J., Hanson, K., Harrison, R., Mears, S., Mihalic, S., Parsons, B., Pugh, C., Schulman, S., Waldron, H., & Sexton, T. (1998). Functional family therapy. In D. S. Elliot (Series Ed.), *Blueprints for violence prevention*. Boulder: Center for the Study and Prevention of Violence, Institute of Behavioral Science, University of Colorado. Boulder: University of Colorado.

Alexander, J. F., & Parsons, B. V. (1982). *Functional family therapy: Principles and procedures*. Carmel, CA: Brooks & Cole.

Andrews, D. A., Zinger, I., Hoge, R. D., Bonta, J., Geandreau, P., & Cullen, F. T. (1990). Does correctional treatment work? *Criminology, 28,* 369–404.

Aniskoiewicz, R. E., & Wysong, E. E. (1987). *Project DARE evaluation report: Kokomo schools, spring 1987*. Kokomo, IN: Department of Sociology, Indiana University at Kokomo.

Aos, S. (2002). The juvenile justice system in Washington State: Recommendations to improve cost-effectiveness. Olympia, WA: Washington State Institute for Public Policy.

Aos, S., Phipps, P., Barnoski, R., & Lieb, R. (1999). *The comparative costs and benefits of programs to reduce crime*. Olympia, WA: Washington State Institute for Public Policy.

Aos, S., Phipps, P., Barnoski, R., & Lieb, R. (2001). *The comparative costs and benefits of programs to reduce crime* (Version 4.0). Olympia, WA: Washington State Institute for Public Policy.

Austin, J. (2000). *Multisite evaluation of boot camp programs: Final report.* Washington, D.C.: Institute on Crime, Justice, and Corrections, George Washington University.

Barnoski, R. (2002). Washington State's implementation of functional family therapy for juvenile offenders: Preliminary findings. Olympia, WA: Washington State Institute for Public Policy.

Barnoski, R. (2004). Assessing risk for re-offense: Validating the Washington State juvenile court assessment. Olympia, WA: Washington State Institute for Public Policy.

Barrish, H. H., Saunder, M., & Montrose, M. W. (1969). Good behavior game: Effects of individual contingencies for group consequences on disruptive behavior in a classroom. *Journal of Applied Behavior Analysis, 2,* 119–124.

Barton, C., Alexander, J., Waldron, H., Turner, C. W., & Warburton, J. (1985). Generalizing treatment effects of Functional Family Therapy: Three replications. *American Journal of Family Therapy, 13,* 16–26.

Becker, H. (1963). Outsiders: Studies in the sociology of deviance. New York: Free Press.

Bernburg, J. G., & Krohn, M. D. (2003). Labeling, life chances, and adult crime: The direct and indirect effects of official intervention in adolescence on crime in early adulthood. *Criminology, 41(4),* 1287–1318.

Berrueta-Clement, J. R., Schweinhart, L. J., & Barnett, W. S. (1984). *Changed lives: The effects of the Perry Preschool Program on youths through age 19.* High/Scope Educational Research Foundation Monograph No. 8. Ypsilanti, MI: High/Scope.

Biema, D. V. (1996, November 11). Just say life skills. *Time,* 70.

Bishop, D., & Frazier, C. (2000). Consequences of transfer. In J. Fagin & F. Zimring (Eds.), *The changing borders of juvenile justice.* Chicago: University of Chicago Press.

Bonnie, R. J., Fulco, C. E., & Liverman, C. T. (Eds.). (1999). *Reducing the burden of injury: Advancing prevention and treatment.* Washington, D.C.: National Academies Press.

Boudouris, J., & Turnbull, B. W. (1985). Shock probation in Iowa. *Journal of Offender Counseling, Services & Rehabilitation, 9,* 53–67.

Blumstein, A., Cohen, J., & Nagin, D. (1978). *Deterrence and incapacitation: Estimating the effects of sanctions on crime rates.* Washington. D.C.: National Academies Press.

Blumstein, A., Cohen, J., Roth, J. A., & Vishers, C. (Eds.). (1986). *Criminal careers and career criminals.* Washington, D.C.: National Academies Press.

Bodwitch, C. (1993). Getting rid of troublemakers: High school disciplinary procedures and the production of dropouts. *Social Problems, 40,* 493–509.

Boruch, R. F., Petrosino, A., & Chalmers, I. (1999, July). *The Campbell Collaboration: A proposal for systematic, multi-national, and continuous reviews of evidence.* Background paper presented at the meeting of the Campbell Collaboration at University College-London, School of Public Policy.

Botvin, G. (1990). Substance abuse prevention: Theory, practice, and effectiveness. In M. Tonry & J. Q. Wilson (Eds.), *Drugs and crime.* Chicago: University of Chicago Press.

Botvin, G., Baker, E., Dusenbury, L. D., Botvin, E. M., & Diaz, T. (1995). Long-term follow-up results of a randomized drug abuse prevention trial in a white middle-class population. *Journal of the American Medical Association, 273,* 1106–1112.

Botvin, G., Baker, E., Dusenbury, L. D., Tortu, S., & Botvin, E. M. (1990). Preventing adolescent drug abuse through a multimodal cognitive-behavioral approach: Results of a three-year study. *Journal of Consulting & Clinical Psychology, 58,* 437–446.

Botvin, G., & Eng, A. (1982). The efficacy of a multicomponent approach to the prevention of cigarette smoking. *Preventive Medicine, 11,* 199–211.

Botvin, G., Mihalic, S. F., & Grotpeter, J. K. (1998). *Blueprints for violence Prevention: Life skills training.* Boulder: Center for the Study and Prevention of Violence, Institute of Behavioral Science, University of Colorado.

Boyle, P. (2001). A DAREing rescue. *Youth Today, 10(4).*

Braithwaite, J. (1998). Restorative justice: Assessing an immodest theory and a pessimistic theory. In M. Tonry (Ed.), *Crime and justice: A review of research* (Vol. 23). Chicago: University of Chicago Press.

Brown, J. M., & Langan, P. A. (1998). *State court sentencing of convicted felons.* Washington, D.C.: Bureau of Justice Statistics, U.S. Department of Justice.

Bry, B. H. (1982). Reducing the incidence of adolescent problems through preventive intervention. *American Journal of Community Psychology, 11,* 252–260.

Camp, G., & Camp, C. (1993). *The corrections yearbook: Adult corrections.* South Salem, N.Y.: Criminal Justice Institute.

Carstens, S. J., Pechia, D. J., & Rohach, L. R. (1989). DARE—Drug Abuse Resistance Education—Is it jerking? Independent School District 281, Robinsdale Area Schools, Minnesota.

Caulkins, J. P., Chiesa, J. R., & Everingham, S. (2000). *Response to NRC assessment of RAND's "Controlling Cocaine" study.* Santa Monica: RAND (MR-1265-DPRC).

Caulkins, J. P., Pacula, R. L., Paddock, S., & Chiesa, J. (2002). *School-based drug prevention: What kind of drug use does it prevent?* Santa Monica: RAND (MR-1459-RWJ).

Caulkins, J. P., Rydell, C. P., Everingham, S., Chiesa, J., & Bushway, S. (1999). *An ounce of prevention, a pound of uncertainty.* Santa Monica: RAND (MR-923-RWJ).

Caulkins, J. P., Rydell, C. P., Schwabe, W., & Chiesa, J. (1997). *Mandatory minimum drug sentences.* Santa Monica: RAND (MR-827-DPRC).

Center for Mental Health Services, U.S. Department of Health and Human Services, Prevention Research Center for the Promotion of Human Development. (n.d.). Available at www.prevention.psu.edu/CMHS.html.

Chaiken, M., & Chaiken, M. R. (1982). *Varieties of criminal behavior.* Santa Monica: RAND (R-2814-NIJ).

Chamberlain, P., & Mihalic, S. (1998). Multidimensional treatment foster care. In D. S. Elliot (Series Ed.), *Blueprints for violence prevention.* Boulder: Center for the Study and Prevention of Violence, Institute of Behavioral Science, University of Colorado.

Chamberlain, P., & Reid, J. B. (1997). Comparison of two community alternatives to incarceration for chronic juvenile offenders. *Journal of Consulting & Clinical Psychology, 6(4),* 624–633.

Chappell, P. (2000). Communities That Care prevention strategies: A research guide to what works. Seattle: Developmental Research and Programs, Inc.

Clark, R. (1995). Situational crime prevention. In M. Tonry & D. Farrington (Eds.), *Building a safer society: Strategic approaches to crime prevention.* Chicago: University of Chicago Press.

Clayton, R. (1987). Project DARE in Lexington: Evaluation of the pilot phase. Unpublished report summarized in *The D.A.R.E. Evaluation Compendium.* Los Angeles: D.A.R.E. Western Regional Training Center.

Clayton, R., Cattarello, R. A., Day, L. E., & Walden, P. (1991). Sensation seeking as a potential validating variable for school-based prevention intervention: A two-year follow-up of D.A.R.E. *Health Communications, 29,* 229–239.

Cloward, R. A., & Ohlin, L. E. (1960). *Delinquency and opportunity: A theory of delinquent gangs.* New York: Free Press.

Cohen, M. A. (1988). Pain, suffering, and jury awards: A study of the cost of crime to victims. *Law & Society Review, 22,* 537–555.

Cohen, M. A., Miller, T. R., & Rossman, S. B. (1994). The costs and consequences of violent behavior in the United States. In A. J. Reiss & J. A. Roth (Eds.), *Understanding and preventing violence: Consequences and control of violence* (Vol. 4). Washington, D.C.: National Academies Press.

Cohen, M. A., Rust, R. T., Steen, S., & Tidd, S. T. (2004). Willingness-to-pay for crime control programs. *Criminology, 42(1)*, 89–109.

Conduct Problems Prevention Group (K. Bierman, J. Cole, K. Dodge, M. Greenberg, J. Lochman, & R. McMahon). (1992). A developmental and clinical model for the prevention of conduct disorder: The FAST Track Program. *Development & Psychopathology, 4*, 509–527.

Conduct Problems Prevention Group (K. Bierman, J. Cole, K. Dodge, M. Greenberg, J. Lochman, & R. McMahon). (1996). Initial impact of the FAST Track prevention trial for conduct problems: I. The high-risk sample. *Journal of Consulting & Clinical Psychology, 67(5)*, 631–647.

Cook, P. J., & Ludwig, J. (2000). *Gun violence: The real costs*. Oxford: Oxford University Press.

Cooper, H., & Hedges, L. V. (Eds). (1994). *The handbook of research synthesis*. New York: Sage.

Correll, J. (1990). *Drug Abuse Resistance Education D.A.R.E.* Washington, D.C.: U.S. Department of Defense.

Crane, B. D, Rivolo, A. R., & Comfort, G. C. (1997). *An empirical examination of counterdrug interdiction program effectiveness*. Washington, D.C.: Institute for Defense Analysis.

Cullen, F. T, Wright, J. P., & Applegate, B. K. (1996). Control in the community. In A. T. Harland (Ed.), *Choosing correctional options that work: Defining the demand and evaluating the supply*. Thousand Oaks, CA: Sage.

Daro, D. O., & Harding, K. A. (1999). Healthy families America: Using research to enhance practice. *The Future of Children, 9(1)* (special issue).

Davies, P. (1999). What is evidence based education? *British Journal of Educational Studies, 47*, 108–121.

Dejong, W. (1987). A short-term evaluation of Project D.A.R.E. (Drug Abuse Resistance Education): Preliminary indications of effectiveness. *Journal of Drug Education, 17*, 279–294.

Dishion, T. J., Andrews, D. W., & Crosby, L. (1995). Adolescent boys and their friends in adolescence: Relationship characteristics, quality and interactional process. *Child Development, 66*, 139–151.

Dishion, T. J., McCord, J., & Poulin, F. (1999). When prevention harms: Peer groups and problem behavior. *American Psychologist, 54*, 755–764.

Dishion, T. J., Poulin, F., & Burraston, B. (2001). Peer group dynamics associated with iatrogenic effects in group interventions with high-risk young adolescents. In C. Erdley & D. W. Nangle (Eds.), *New directions for child and adolescent development: The role of friendship in psychological adjustment*. San Francisco: Jossey-bass.

Dolan, L., Turkan, J., Wethamer-Larsson, L., & Kellam, S. (1989). *The Good Behavior Game manual*. Baltimore: Prevention Program.

Donnermeyer, J. F. (1998). Prevention education and substance use. *Journal of School Health, 68.*

Duggan, A. K., McFarlane, E. C., Windham, A. M., Rohde, C. A., Salkever, D. S., Fuddy, L., Rosenberg, L. A., Buchbinder, S. B., & Sia. C. J. (1999). Evaluation of Hawaii's Healthy Start Program. *Future of Children 9(1)*, 66–90.

Dukes, R., Stein, J., & Ullman, J. (1996). The long term effects of DARE. *Evaluation Review, 20*, 49–66.

Dukes, R., Stein, J., & Ullman, J. (1997). The long term effects of DARE. *Evaluation Review, 21*, 473–500.

Dyal, D. Y.(1995). Ten organizational practices of public health: A historical perspective. *American Journal of Preventive Medicine, 11*, 6–8.

Eddy, J. M., Reid, J. B., & Fetrow, R. A. (2000). An elementary school-based prevention program targeting modifiable antecedents of youth delinquency and violence: Linking the Interests of Families and Teachers (LIFT). *Journal of Emotional & Behavioral Disorders, 8(3)*, 165–176.

Edelman, P. (2002). American government and the politics of youth. In M. K. Rosenheim, F. E. Zimring, D. S. Tanenhaus & B. Dohrn (Eds.), *A century of juvenile justice*. Chicago: University of Chicago Press.

Ellickson, P. L., Bell, R. M., & McGuigan, K. (1993). Preventing adolescent drug use: Long-term impacts of a junior high program. *American Journal of Public Health, 83(6)*, 856–861.

Elliot, D. S. (1997). *Blueprints for violence prevention*. Boulder: Center for the Study and Prevention of Violence, Institute of Behavioral Science, University of Colorado.

Elliot, D. S., & Ageton, S. A. (1980). Reconciling race and class differences in self-reported and official estimates of delinquency. *American Sociological Review, 49*, 95–100.

Elliot, D. S., Huizinga, D., & Menard, S. (1989). Multiple problem youth: Delinquency, substance use and mental health problems. New York: Springer-Verlag.

Elliot, D. S., & Menard, S. (1996). Delinquent friends and delinquent behavior: Temporal and developmental patterns. In J. D. Hawkins (Ed.), *Current theories of crime and deviance*. Newbury Park, CA: Sage Publications.

Empey, La Mar T. (1979). *American delinquency: The future of childhood and juvenile justice*. Charlottesville: University of Virginia Press.

Ennett, S. T., Tobler, N. S., Ringwalt, C. L., & Flewelling, R. L. (1994). How effective is drug abuse resistance education? A meta-analysis of Project

D.A.R.E. outcome evaluations. *American Journal of Public Health, 84,* 1394–1401.

Fagan, J. (1995). Separating the men from the boys: The comparative advantage of juvenile versus criminal court sanctions on recidivism among adolescent felony offenders. In J. C. Howell, B. Krisberg, J. D. Hawkins, & J. J. Wilson (Eds.), *A sourcebook: Serious violent and chronic juvenile offenders.* Thousand Oaks, CA: Sage.

Faine, J. R., & Bohlander, E. (1988). Drug abuse resistance education: An assessment of 1987–88 Kentucky State Police D.A.R.E. Program. Bowling Green. KY: Social Research Laboratory, Western Kentucky University.

Farrington, D. P., & Petrosino, A. (2000). The Campbell Collaboration Crime and Justice Group. *Annals of the American Academy of Political & Social Science, 578,* 3549.

Feiner, R. D., & Adan, A. M. (1988). The School Transitional Enviroment Project: An ecological intervention and evaluation. In R. H. Price, E. L. Cowen, R. P. Lorion, & J. Ramos-McKay (Eds.), *14 ounces of prevention: A casebook for practitioners.* Washington, D.C.: American Psychological Association.

Feld, B. C. (1998). The juvenile court. In M. Tonry (Ed.), *The handbook of crime and punishment.* New York: Oxford University Press.

Finckenaur, J. O., & Gavin, P. W. (1999). *Scared straight.* Long Grove IL: Waveland Press.

Gendreau, P. J., Goggin, C., Cullen, F. T., & Andrews, D. A. (2000). *The effects of community sanctions and incarceration on recidivism.* Ottawa: Corrections Service of Canada.

Glass, S. (1997, March 3). Don't you D.A.R.E. *New Republic,* 18–28.

Glueck, S., & Glueck, E. (1950). *Unraveling juvenile delinquency.* New York: Commonwealth Fund.

Gold, M. R., Siegel, J. E., Russell, L. B., & Weinstein, M. C. (Eds.). (1996). *Cost-effectiveness in health and medicine.* New York: Oxford University Press.

Goldberg, L., Elliot, D., Clarke, G. N., MacKinnon, D. P., Moe, E., Zoref, L., Green, C., Wolf, S., Greffath, E., Miller, D. J., & Lapin, A. (1996). Effects of a multidimensional anabolic steroid prevention intervention: The Adolescents Training and Learning to Avoid Steroids (ATLAS) Program. *Journal of the American Medical Association, 276(19),* 1555–1562.

Gottfredson, D. C. (1990). Changing school structures to benefit high-risk youths. Troubled and troubling youth: Multidisciplinary perspectives. Newbury Park, CA: Sage.

Gottfredson, D. C. (2001). *Schools and delinquency.* New York: Cambridge University Press.

Gottfredson, D. C., Wilson, D., & Najaka, S. S. (2002). School-based crime prevention. In L. W. Sherman, D. P. Farrington, B. C. Welsh & D. L. MacKenzie (Eds.). *Evidenced-based crime prevention.* London: Routledge.

Gottfredson, G. D. (1987). Peer group interventions to reduce the risk of delinquent behavior: A selective review and new evaluation. *Criminology, 25(3),* 671–714.

Greenberg, M. T., Domitrovich, C., & Bumbarger, B. (1999). *Preventing mental disorders in school-aged children: A review of the effectiveness of prevention programs.* Washington, D.C.: U.S. Department of Health & Human Services.

Greenberg, M. T., Kusche, C., & Mihalic, S. (1998). Promoting alternative thinking strategies (PATHS). In D. S. Elliot (Series Ed.), *Blueprints for violence prevention.* Boulder: Center for the Study and Prevention of Violence, Institute of Behavioral Science, University of Colorado.

Greenwood, P. W. (2002). Juvenile crime and juvenile justice. In J. Q. Wilson & J. Petersilia (Eds.), *Crime.* Oakland: ICS Press.

Greenwood, P. W., & Abrahamse, A. F. (1982). *Selective incapacitation.* Santa Monica: RAND (R-2815-NIJ).

Greenwood, P. W., Caulkins, J. P., Wong, J. S., & Cicchetti, S. (2003). *The Deschutes County Community Youth Investment Program.* Agoura, CA: Greenwood & Associates.

Greenwood, P. W., & Hawken, A. (2000). *An assessment of the effects of California's Three Strikes law.* Agoura, CA: Greenwood & Associates.

Greenwood, P. W., Model, K. E., Rydell, C. P., & Chiesa, J. (1996). *Diverting children from a life of crime: Measuring costs and benefits.* Santa Monica: RAND (MR-699-UCB/RC/IF).

Greenwood, P. W., Rydell, C. P., Abrahamse, A. F., Caulkins, J. P., Chiesa, J. C., Model, K. E., & Klein, S. P. (1994). *Three strikes and you're out: Estimated benefits and costs of California's new mandatory sentencing law.* Santa Monica: RAND (MR-509-RC).

Greenwood, P. W., & Turner, S. (1993). Evaluation of the Paint Creek Youth Center: A residential facility for serious delinquents. *Criminology, 31(2),* 263–279.

Greenwood, P. W., Wasserman, J., Davis, L. M., Flora, J. A., Howard, K. A., Schleicher, N., Abrahamse, A., Jacobson, P. D., Marshall, G., Oken, C., & Chiesa, L. (2001). *The California Wellness Foundation's Violence Prevention Initiative.* Santa Monica: RAND (MR-1342.0-TCWF).

Grisso, T. (2004). Double jeopardy: Adolescent offenders with mental disorders. Chicago: University of Chicago Press

Grisso, T., & Underwood, L. A. (2004). *Screening and assessing mental health and substance use disorders among youth in the juvenile justice system.*

Washington, D.C.: Office of Juvenile Justice and Delinquency Prevention, U.S. Department of Justice.

Grossberg, M. (2002). Changing conceptions of child welfare in the United States, 1820–1935. In M. K. Rosenheim, F. E. Zimring, D. S. Tanenhaus & B. Dohrn (Eds.), *A century of juvenile justice*. Chicago: University of Chicago Press.

Hahn, R. A., Bilukha, O., Crosby, A., Fullilive, M. T., Lieberman, A., Moscicki, E. K., Snyder, S., Tuma, F., Schofield, A., Corso, P. S., & Briss, P. (2003). *First reports evaluating the effectiveness of strategies for preventing violence: Early childhood home visitation*. Atlanta: CDC.

Harrell, A. V., Cavanaugh, S., & Sridharan, S. (1998). *Impact of the Children at Risk Program: Comprehensive final report II*. Washington, D.C.: Urban Institute.

Hawkins, J. D., & Catalano, R. F. (1992). *Communities that care*. San Francisco: Jossey-Bass.

Hawkins, J. D., Catalano, R. F., & Arthur, M. W. (2002). Promoting science-based prevention in communities. *Addictive Behaviors, 27(6)*, 951–76.

Hawkins, J. D., Catalano, R. F., & Brewer, D. D. (1995). Preventing serious, violent and chronic offending: Effective strategies from conception to age 6. In J. C. B. Howell, J. D. Krisberg, J. J. Hawkins, & J. J. Wilson (Eds.), *Sourcebook on serious, violent and chronic juvenile offenders*. Thousand Oaks, CA: Sage.

Hawkins, J. D., Catalano, R. F., Kosterman, R., Hill, K. (1999). Preventing adolescent health-risk behaviors by strengthening protection during childhood. *Archives of Pediatric & Adolescent Medicine, 153*, 226–234.

Hawkins, J. D., Herrenkohl, T., Farrington, D. P., Brower, D., Catalano, R. F., & Harachi, T. (1998). A review of predictors of youth violence. In R. Loeber & D. Farrington (Eds.), *Serious and violent juvenile offenders*. Thousand Oaks, CA: Sage.

Healy, W. (1915). *The individual delinquent*. Boston: Little, Brown.

Henggeler, S. W., Cunningham, P. B., Pickrel, S. G., Schoenwald, S. K., & Brondino, M. J. (1996). Multisystemic therapy: An effective violence prevention approach to serious juvenile offenders. *Journal of Adolescence, 19*, 47–61.

Henggler, S. W., Mihalic, S. F., Rone, L., Thomas, C., & Timmons-Mitchel, J. (1998). Multisystemic therapy. In D. S. Elliot (Series Ed.), *Blueprints for violence prevention* (Bk. 6). Boulder: Center for the Study and Prevention of Violence, Institute of Behavioral Science, University of Colorado.

Hirschi, T. (1980). Labeling theory and juvenile delinquency: An assessment of the evidence. In W. Grove (Ed.), *The labeling of deviance: Evaluating a perspective* (2d ed.). New York: Wiley.

Johnson, D. L., & Walker, T. (1987). Primary prevention of behavior problems in Mexican-American children. *American Journal of Community Psychology*, *15*, 375–385.

Jones, M. B., & Offord, M. D. (1989). Reduction of anti-social behavior in poor children by non-school skill development. *Journal of Child Psychology & Psychiatry*, *30*, 737–750.

Juvenile Justice Update. (2004, April / May). *National study concludes school-based drug testing does not have impact on drug use*. Kingston, NJ: Civic Research Institute.

Karoly, L. A., Greenwood, P. W., Everingham, S. S., Hoube, J., Kilburn, M. R., Rydell, C. P., Sanders, M., & Chiesa, J. (1998). *Investing in our children*. Santa Monica: RAND (MR-898-TCWF).

Kennedy, D., Braga, A. A., Piehl, A. M., & Waring, E. J. (2001). *Reducing gun violence: The Boston Gun Project's operation ceasefire*. Washington, D.C.: National Institute of Justice, NCJ 18874, U.S. Department of Justice.

Kitzman, H., Olds, D., Sidora, K., Henderson, C., Hanks, C., Cole, R., Luckey, D., Bondy, J., Cole, K., & Glazner, J. (2000). Enduring effects of Nurse Home Visitation on maternal life course: A 3-year follow-up of a randomized trial. *Journal of the American Medical Association, 283(15)*, 1983–1989.

Klein, M. (1971). *Street gangs and street workers*. Englewood Cliffs, NJ: Prentice-Hall.

Korfmacher, J., O'Brian, R., Hiatt, S., & Olds, D. (1999). Differences in program implementation between nurses and paraprofessionals in prenatal and infancy home visitation: A randomized trial. *American Journal of Public Health, 89(12)*, 1847–1851.

Kosterman, R., Hawkins, J. D., Spoth, R., Haggerty, K., & Zhu, K. (1997). Effects of a preventive parent training intervention on observed family interactions: Proximal outcomes from preparing for the drug free years. *Journal of Community Psychology, 25(3)*, 277–292.

Laub, J. H. (2002). A century of delinquency research and delinquency theory. In M. K. Rosenheim, F. E. Zimring, D. S. Tanenhaus & B. Dohrn (Eds.), *A century of juvenile justice*. Chicago: University of Chicago Press.

Lally, J. R., Mangione, P. L., & Honig, A. S. (1988). The Syracuse University Family Development Research Program: Long-range impact of an early intervention with low-income children and their families. In D. R. Powell (Ed.), Parent education as an early childhood intervention: Emerging directions in theory, research and practice. *Annual Advances in Applied Developmental Psychology* (Vol. 3). Norwood, NJ: Ablex Publishing.

Landsverk, J., Carrilio, T., Connelly, C. D., Ganger, W. C., Slymen, D. J., Newton, R. R., Leslie, L., & Jones, C. (2002). *Healthy Families San Diego clinical trial: Technical report.* San Diego: Child and Adolescent Services Research Center, San Diego Children's Hospital and Health Center.

Lattimore, B. C., Mihalic, S. F., Grotpeter, J. K., Taggert, R. (1998). The Quantum Opportunities Program. In D. S. Elliot (Series Ed.), *Blueprints for violence prevention.* Boulder: Center for the Study and Prevention of Violence, Institute of Behavioral Science, University of Colorado.

Lemert, E. (1967). *Human deviance, social problems and social control.* Englewood Cliffs, NJ: Prentice-Hall

Lewis, R. V. (1983). California style: Evaluation of the San Quentin SQUIRES Program. *Criminal Justice & Behavior, 10(2)*, 209–226.

Lipsey, M. W. (1992). Juvenile delinquency treatment: A meta-analytic inquiry into the variability of effects. In T. D. Cook, H. Cooper, D. A. Condray, H. Hartman, L. V. Hodges, R. J. Light, T. A. Louis, & F. Mosteller (Eds.), *Meta-analysis for explanation: A casebook.* New York: Sage.

Lipsey, M. W. (2005). Peer aggregation and treatment efficacy. In K. A. Dodge & T. Dishion (Eds.), *Deviant by Design.* New York: Guilford Press.

Lipsey, M. W., & Derzon, J. H. (1998). Predictors of violent and serious delinquency in adolescence and early adulthood. In R. Loeber & D. Farrington (Eds.), *Serious and violent juvenile offenders.* Thousand Oaks, CA: Sage.

Lipsey, M. W., & Wilson, D. (1998). Effective intervention for serious juvenile offenders: A synthesis of research. In R. Loeber & D. Farrington (Eds.), *Serious and violent juvenile offenders.* Thousand Oaks, CA: Sage.

Lipsey, M. W., & Wilson, D. (2001). *Practical meta-analysis.* Thousand Oaks, CA, Sage.

Lipton, D., Martinson, R., & Wilks, J. (1975). The effectiveness of correctional treatment: A survey of treatment evaluation studies. New York: Praeger.

Lungren, D. (1998). Three strikes and you're out: Its impact on the California criminal justice system after four years. Retrieved July 24, 2001, from www.threestrikes.org/studies.html.

MacKenzie, D. L. (1997). Criminal justice and crime prevention. In L. W. Sherman, D. Gottfredson, D. MacKenzie, J. Eck, P. Reuter & S. Bushway (Eds.), *Preventing crime: What works, what doesn't, what's promising.* Washington, D.C.: Office of Justice Programs, U.S. Department of Justice.

MacKenzie, D. L. (2002). Reducing the criminal activities of known offenders and delinquents: Crime prevention in courts and corrections. In L. W. Sherman, D. P. Farrington, B. C. Welsh & D. L. MacKenzie (Eds.), *Evidenced-based crime prevention.* London: Routledge.

MacKenzie, D. L., Brame, R., McDowall, D., & Souryal, C. (1995). Boot camp prisons and recidivism in eight states. *Criminology, 33(3)*, 327–357.

Manski, C. F., J. V. Pepper & C. V. Petrie (Eds.). (2001). *Informing America's policy on illegal drugs: What we don't know keeps hurting us*. Washington, D.C.: National Academies Press.

Manski, C. F., J. V. Pepper & Y. F. Thomas (Eds.). (1999). *Assessment of two cost-effectiveness studies on cocaine control policy*. Washington, D.C., National Academies Press.

Martinson, R. (1974). What works? Questions and answers about prison reform. *Public Interest, 10*, 22–54.

Mayhew, P., Clark, R. V., & Elliot, D. (1989). Motorcycle theft, helmet legislation and displacement. *Howard Journal of Criminal Justice, 28*, 1–8.

McCord, J. (1992). The Cambridge-Somerville study: A pioneering longitudinal-experimental study of delinquency prevention. In J. McCord & R. Tremblay (Eds.), *Preventing anti-social behavior: Interventions from birth through adolescence*. New York: Guilford Press.

McCord, J. (1997, April). *Some unanticipated consequences of summer camps*. Paper presented at the biennial meeting of the Society for Research in Child Development, Washington, D.C.

McDonald, R. M., Towberman, D. B., & Hague, J. L. (1990). Vol. 2: *1989 impact assessment of Drug Abuse Resistance Education in the Commonwealth of Virginia*. Richmond: Virginia Institute for Research in Justice and Risk Administration, Commonwealth University.

Mendel, R. A. (2001). Less hype, more help: Reducing juvenile crime, what works — and what doesn't. Washington D.C.: American Youth Policy Forum.

Mercy, J. A., & O'Carrol, P. W. (1988). New directions in violence prediction: The public health arena. Special issue: The prediction of interpersonal criminal violence. *Violence & Victims, 3(4)*, 285–301.

Mihalic, S., & Aultman-Bettridge, T. (2002). A guide to effective school-based prevention programs. In W. L. Tulk (Ed.), *Policing and school crime*. Englewood Cliffs, NJ: Prentice-Hall.

Mihalik, S., Fagan, A., Irwin, K., Ballard, D., & Elliot, D. (2002). *Blueprints for violence prevention replications: Factors for implementation success*. Boulder: Center for the Study and Prevention of Violence, Institute of Behavioral Science, University of Colorado.

Milenson, M. L. (1997). Demanding medical excellence: Doctors and accountability in the information age. Chicago: University of Chicago Press.

Miller, D. W. (2001, October 19). DARE Reinvents Itself—With help from its social-science critics. *Chronicle of Higher Education*.

Miller, T., Cohen, M., & Wiersema, B. (1996). *Victims, costs, and consequences: A new look*. Washington, D.C.: National Institute of Justice, NCJ 155282, U.S. Department of Justice.

Moffit, T. E., Caspi, A., Rutter, M., & Silva, P. A. (2001). Sex differences in antisocial behavior: Conduct disorder, delinquency and violence in the Dunedin Longitudinal Study. Cambridge: Cambridge University Press.

Nagin, D., Laub, J., & Sampson, R. (1998). Trajectories of change in criminal offending: Good marriages and the desistance process. *American Sociological Review, 63*, 225–239.

Nagin, D., Fergusson, D., & Horwood, J. (2000). Offending trajectories in a New Zealand cohort. *Criminology, 38*, 525–552.

OJJDP. (1997). *Proposed comprehensive plan for fiscal 1998*. Washington, D.C.: Office of Juvenile Justice and Delinquency Prevention, U.S. Department of Justice.

Olds, D. L. (1996, November 16). *Reducing risks for childhood-onset conduct disorder with prenatal and early childhood home visitation*. Paper presented at the American Public Health Association Pre-Conference Workshop: Prevention Science and Families: Mental Health Research and Public Health Policy Implications, New York.

Olds, D. L., Eckenrode, J., Henderson, C. R., Kizman, H., Powers, J., Cole, R., Sidora, K., Morris, P., Pettit, L. M., & Luckey, D. W. (1997). Long-term effects of home visitation on maternal life course and child abuse and neglect: Fifteen-year follow-up of a randomized trial. *Journal of the American Medical Association, 278*, 637–643.

Olds, D. L., Henderson Jr., C. R., Cole, R., Eckenrode, J., Kitzman, H., Luckey, D., Pettitt, L., Sidora, K., Morris, P., & Powers, J. (1998). Long-term effects of nurse home visitation on children's criminal and antisocial behavior: 15-year follow-up of a randomized trial. *Journal of the American Medical Association, 280*, 1238–1244.

Olds, D. L., Henderson, Jr., C. R., Tatelbaum, R., & Chamberlain, R. (1986). Improving the delivery of prenatal care and outcomes of pregnancy: A randomized trial of nurse home visitation. *Pediatrics, 77(1)*, 16–28.

Olds, D. L., Hill, P. L., Mihalic, S. F., & O'Brien, R. A. (1998). Prenatal and infancy home visitation by nurses. In D. S. Elliot (Series Ed.), *Blueprints for violence prevention*. Boulder: Center for the Study and Prevention of Violence, Institute of Behavioral Science, University of Colorado.

Olds, D. L., Robinson, J., O'Brien, R., Luckey, D. W., Pettitt, L. M., Henderson, C. R., Ng, R. K., Sheff, K. L., Korfmacher, J., Hiatt, S., & Talmi, A. (2002). Home visiting by paraprofessionals and by nurses: A randomized controlled trial. *Pediatrics, 110(3)*, 486–496.

Olweus, D., Limber, S., & Mihalic, S. (1998). Bullying Prevention Program. In D. S. Elliot (Series Ed.), *Blueprints for violence prevention*. Boulder: Center for the Study and Prevention of Violence, Institute of Behavioral Science, University of Colorado.

Parent, D. (2003). *Correctional boot camps: Lessons from a decade of research.* Washington, D.C.: National Institute of Justice, NCJ 197018, U.S. Department of Justice.

Park, J., Kosterman, R., Hawkins, J. D., Haggerty, K. P., Duncan, T. E., Duncan, S. C., & Spoth, R. (2000). Effects of the "Preparing for the Drug Free Years" curriculum on growth in alcohol use and risk for alcohol use in early adolescence. *Prevention Science, 1(3),* 125–138.

Paternoster, R., & Iovanni, L. (1989). The labeling perspective and delinquency: An elaboration of the theory and assessment of the evidence. *Justice Quarterly, 6,* 359–394.

Patterson, G. (1982). A social learning approach to family intervention: Coercive family process. Eugene, OR: Castalia.

Peters, M., Thomas, D., & Zamberlan, C. (1997). *Boot camps for juvenile offenders.* Washington, D.C.: Office of Juvenile Justice and Delinquency Prevention, NCJ 164258, U.S. Department of Justice.

Pentz, M. A., Mihalic, S. F., & Grotpeter, J. K. (1998). The Midwestern Prevention Project. In D. S. Elliot (Series Ed.), *Blueprints for violence prevention.* Boulder: Center for the Study and Prevention of Violence, Institute of Behavioral Science, University of Colorado.

Petrosino, A. (1997). What Works? Revisited again: A meta-analysis of randomized field experiments in individual level interventions. Newark, NJ: Rutgers University Press.

Posey, R., Wong, S., Catalano, R., Hawkins, D., Dusenbury, L., & Chappell, P. (1996). *Communities That Care prevention strategies: A research guide to what works.* Seattle: Social Development Research Group.

Puzzanchera, C., Stahl, A. L., Finnegan, T. A., Tierney, N., & Snyder, H. N. (2003). Juvenile court statistics 1999. Pittsburgh: National Center for Juvenile Justice, NCJ 201241.

Raphael, S., & Ludwig, J. (2003). Prison Sentence enhancements: The case of Project Exile. In J. Ludwig & P. J. Cook (Eds.), *Evaluating gun policy.* Washington, D.C.: Brookings Institution.

Reiss Jr., A. J., & Roth, J. A. (1993). *Understanding and preventing violence.* Washington, D.C.: National Academies Press.

Reuter, P., MacCoun, R., Murphy, P. J., Abrahamse, A. F., & Simon, B. (1990). *Money from Crime: A study of the economics of drug dealing in Washington, D.C.* Santa Monica: RAND (R-3894-RF).

Reyes, O., & Jason, L. A. (1991). An evaluation of a high school dropout prevention program. *Journal of Community Psychology, 10,* 277–290.

Ringwalt, C., Curtin, T. T., & Rosenbaum, D. P. (1990). *A first year evaluation of DARE in Illinois.* Chicago: Center for Research in Law and Justice, University of Illinois at Chicago.

Ringwalt, C., Ennett, S. T., & Holt, K. D. (1991). An outcome evaluation of Project D.A.R.E. *Health Education Research, 6,* 327–337.

Ringwalt, C., Ennett, S., Vincus, A., Thorne, J., Rohrbach, L. A., & Simons-Rudolph, A. (2002). The prevalence of effective substance use prevention in U.S. middle schools. *Prevention Science, 3(4).*

Ringwalt, C., Greene, J. M., Salt, S. T., Iachan, R., & Clayton, R. R. (1994). *Past and Future Directions of the D.A.R.E. Program.* Research Triangle Park, NC: Research Triangle Institute.

Robbins, M. S., & Szapocznik, J. (2000). *Brief strategic family therapy.* Washington, D.C.: Office of Juvenile Justice and Delinquency Prevention, NCJ 179825, U.S. Department of Justice.

Rosenbaum, D. P., Flewelling, R. L., Baily, S. L., Ringwalt, C. L., & Wilkinson, D. L. (1994). Cops in the classroom: A longitudinal evaluation of Drug Abuse Resistance Education (DARE). *Journal of Research in Crime & Delinquency, 31,* 3–31.

Rosenbaum, D. P., & Hanson, G. S. (1998). Assessing the effects of school-based drug education: A six-year multi-level analysis of Project D.A.R.E. *Journal of Research in Crime & Delinquency, 35(4),* 381–412.

Rosenbaum, D. P. (2002). Drug Abuse Resistance Education (D.A.R.E.). In *Encyclopedia of Juvenile Justice.* Thousand Oaks, CA: Sage.

Rosenheim, M. K., F. E. Zimring, D. S. Tanenhaus & B. Dohrn (Eds.). (2002). *A century of juvenile justice.* Chicago: University of Chicago Press.

Rydell, C. P., & Everingham, S. S. (1994). *Controlling cocaine: Supply versus demand programs.* Santa Monica: RAND (MR-331).

Sampson, R. J., & Laub, J. H. (1993). *Crime in the making: Pathways and turning points through life.* Cambridge: Harvard University Press.

Schaps, E., Bartolo, R. D., Moskowitz, J., Palley, C. S., & Churgin, S. (1981, Winter). A review of 127 drug abuse prevention program evaluations. *Journal of Drug Issues,* 17–43.

Schinke, S. P., & Gilchrist, L. D. (1983). Primary prevention of tobacco smoking. *Journal of School Health, 53,* 416–419.

Schlossman, S. (1977). *Love and the American delinquent.* Chicago: University of Chicago Press.

Schlossman, S. (1983). Studies in the history of early 20th century delinquency prevention. Santa Monica: RAND (N-1945-NIE).

Schlossman, S., Zellman, G., & Shavelson, R. (1984). *Delinquency prevention in South Chicago.* Santa Monica: RAND (R-3142-NIE).

Schweinhart, L. J., Barnes, H. V., & Weikart, D. P. (1993). *Significant benefits: The High/Scope Perry Preschool Study through age 27.* Ypsilanti, MI: High/Scope Press.

Seitz, V., Rosenbaum, L. K., & Apfel, N. H. (1985). Effects of family support intervention: A ten-year follow-up. *Child Development, 65,* 677–683.

Shadish, W., Cook, T. D., & Campbell, D. T. (2002). Experimental and quasi-experimental designs for generalized causal inference. Boston: Houghton Mifflin.

Shadish, W., & Meyers, D. (2002). Campbell Collaboration Research Design Policy Brief.

Shadish, W., & Ragsdale, K. (1996). Random versus nonrandom assignment in controlled experiments. *Journal of Consulting & Clinical Psychology, 64,* 1290–1305.

Shaw, C. R., & McKay, H. D. (1931). Social factors in juvenile delinquency. In *Report on the causes of crime* (vol. 2). National Commission on Law Observance and Enforcement. Washington, D.C.: Government Printing Office.

Shaw, C. R., & McKay, H. D. (1942). *Juvenile delinquency and urban areas.* Chicago: University of Chicago Press.

Sherman, L. W., Gottfredson, D., MacKenzie, D., Eck, J., Reuter, P., & Bushway, S. (1997). *Preventing crime: What works, what doesn't, what's promising.* Washington, D.C.: Office of Justice Programs, U.S. Department of Justice.

Shure, M. B. (1993). Interpersonal problem solving and prevention: A five-year longitudinal study—kindergarten through grade 4. Final report MH-40801. Washington, D.C.: National Institute of Mental Health.

Shure, M. B., & Spivack, G. (1982). Interpersonal problem solving in young children: A cognitive approach to prevention. *American Journal of Community Psychology, 10,* 341–355.

Slavin, R. E. (1989). When does cooperative learning increase student achievement? *Psychological Bulletin, 94,* 429–445.

Slavin, R. E. (1990). Achievement effects of ability grouping in secondary schools: A best evidence synthesis. *Review of Educational Research, 60,* 471–499.

Sloboda, Z., Hawthorne, R., Tonkin, P., Stephens, R. C., Marquette, J., Snell, A., Williams, J. E., Michelle Henry, S., & Huskins, D. (2003). *Building and assessing an evidence-based substance abuse prevention program delivered by D.A.R.E. Officers: Year 1.* Paper presented at the meeting of the Institute for Health and Social Policy, University of Akron, Akron, OH.

Snyder, H. (2002). *Juvenile arrests in 1999.* Washington, D.C.: Office of Juvenile Justice and Delinquency Prevention, U.S. Department of Justice.

Sontheimer, H., & Goodstein, L. (1993). Evaluation of juvenile intensive aftercare. *Justice Quarterly, 10,* 197–227.

Spelman, W. (2000). The limited importance of prison expansion. In A. Blumstein & L. Wallman (Eds.), *The crime drop in America*. Cambridge: Cambridge University Press.

Spoth, R., Reyes, M., Redmond, C., & Shin, C. (1998). Assessing a public health approach to delay onset and progression of adolescent substance use: Latent transition and loglinear analyses of longitudinal family preventive intervention outcomes. Ames, IA: Social and Behavioral Research Center for Rural Health.

Strayhorn, J. M., & Weidman, C. S. (1991). Follow-up of one year after parent-child interaction training: Effects on behavior of preschool children. *Journal of the American Academy of Child & Adolescent Psychiatry, 30*, 138–143.

Sutherland, E. H., & Cressey, D. R. (1955). *Principles of Criminology* (5th ed.). Philadelphia: Lippincott.

Swisher, J. D. (1979). Prevention issues. In R. L. DuPont, A. Goldstein, J. O'Donnell (Eds.), *Handbook on drug abuse*. Washington, D.C.: National Institute on Drug Abuse.

Swisher, J. D., & Hu, T. W. (1983). Alternatives to drug abuse: Some are and some are not. In T. J. Glynn, C. G. Leukefeld & J. P. Ludford (Eds.), *Preventing adolescent drug abuse: Intervention strategies*. DHHS Publication no. (ADM) 83-1280. Washington, D.C.: National Institute on Drug Abuse, U.S. Public Health Service.

Szapocznik, J., & Williams, R. A.(2000). Brief strategic family therapy: Twenty-five years of interplay among theory, research and practice in adolescent behavior problems and drug abuse. *Clinical Child & Family Psychology Review, 3(2)*, 117–134.

Tanenhaus, D. S. (2002). The evolution of juvenile courts in the early twentieth century: Beyond the myth of immaculate conception. In M. K. Rosenheim, F. E. Zimring, D. S. Tanenhaus & B. Dohrn (Eds.), *A century of juvenile justice*. Chicago: University of Chicago Press.

Taylor, R. B. (2002). Physical environment, crime, fear and resident-based control. In J. Q. Wilson & J. Petersilia (Eds.), *Crime: Public policies for crime control*. Oakland, CA: ICS Press.

Thornberry, T. P. (1998). Membership in youth gangs and involvement in serious and violent juvenile offending. In R. Loeber & D. Farrington (Eds.), *Serious & violent juvenile offenders*. Thousand Oaks, CA: Sage.

Tierney, J. B., Resch, N. L. (1995). *Making a difference: An impact study of Big Brothers Big Sisters*. Philadelphia: Public/Private Ventures.

Title, C. (1980). Labeling and crime: An empirical evaluation. In W. Grove (Ed.), *The labeling of deviance: Evaluating a perspective* (2d ed.). New York: Wiley.

Tolan, P. (2002). Crime prevention: Focus on youth. In J. Q. Wilson & J. Petersilia (Eds.), *Crime: Public policies for crime control*. Oakland, CA: ICS Press.

Tolan, P., & Gorman-Smith, D. (1998). Development of serious and violent offending careers in serious and violent juvenile offenders. In R. Loeber & D. Farrington (Eds.), *Serious and violent juvenile offenders*. Thousand Oaks, CA: Sage.

Tolan, P., & Guerra, N. G. (1994). *What works in reducing adolescent violence*. Boulder: Center for the Study and Prevention of Violence, Institute of Behavioral Science, University of Colorado.

Torbet, P., & Szymanski, L. (1998). *State legislative responses to violent juvenile crime: 1996–97 Update*. Washington, D.C.: Office of Juvenile Justice and Delinquency Prevention, U.S. Department of Justice.

Tremblay, R. E., Vitaro, F., Bertrand, L., LeBlanc, M., Beauchesne, H., Bioleau, H., & David, L. (1992). Parent and child training to prevent early onset of delinquency: The Montreal longitudinal experimental study. In J. McCord & R. Tremblay (Eds.), *Preventing anti-social behavior: Interventions from birth through adolescence*. New York: Guilford Press.

Tremblay, R. E., Vitaro, F., Bertrand, L., LeBlanc, M., Beauchesne, H., Bioleau, H., & David, L. (1996). From childhood physical aggression to adolescent maladjustment: The Montreal Prevention Experiment. In R. D. Peters & R. J. McMahon (Eds.), *Preventing childhood disorders, substance abuse and delinquency*. Thousand Oaks, CA: Sage.

Turner, S., Fain, T., Greenwood, P. W., Chen, Y., & Chiese, J. (2002). *Report on evaluation of Federal Violent Offender Truth in Sentencing Law*. Santa Monica: RAND (DRU-2634-NIJ).

U.S. Department of Education, Safe and Drug-Free Schools Program. (1998). *Notice of final principles of effectiveness*. 63 Fed. Reg. 29901–29906.

U.S. Department of Health and Human Services. (2001). *Youth violence: A report of the Surgeon General*. Rockville, MD: U.S. Department of Health and Human Services.

Von Hirsch, A. (1998). Penal theories. In M. Tonry (Ed.), *Handbook of crime and punishment*. New York: Oxford University Press.

Walker, H. M., Severson, H. H., & Feil, E. G. (1995). *The Early Screening Project: A proven child-find process*. Longmont, CO: Sopris West.

Wall Street Journal. (1993, September 28). "Bad Boys."

Webster-Stratton, C. (2001). The Incredible Years: Parent, teacher and child training series. In D. S. Elliot (Series Ed.), *Blueprints for violence prevention*. Boulder: Center for the Study and Prevention of Violence, Institute of Behavioral Science, University of Colorado.

Webster-Stratton, C. (1998). Preventing conduct problems in Head Start children: Strengthening parent competencies. *Journal of Consulting & Clinical Psychology, 66*, 715–730.

Webster-Stratton, C., & Hammond, M. (1997). Treating children with early-onset conduct problems: A comparison of child and parent training interventions. *Journal of Consulting & Clinical Psychology, 65*, 93–109.

Webster-Stratton, C., & Reid, J. (1999). *Treating children with early-onset conduct problems: The importance of teacher training.* Paper presented at a meeting of the Association for the Advancement of Behavior Therapy, Toronto.

Weisburd, D., Lum, C. M., & Petrosino, A. (2001). Does research design affect study outcomes in criminal justice? *Annals of the American Academy of Political & Social Science, 578*, 50–70.

Welsh, B. C., D. P. Farrington & L. W. Sherman (Eds.). (2000). *Costs and benefits of preventing crime: Economic costs and benefits.* Westview Press.

Welsh, B. C., & Hoshi, A. (2002). Communities and crime prevention. In L. W. Sherman, D. P. Farrington, B. C. Welsh & D. L. MacKenzie (Eds.), *Evidence-based crime prevention.* New York: Routledge.

Windlesham, L. (1998). *Politics, punishment and populism.* New York: Oxford University Press.

Yamaguchi, R., Johnston, L. D., & O'Malley, P. M. (2003). Relationship between student illicit drug use and school drug-testing policies. *Journal of School Health, 73(4)*.

Yoshikawa, H. (1994). Prevention as cumulative protection: Effects of early family support and education on chronic delinquency and its risks. *Psychological Bulletin, 115(1)*, 1–26.

Zhang, S. C. (1999). *An evaluation of the Los Angeles County juvenile drug treatment boot camp.* San Marco: California State University and the National Institute of Justice, NCJ 189787, U.S. Department of Justice.

Zimring, F. E. (2002). The common thread: Diversion in the jurisprudence of the juvenile courts. In M. K. Rosenheim, F. E. Zimring, D. S. Tanenhaus & B. Dohrn (Eds.), *A century of juvenile justice.* Chicago: University of Chicago Press.

Zimring, F. E., & Hawkins, G. (1995). *Incapacitation: Penal confinement and the restraint of crime.* New York: Oxford University Press.

Zimring, F. E., & Hawkins, G. (1997). *Crime is not the problem.* New York: Oxford University Press.

Zimring, F. E., Hawkins, G., & Kamin, S. (2001). *Punishment and democracy: Three strikes and you're out in California.* New York: Oxford University Press.

Zimring, F. E., Kamin, S., & Hawkins, G. (1999). *Crime 1and punishment in California.* Berkeley: Institute for Governmental Studies, University of California at Berkeley.

Zuger, A. (1997, December 16). New way of doctoring: By the book. *New York Times.*

Index

accountability, culture of, 115–16
Achenback Child Behavior Checklist, 32
active street time, 31
Adaptive and Maladaptive Teacher Rating Scales, 32
adjudicated delinquents, prevention programs for, 70–73, 71t
adolescents, prevention programs for, 61–70, 63–65t
adult crime, juvenile records and, 3. *See also* crimes
agencies: capabilities of, 172; constituents of, 172; missions of, 172
Alexander, Jim, 165
alternative recreation, 86
American Medical Association, 20
Anti-Drug Abuse Act (1986), 158
Aos, Steve, 42
Armed Career Criminal Act (1984), 157–58
arrest data, 31
Athletes Training and Learning to Avoid Steroids (ATLAS), 68
at-risk youths: approaches to intervening with, 15–16; family characteristics data for, 32

balanced and restorative justice (BARJ), 189, 190
Barr, Bob, 164, 165
BASIC program, 60; replication of, 82–83
behavioral token programs, 88
behavior rating sales, 32
benefits, measurement considerations for, 37–38
Big Brothers and Big Sisters (BBBS) mentoring program, 67; cost-benefit calculations for, 79–81, 80t; cost of, 74; number of convictions prevented by, 75
block grants, 163–64
Blueprints project, 37, 41–42, 45
boot camps, 88, 97–100, 167; characteristics and outcomes of, 99t; comparative advantage of, 115; latent functions and, 114
Boston Gun Project, 175
Botvin, Gill, 165

BPP. *See* Bullying Prevention Program (BPP)

Brief Strategic Family Therapy (BSFT), 68–69

Brown, Lee, 126–27

BSFT. *See* Brief Strategic Family Therapy (BSFT)

Bullying Prevention Program (BPP), 69

Bunning, Jim, 161

Burnam, Audrey, 128–29

Bush, George H. W., Sr., 165

Cambridge-Somerville experimental program, 24

Campbell Collaboration (C2), 35–36

capabilities, of agencies, 172

CASASTART, 69

Catalano, Richard, 40

Caulkins, Jon, 128, 129

CBA. *See* cost-benefit analysis (CBA)

CBC. *See* Congressional Black Caucus (CBC)

CEA. *See* cost-effectiveness analysis (CEA)

Chicago Area Project (CAP), 22–23

children, prevention programs for, 51–56, 53t; benefits of, 77–78. *See also* elementary-school-age children

Children's Bureau, 20

classroom-management techniques, 58

Clinton, Bill, 158, 162

cocaine, controlling, cost-effectiveness analysis of, 124–29, 140

communities, role of, delinquency and, 21–23

Communities That Care (CTC) model, 26, 40

community-based programs, 88, 89–90

Community Oriented Policing Services (COPS), 165

community policing, 160

Community Youth Investment Program (CYIP), 139–40

Compensatory Education Programs, 56, 61

confinement, 188

Congressional Black Caucus (CBC), 156, 159–60

constituents, of agencies, 172

contingent valuation (CV), 38–39, 145

Continuous Progress Programs, 56, 61

Contract with America, 162–64

convictions: number of prevented, by type of prevention program, 75–76, 75f; prevented, cost of, 76–77, 76f

Convicts against Prison Sentences, 103

Cooperative Learning Programs, 56, 61

COPS. *See* Community Oriented Policing Services (COPS)

cost-benefit analysis (CBA), 32; funding among alternative programs and, 141–46; for resource allocation, 148; summary of, 152–54

cost-effectiveness analysis (CEA): conducting, 120–23; controlling cocaine example of, 124–29; of juvenile-delinquency prevention,

138–41; origins and evolution of, 120; outcome measure in, 121; savings estimates and, 122–23; summary of, 151–54; of Three Strikes laws, 129–38

cost-effectiveness measures, for resource allocation, 148

cost-effectiveness ratio, 121, 123; for Three Strikes law, 134–35, 135f

"creaming" selection process, 34

crime-prevention programs, Republican vs. Democrat views of, 160–61

crime rates, sentencing laws and, 4

crimes: adult, 3; anticipatory dimensions of, 11, 12; community impact and, 6–7; incapacitation approaches to, 11; intervention approaches to, 11–12; property, 7; proxy measures for, 29; reactive dimensions of, 10–11, 12; types of responses to, 10–11, 11t; violent, 3–4

criminal-justice programs, vs. health and human service agency programs, 174

criminal-justice system, 172; capabilities of, 173; constituencies of, 175–76; control and, 173; focus of, 173; monitoring and, 173; organization of, 176; principles for assigning prevention responsibilities and, 178–79; response by, to enhance delinquency prevention, 174–75; risk assessment and, 173

culture of accountability, 115–16

custodial programs, characteristics of effective, 188–89

CYIP. *See* Community Youth Investment Program (CYIP)

DARE. *See* Drug Awareness Resistance Program (DARE)

deinstitutionalization, as prevention strategy, 23–24

delinquency: causes of, 21; Great Society programs and, 23; proxy measures for, 29; role of communities and, 21–23; role of neighborhoods and, 21–23

delinquency prevention, 4; boundaries of, 13; categorizing literature on, 40–44; crime control and, 10–12; current theories of, 25; defined, 5–6; dividing line between control interventions and, 14, 15t; dividing line between treatment and, 13–14; education and, 8; future of, 181–82; history of, in United States, 4–5; schools and, 16; shortcomings in, as field of study, 8; youth development and, 12. *See also* delinquency-prevention policies; delinquency-prevention programs; prevention

delinquency-prevention policies, evolution of, 12–13. *See also* delinquency prevention

delinquency-prevention programs, 13; outcome measures for, 30t; RAND cost-effectiveness analysis of, 138–41. *See also* prevention programs

delinquents, 7; prevention programs for adjudicated, 70–73, 71t

Democratic Party, views on prevention programs by, 160–61

Department of Education, 171

Department of Health and Human Services (HHS), 171. *See also* health and human service (HHS) agencies
Department of Justice, 171
Deschutes County, Oregon, 167
deviant labeling, 169–71, 177
deviant peer contagion, 88, 177
DiIulio, John, 64
discount rates, political, 140
diversion, as prevention strategy, 23–24
Drug Awareness Resistance Program (DARE), 13, 86–87, 90–97; comparative advantage of, 115; curriculum, 92; evaluations of, 93–96; explanations for persistence of, 111–13; latent functions and, 114; lessons learned from, 96–97; political allocations and, 147–48; prevalence of, 92–93
drug testing, school-based, 86, 87

early release, 88
Education. *See* Department of Education
education, delinquency prevention and, 8
effectiveness, measuring, 147–48
effect size, 148; problems in using, for choosing prevention programs, 151; proven and promising programs ranked by, 150–51, 150t
elementary-school-age children: home visitation for, 59; parent training for, 59; prevention programs for, 56–61, 57t
Elliot, Thomas, 21

evaluation designs, 33–35; impact of, on outcomes, 35–36
Everingham, Susan, 124
"evidence-based medicine" movement, 35
experiments, randomized, 28–29, 33

failed prevention programs, 84–85; criteria for identifying, 85–86; explanations for persistence of, 111–13; primary, 86–87; secondary, 87–88; tertiary, 88–90. *See also* prevention programs; promising prevention programs
family-based interventions, 16
family characteristics data, 32
family reform schools, 18
FAST Track, 58, 59–60
Federal Crime Bill (1994), 4; legislative history of, 157–67; passage and implementation of, 156
federal jurisdictions, movement toward, 180–81
FFT. *See* Functional Family Therapy (FFT)
field experiments, randomized, 28–29, 33
Finkenauer, James, 103
foster care, 179–80
Functional Family Therapy (FFT), 40, 70–72, 178; cost-benefit calculations for, 79–81, 80t; cost of, 75; cost of conviction prevented by, 76–77; evaluations of, 82; replication of, 82

Gingrich, Newt, 162
goals, of prevention programs, 29–30
Goddard, Henry, 21

Good Behavior Game, 58
Gordon, Don, 165
Gottfredson, Denise, 56
government, prevention and, 7–9
Great Society programs, delinquency and, 23
Guerra, Nancy, 40

Hansen, William, 91
Hawaii Healthy Start Program, 107, 109
Hawkins, David, 40, 144
health and human service (HHS) agencies: capabilities of, 173; constituencies of, 175–76; missions of, 172; organization of, 176; principles for assigning prevention responsibilities and, 178–79; response by, to enhance delinquency prevention, 174–75. *See also* Department of Health and Human Services (HHS)
health and human service (HHS) agency programs, vs. criminal-justice programs, 174
Healthy Families America (HFA): enrollment in, 108; latent functions and, 114–15; vs. NFP, 108; overview of, 107; positive outcomes for, 109–10; principles of, 107–8; randomized clinical trials of, 109–10; Research Network of, 108–9; summary of, 110–11
Healy, William, 21
HFA. *See* Healthy Families America (HFA)
Hitch, Charles, 120
home-visitation programs, 52–54; competition between proven and

unproven models in prenatal and infancy, 104–11; for school-age children, 59; violence prevention and, 111
House of Refuge. *See* New York House of Refuge

I Can Problem Solve program, 58
Iguchi, Martin, 128–29
incapacitation approaches, to crimes, 11
incarceration rates, for juveniles and young adults, 184, 185f
Incredible Years Program, The, 60–61; replication of, 82–83
individual counseling, 88, 89
infants: home visitation programs for, 104; prevention programs for, 51–56, 53t
In re Gault, 23–24
Institute for Defense Analysis (IDA), controlling cocaine study and, 127–29
institutional placements, 18–19
intake screening, of juvenile cases, 185–87
Intensive Protective Supervision (IPS), 73; cost-benefit calculations for, 79–81, 80t
intervention approaches, to crimes, 11–12
interventions: measuring, 28–29; measuring future benefits of, 37–38; primary, 12; secondary, 12; tertiary, 12
Iowa Strengthening Families Program (ISFP), 68
IPS. *See* Intensive Protective Supervision (IPS)

ISFP. *See* Iowa Strengthening Families Program (ISFP)

judgmental designs, 33–34
jury awards, 38–39
Justice, Department of. *See* Department of Justice
juvenile arrests, 184, 185f
Juvenile Awareness Project, 101, 103–4
juvenile courts, 15, 183; conflicting demands on, 189; incarceration rates of, 183–85; intake screening and, 185–87; lessons for, 190–92; mission and morale in, 183–87; mission creep in, 184; progressive movement and, 19–21; punitive sanctions by, 189–90; rationales of, 23; role of, 192–94; volume of cases for, 184–86, 186f
juvenile-delinquency prevention, cost-effectiveness analysis of, 138–41
Juvenile Justice and Delinquency Prevention Act (1974), 24
Juvenile Justice and Delinquency Prevention Act (1992), 25–26
juvenile offenders, 3; incarceration rates for, 184, 185f; institutional placement of, 18–19
juvenile records, adult crime and, 3

latent functions, influence of, 114–15
Law Enforcement Grants program, 165
leadership, 86
Levant, Glen, 112
leverage, delinquency prevention and, 34–35

Life Skills Training (LST), 67–68, 97; cost-benefit calculations for, 79–81, 80t; net taxpayer benefits for, 79; replication of, 82
LIFT. *See* Linking the Interests of Families and Teachers (LIFT)
Lindsey, Benjamin, 21
Linking the Interests of Families and Teachers (LIFT), 59
Lipsey, Mark, 40

management techniques, classroom, 58
Massachusetts Industrial School, 18
McKay, Henry, 22
measurements, for interventions, 28–29
mediation, 86
Midnight Basketball program, 165
Midwestern Prevention Project (MPP), 70
milieu therapy, 88
Miller, Jerome, 17
mission creep, in juvenile courts, 184
missions, 172; of health and human service agencies, 172; of juvenile courts, 183–87; of school systems, 173
Montreal Preventive Treatment Program (PTP), 59
morale, in juvenile courts, 183–87
MPP. *See* Midwestern Prevention Project (MPP)
MST. *See* Multisystemic Therapy (MST)
MTFC. *See* Multidimensional Treatment Foster Care (MTFC)
Multidimensional Treatment Foster Care (MTFC), 70, 72–73, 178;

cost-benefit calculations for, 79–81, 80t; cost effectiveness of, 115; cost of, 75; cost of conviction prevented by, 76–77; effect size of, 150; replication of, 82

Multisystemic Therapy (MST), 40, 72, 178; cost-benefit calculations for, 79–81, 80t; cost of, 75–76; cost of conviction prevented by, 76–77; effect size of, 150; replication of, 82

National Center for children, Families and Communities (NCCFC), 105

National Committee to Prevent Child Abuse (Prevent Child Abuse America), 107

National Rifle Association (NRA), 156, 161

needs assessment, 148–49

neighborhoods, role of, delinquency and, 21–23

Nelles, Fred, 20

New York House of Refuge, 4, 18

NFP. *See* Nurse Family Partnership (NFP)

Nicola, George, 102

nonexperimental designs, 33–34

NRA. *See* National Rifle Association (NRA)

Nurse Family Partnership (NFP), 114, 164; benefits of, 77; conditions for new sites for, 105–7; convictions prevented by, 76–77; effect size of, 151; elements of, 104; vs. HFA, 108; net taxpayer benefits for, 79; randomized clinical trials for, 105; range of net benefits for,

estimated by WSIPP, 143–44, 143t; replication of, 82, 105; savings for, compared with other savings, 76, 77f; summary of, 110–11

Nurse Home Visitation Program, 13, 37, 41, 48, 52–54, 164; cost-benefit analysis of, 142–43; cost-benefit calculations for, 79–81, 80t; cost of, 77; positive outcomes of, 142

Office of Juvenile and Delinquency Prevention (OJJDP), 24

Office of Juvenile Justice and Delinquency Prevention, 15

Olds, David, 13, 37, 41, 48, 52, 104, 164

orphan trains, 19

outcomes, 29; impact of research design on, 35–36; key decisions in analyzing, 36–40

Parent-Child Development Center Program, 55

Parent-Child Interaction Training Program, 54–55

parenting programs, 41

parent training, for school-age children, 59–61

PATHS. *See* Promoting Alternative Thinking Strategies (PATHS)

Patterson, Jerry, 165

PDFY. *See* Preparing for the Drug Free Years (PDFY)

peer counseling, 86

peer-group norms, shifting, 87

Perry Preschool (PP) Program, 13, 41, 54, 164; benefits of, 77; cost-benefit calculations for, 79–81, 80t; net taxpayer benefits for, 79;

Perry Preschool (PP) Program (*cont.*)
   savings for, compared with other
   savings, 76, 77f
perverse rewards, of prevention programs, 34, 168–69
police, 4
policies. *See* delinquency-prevention
   policies, evolution of
political discount rates, 140
Positive Youth Development, 67
PP. *See* Perry Preschool (PP) Program
Prenatal/Early Infancy Project, 52
Preparing for the Drug Free Years
   (PDFY), 68
Prevent Child Abuse America
   (National Committee to Prevent
   Child Abuse), 107
*Preventing Crime: What Works, What
   Doesn't, and What's Promising,* 41
prevention, 4; defined, 5–6; government and, 7–9; in 1980s and
   1990s, 24–27; political liabilities
   of, 167–69; strategies for, 23–24.
   See also delinquency prevention
prevention practice: evolution of,
   16–17; history of, 15–16
prevention programs: cost-benefit
   analysis for, 148; cost/benefit
   analysis of, 32; cost-effectiveness
   measures for, 148; cost of, per conviction prevented, 76–77, 76f;
   criteria for allocating resources for,
   147–51; deviant labeling and, 169–
   71; goals of, 29–30; markers for
   measuring effectiveness of, 46–
   47; needs assessment for, 148–49;
   number of convictions prevented
   by, 75–76, 75f; organizing and
   categorizing, 51; perverse incentive

features of, 168–69; RAND cost-
   effectiveness analysis of, 138–41;
   range of net benefits for, estimated
   by WSIPP, 143–44, 143t; reasons
   for different conclusions by reviewers for, 44–48; reducing risk
   factors and, 25; reporting impact
   of, 47–48; Republican vs. Democrat views of, 160–61; reviews of,
   43–44; for risk factors, 49–50;
   running of, 188; underevaluation
   of, 89. *See also* failed prevention
   programs; promising prevention
   programs
prevention responsibilities, principles
   for assigning, 176–80
preventions: primary, 192; secondary,
   192
Preventive Intervention program, 66
primary interventions, 12
primary preventions, 192
prison construction, 63, 165–66
prisons, 4
probation officers, 20
programs. *See* delinquency-
   prevention programs
progressive movement, juvenile
   courts and, 19–21
Project ALERT, 97
Project EXILE, 175
Project Northland, 69–70
Project PATHE, 13, 62
Project Safe Neighborhoods, 175
Project SMART, 91
Project STATUS, 62
promising prevention programs, 80t;
   for adjudicated delinquents, 70–
   73, 71t; for adolescents, 61–70,
   63–65t; cost and benefits of, 73–

79; cost-benefit calculations for, 79–81; for elementary-school-age children, 56–61, 57t; identifying, 50–51; for infancy and early childhood, 51–56, 53t, 77–78. *See also* failed prevention programs; prevention programs

Promoting Alternative Thinking Strategies (PATHS), 58–59

property crimes, community impact and, 7. *See also* crimes

PTP. *See* Montreal Preventive Treatment Program (PTP)

quality of life, measuring, 38

Quantum Opportunities Program (QOP), 41, 48, 66–67; cost-benefit calculations for, 79–81, 80t; cost of, 74–75; effect size of, 150–51

quasi-experimental designs, 33–34

RAND: Controlling Cocaine study of, 124–29; cost-effectiveness analysis of juvenile-delinquency prevention and, 138–41; Three Strikes cost-effectiveness analysis by, 129–38

randomized experiments, 28–29, 33

recidivism, 151

reentry programs, 22

reformatories, 18

Reiss, Albert, 40

Reno, Janet, 159

Republican Party, views on prevention programs by, 160–61

research designs. *See* evaluation designs

residential programs, 88

resource allocation, criteria for, for prevention programs, 147–48

responsibilities. *See* prevention responsibilities, principles for assigning

return on investment, 32. *See also* cost-benefit analysis (CBA)

reviews: of prevention programs, 43–44; reasons for different conclusions of, 44–48

risk factors: prevention programs for, 49–50; reducing, prevention programs and, 25

Robinson, Laurie, 113

Roth, Jeff, 40

Rydell, Peter, 124, 131

savings estimates, cost-effectiveness analysis and, 122–23

Scared Straight, 85, 87–88, 100–104, 167; political allocations and, 147–48

Schelling, Tom, 38

school-based drug testing, 86, 87

schools, delinquency prevention and, 16

school systems, missions of, 173

School Transitional Environmental Program (STEP), 62–66

Scientific Methods Score (SMS), University of Maryland, 41, 43

Seattle Social Development Program (SSDP), 58, 61; cost-benefit calculations for, 79–81, 80t

secondary interventions, 12

secondary preventions, 192

self-reported data, 30–31

sensitivity analysis, 123

sentencing laws, crime rates and, 4

Shapiro, Arnold, 102
Shaw, Clifford, 22, 89
Sheppard-Towner Act, 20
skill-development programs, 58
Smith, Lamar, 165
social casework waiver to adult court, 88, 89
social competency instruction, 86
SQUIRES program, 103
SSDP. *See* Seattle Social Development Program (SSDP)
standardized mean difference effect size, 36
state jurisdictions, movement towards, 180–81
STEP. *See* School Transitional Environmental Program (STEP)
surveys, victim, 38
Syracuse Family Development Project, 13
Syracuse University Family Development Research Project, 54

tertiary interventions, 12
Thrasher, Frederic, 21
Three Strikes laws, 41, 140; characteristics of, 130; cost-effectiveness analysis of, 129–38; explanations for persistence of, 112–13; Federal Crime Bill of 1994 and, 160
time incarcerated, 31
Tolan, Patrick, 40
transient behavior change, phenomenon of, 37

United States, history of delinquency prevention in, 4–5

victim costs, by crime, 38–39, 38t
victim surveys, 38
violence prevention, home-visitation programs and, 11. *See also* prevention
Violent Crime Reduction Trust Fund, 163
violent crimes, 3–4; community impact and, 7. *See also* crimes
vocational programs, 88, 89

Washington State Institute for Public Policy (WSIPP), 37, 42; range of net benefits for prevention programs estimated by, 143–44, 143t
What Works in Reducing Adolescent Violence (Tolan and Guerra), 40
Whittier School, 20
wilderness challenge programs, 88, 89
willingness to pay (WTP), estimating, 144–45
WSIPP. *See* Washington State Institute for Public Policy (WSIPP)
WTP. *See* willingness to pay (WTP)

Yale Child Welfare Project, 54
Yoshikawa, Hirokazu, 40
young adults, incarceration rates for, 184, 185f
youth development, delinquent prevention programs vs. other programs, 12
youths. *See* delinquents; elementary-school-age children; juvenile offenders

Zimring, Franklin E., 144